The Theater Will Rock

The Theater Will Rock

A History of the Rock Musical,
from *Hair* to *Hedwig*

Elizabeth L. Wollman

THE UNIVERSITY OF MICHIGAN PRESS

Ann Arbor

For Andrew and Paulina

2009   2008   2007   2006   4   3   2   1

A CIP catalog record for this book is available from the British Library.

Library of Congress Cataloging-in-Publication Data

Wollman, Elizabeth L., 1969–
     The theater will rock : a history of the rock musical : from Hair
to Hedwig / Elizabeth L. Wollman.
          p.   cm.
     Includes bibliographical references (p.   ) and index.
     ISBN-13: 978-0-472-11576-1 (cloth : alk. paper)
     ISBN-10: 0-472-11576-6 (cloth : alk. paper)
     1. Musicals—History and criticism.   2. Rock music—History
and criticism.   I. MacDermot, Galt. Hair.   II. Trask, Stephen.
Hedwig and the Angry Inch.   III. Title.

ML1711.8.N3W65   2006
782.1'416609—dc22   2006010056

Acknowledgments

MANY PEOPLE ASSISTED in the completion of this project. I must first thank my informants: Martha Banta, Richard Barone, Carla Bianco, Catherine Campbell, Michael Cerveris, Bill Compton, Tom D'Ambrosio, Nina Machlin Dayton, Natascia Díaz, Martha Donaldson, Paul Scott Goodman, Walter Michael Harris, Clifford Lee Johnson III, Marjorie LiPari, Galt MacDermot, Heather MacRae, Evelyn McDonnell, Ken Mandelbaum, Annmarie Milazzo, James LL. Morrison, Natalie Mosco, Tom O'Horgan, James Rado, Bill Schelble, Connie Schlier, Stephen Schwartz, Leigh Silverman, Mark Stewart, Don Summa, Steve Sweetland, Steve Swenson, Stephen Trask, Jack Viertel, Tom Viertel, and Billy Zavelson; without their willingness to be interviewed, their wisdom, and their candid insights, this book could not have been written. Thanks also to the members of my dissertation committee for the many comments made during the writing of what turned out to be the first draft of this book: Peter Manuel, John Graziano, Judy Milhous, Andrew Tomasello, David Savran, and Stephen Blum. Additional thanks go to Judy and to Rob Hume for the crash course in indexing.

I am grateful to the staff at the New York Public Library for the Performing Arts for helping me secure rights to photographs, as well as for digging up myriad archived clippings folders. Tom Lisanti from the permissions department was particularly helpul. The members of the Fine and Performing Arts Department at Baruch College, as well as many of the college's administrators, have lent their advice, support, and friendship; particular mention is due to Christopher Bruhn, Myrna Chase, Skip Dietrich, Mikhail Gershovich, Gary Hentzi, Philip Lambert, David Potash, Gene Scholtens, Leonard Sussman, and Andrew Tomasello.

LeAnn Fields, Rebecca Mostov, and Marcia La Brenz at the University of Michigan Press have acted as fearless guides for this first-time author; I deeply appreciate their good humor and the skill with which they have handled my manuscript. Three anonymous readers of earlier drafts made comments that were enormously helpful; one reader in particular suggested the current format for this book, for which I am eternally beholden. Dagmar and Marcia Hudson were particularly kind in helping me obtain the rights to use pictures from *Dude, Your Own Thing*, and *Ain't Supposed to Die a Natural Death*. John Michael Cox, Jr., identified the actors in the *Dude* photo for me.

Many friends, colleagues, and family members offered advice, guidance, and camaraderie along the way. I thank Meena Bose; Jak Cheng; Jim, Gail, and Jennifer Dunn; Joanne Hoffman; Marion Jacobson; Nancy Langer; Ann Lyons; Sandra Mardenfeld; Lisa Miller; Jason Oakes; Shuli Passow; Elijah Pluchino; Josh Saltman; Joe Sampson; Mark Stein; Steve and Jessica Swenson; and Paul Yoon. The exceptionally talented Laurice Perez deserves special mention; knowing that my daughter is in her capable hands on weekday mornings and afternoons has allowed me precious worry-free time during which I have been able to work on this book.

I am forever grateful for the support of my parents, Barbara and Michael, who instilled in me a love for music and the theater, and an interest in supporting the performing arts; my sister Jessica, who patiently listened to me read many a long passage from this book, and who always offered honest, intelligent advice (about the book and countless other topics); and my brother-in-law, Dan, who on many occasions listened to (and usually clarified) my rambling theories on popular music history and performance. Finally, I thank my husband Andrew and our daughter Paulina for their unending patience, support, encouragement, and love.

Earlier versions of portions of this work have appeared in the following publications:

Sections of interlude 1 and chapter 5 appeared in *Bad Music: The Music We Love to Hate*, edited by Christopher Washburne and Maiken Derno (Routledge, 2004).

Material from interludes 3 and 4 appeared in "The Economic Development of the 'New' Times Square and Its Impact on the Broadway Musical," *American Music* 20, no. 4 (2002).

Contents

Introduction

ROCK MUSIC HAS ALWAYS HAD AN UNEASY RELATIONSHIP with the American musical theater. Before the rise of rock 'n' roll in the 1950s, theater composers routinely acknowledged popular idioms—jazz and ragtime, for example—by appropriating them for theatrical purposes shortly after their emergence. Yet, while there have been repeated attempts over the past half-century to unite rock music with musical theater, their sociological, ideological, and aesthetic divergences have made such unions especially tricky.

Although rock 'n' roll was introduced in the United States in the mid-1950s, and became increasingly sophisticated and influential in the following decade, most of those who were then creating American musicals dismissed the new popular style as a noisy, vulgar fad. A few musical theater composers experimented with rock 'n' roll through the 1950s and 1960s, especially once it became clear that the music was not only not going away, but was outselling Tin Pan Alley fare. Nevertheless, it was not until 1967 that *Hair,* the first critically and commercially successful rock musical, opened at Joseph Papp's new Public Theater in the East Village neighborhood of New York City.

When *Hair* transferred from Off Broadway to Broadway in 1968, its phenomenal popularity and impact led some theater critics to proclaim that rock music's influence would revolutionize the musical theater, which by then had begun to decline in popularity among the American people. And indeed, the rock musical has become something of a staple in New York City. Almost every season since *Hair* arrived at the Biltmore, at least a few musicals that borrow heavily from contemporary popular genres have appeared on, Off, or Off-Off-Broadway to wildly varying degrees of commercial and critical success.

Yet despite their constant presence, staged rock musicals remain somewhat marginal, and their status problematic. In the first place, the business of theater is a risky endeavor, and as is the case with musicals in general, far more staged rock musicals fail than succeed. For every success—like *Hair, Rent,* or *Hedwig and the Angry Inch*—there have been countless flops—like *Dude, Via Galactica, The House of Leather,* and *The Legend of Johnny Pot*—most of which were openly scorned by theater critics and blithely disregarded by theatergoers. In the second place, while the influence of post-1950s popular music on the American musical theater has been profound, it has also, in many cases, been loudly lamented by theater critics and historians. For example, the now-typical use of electric instruments and amplification systems in the theater are begrudgingly seen as necessary evils that attract wider audiences while simultaneously destroying the purity of the musical as it was during its golden age from the 1930s through the 1950s. In the third, and perhaps most important case, no one seems quite sure of what, exactly, a "rock musical" is.

Definitions and Their Discontents

As Scott Warfield writes in "From *Hair* to *Rent:* Is 'Rock' a Four-Letter Word on Broadway?" despite widespread use of the term since its inception in the late 1960s, no formal definition of "rock musical" has ever appeared in print.[1] The term, inadvertently coined by the creative team of *Hair* when they jokingly subtitled their creation *The American Tribal Love-Rock Musical,* has been applied with maddening unpredictability ever since, and thus remains elusive, inconsistent, protean, and contradictory. Many musicals that reveal even trace hints of contemporary popular music influence have been dubbed rock musicals by theater critics and historians, many of whom are unfamiliar with popular music trends to begin with. Conversely, there have been many musicals with scores that borrow a great deal from rock music, but have never been identified as such by their producers or press agents because of a common industry fear that labeling any show a rock musical will significantly limit its potential audience.

The elusiveness of a definition for rock musicals should come as no surprise; the terms *rock 'n' roll, rock,* and *pop,* after all, have also proven exasperatingly difficult to define, especially in relationship to one another.

These terms carry with them not only musical and sociological connotations, but also ideological ones that are at once highly subjective and powerfully entrenched.[2] Making matters worse is the fact that these terms are often used interchangeably with one another: one critic's rock 'n' roll is another critic's "rock"; one fan's "rock" is another fan's "pop."

Because the term *rock* is so elusive, it follows that the term *rock musical*—as well as offshoots like *rock opera, pop musical,* and *pop opera*—is as well. Some of these terms are more easily distinguishable than others. *Rock opera,* for example, is fairly easily differentiated from *rock musical* in that the former tends to refer to dramatic productions that are sung-through, whereas the latter generally refers to dramatic productions that include spoken dialogue. *Jesus Christ Superstar,* which features no spoken dialogue, is thus a rock opera; *Hair,* which features a great deal of spoken dialogue, is a rock musical.

The terms *rock musical* and *pop musical,* however, are harder to define and to distinguish from each other for the same subjective reasons that the terms *rock* and *pop* resist clear-cut definitions. In the half-century since its inception, rock 'n' roll and its offshoots have morphed, mutated, and multiplied, becoming so intermingled along the way that while they may be ideologically separate, they are often stylistically impossible to differentiate. Further, so many of these interrelated forms have found their ways onto the stages of musical theater productions at this point that the term *rock musical* seems impossible to define.

Warfield notes, however, that despite the casual and often contradictory usages of the term *rock musical,* one can identify several staged productions that have been most strongly associated with it; these musicals can be used to pinpoint a few categories that help to clarify the term. Warfield offers four types of shows that are most often labeled rock musicals. The first, "self-identified" rock musicals, includes shows that have been called rock musicals by creators or producers, either in official subtitles (as in *Your Own Thing: A New Rock Musical*) or in ad campaigns. The second category consists of works that were released as concept albums before they were brought to the stage (for example *Jesus Christ Superstar* and *The Who's Tommy*). The third—and by far the largest, most subjective category—is for works that were never called rock musicals by their creators or producers, but which nevertheless revealed enough influence from contemporary popular genres to earn the label in the press, in theater histories, or among musical theater aficionados (for example, *Rent*). The final category is for nostalgic musicals that draw primarily from the earliest styles of rock 'n' roll, for example *Grease*, *Little Shop of Horrors*, and the Leiber and Stoller revue *Smokey Joe's Café*. As Warfield acknowledges, these categories must be flexible, since many musicals straddle the boundaries or fit comfortably into more than one, and especially since the term *rock musical* is applied so randomly, and so often.[3]

Because of the many elusive terms that are regularly applied to musicals in the press, and among industry members and fans—and that thus appear regularly throughout this study—I have taken pains to avoid a number of semantic obstacles. In the following pages, I distinguish *rock 'n' roll*, *popular music*, and *rock* from one another. I use the first term in reference to the rhythm-and-blues-influenced genre of popular music that developed in the mid-1950s and fueled the development of the broader, less easily defined genre *rock* in the mid-1960s. *Popular music*, the broadest of the three terms, is used for more general discussions, or for music that defies more specific descriptors.

The American Musical: History and State of Research

The specific origins of the modern musical—which has roots in comic opera, operetta, music hall, melodrama, minstrelsy, vaudeville, and burlesque—are both confused and contested. What is often cited as the first American musical, *The Black Crook*, opened in New York City in September 1866. This piece, which enjoyed rave reviews and a healthy commercial run, offered "melodrama, romance, comedy, dance, songs, specialty acts, spectacular scenic effects, elaborate costumes, and legs, legs, legs," but very little in the way of a cohesive narrative.[4] *The Black Crook* served as a prototype for the American musical as it developed through the very early twentieth century.

For decades after the premiere of *The Black Crook*, musicals were most akin to vaudeville shows: they were vehicles for popular songs and specialty acts, which were subject to change nightly, and which were loosely connected through the thinnest and most ridiculous of plots. During the middle to late 1920s, however, a number of young composers and songwriting teams—including George and Ira Gershwin, Richard Rodgers and

Lorenz Hart, Vincent Youmans, Jerome Kern and Oscar Hammerstein II, Irving Berlin, and Cole Porter—began to create theater pieces that more fully integrated songs and plots.[5] The American musical matured between the world wars and into the 1950s, when theater composers and lyricists like Richard Rodgers and Oscar Hammerstein II, Alan Jay Lerner and Frederick Loewe, Frank Loesser, and Leonard Bernstein moved beyond frivolous boy-meets-girl storylines toward the development of "musical dramas," in which songs and dance numbers helped define increasingly complex characters and propel newly sophisticated narratives. This "integrated" musical play flourished until the rise of rock 'n' roll caused a rift between American popular music and the musical theater.

Despite its rich history, its populist appeal, and its continuous reflection of the changing sociocultural moods of the nation, the American musical has long been ignored as an area for scholarly investigation, possibly because its mainstream appeal makes it seem too musically and dramatically low-brow to interest critics of the so-called high arts, and too conventional to win the affections of culture critics who focus on popular musical forms like jazz and rock.[6] There is some indication that this may be changing: since the mid-1990s, an increasing number of scholarly studies have begun to appear that suggest a growing interest in the American musical.[7] Nevertheless, aside from the many articles that appear each season in the popular press, most of the written works on the American musical remain strictly linear histories.[8]

Although rock musicals have been considered in a number of these histories, their treatment is generally superficial, and almost always negative. Most historians tend to cite what they see as the shortcomings of the rock musical. Traditionalists, especially, take particular issue with its reliance on amplification and electric instrumentation, and its resultant loud volumes.[9]

In contrast with the American musical, a great deal of scholarly work has been written about rock music's sociohistorical development, performance approach, and aesthetics. Unlike the musical theater's precarious position on the high/low culture continuum, rock music rivals traditional high culture, by "replicating within itself a full hierarchy of tastes from low-brow to high-brow."[10] The staged rock musical clearly occupies the lowest rung of such a continuum in the eyes of many rock journalists and historians, a few of whom have written about staged rock musicals with the utmost contempt, and a majority of whom simply ignore them entirely.

Setting the Scene

The backdrop of this study—Broadway, Off Broadway, and Off-Off-Broadway during the second half of the twentieth century—was by no means chosen at random. New York City has been the theater capital of the United States since roughly 1825, when its population surpassed that of the country's former theater capital, Philadelphia. Since the latter part of the nineteenth century, New York's commercial theater district, located on and around Broadway in midtown Manhattan, has been home to the largest collection of professional theaters in the nation.

In the early twentieth century, the city also became home to a number of comparatively small, noncommercial theaters and theater companies that comprised what was then called the little theater movement. In the early 1950s, some of these smaller theaters became known as "Off Broadway" houses.[11] As Off Broadway theater became increasingly influential and commercial through the 1950s and early 1960s, the even less commercial, decidedly more experimental Off-Off-Broadway movement was born. Although many people who write about the American theater tend to treat these three realms separately—with, for example, histories of Broadway virtually ignoring Off and Off-Off-Broadway—they are in fact interconnected entities that have exerted a great deal of influence on one another at different times in their histories.

This is particularly the case when it comes to rock musicals. Because rock music was initially—and, some would argue, remains—unwelcome on the Broadway stage, creators of rock musicals have consistently nurtured their shows in the Off and Off-Off-Broadway realms. In a significant number of cases, rock musicals that premiere in smaller theaters are transferred to Broadway houses only after their commercial success justifies such a costly and risky move. In this respect, the rock musical differs markedly from the traditional American musical, which is most firmly rooted in the commercial theater, and which, at least historically, owes relatively little to Off and Off-Off-Broadway.

Hair, the theatrical production whence the term *rock musical* originates, serves as an excellent example of the ways in which the development of the rock musical is connected to all three theatrical realms. *Hair* was written in the mid-1960s—a time when Broadway was suffering economically and artistically—by two former Broadway actors who had become involved in the then-flourishing experimental realm of Off-Off-

Broadway. The musical was first produced Off Broadway in 1967 as the inaugural production of the Public Theater; its markedly experimental, hugely successful Broadway incarnation was directed in 1968 by the Off-Off-Broadway director Tom O'Horgan.

Hair is not unique in this respect. Other rock musicals—*Rent*, for example—originated Off or Off-Off-Broadway and were later moved to Broadway houses. An equal number—for example, the failed *Dude* (1972) and the interactive *Rocky Horror Show* (2000)—reflected stylistic influences of Off or Off-Off-Broadway, even though these musicals were developed specifically for commercial runs in Broadway houses. Because the staged rock musical was developed in New York City and continues to appear with frequency there, any consideration of its development must necessarily relate back to the city's interconnected theater communities.

On with the Show

This book traces the history of rock's impact on the American musical theater, and identifies the theatrical highs and lows that have resulted from that union, between the mid-1950s and the turn of the century. The book is divided into chapters, in which I discuss particular shows chronologically and in detail. These chapters are interspersed with interludes, which focus on broader issues surrounding rock, the musical theater, and their relationship; because the interludes are more analytical in nature, musicals that are discussed within them are not necessarily presented chronologically. It is my hope that the structure of this book will allow readers interested in a straightforward history to read the chapters and skip the interludes; those interested in both history and interpretation can read chapters and interludes in whatever order they choose.

The first chapter examines early attempts at fusing rock 'n' roll with musical theater fare, a fusion that was more often the result of perceived necessity on the part of theater producers than of composers' interest in or respect for the new popular style. The first interlude examines issues of authenticity as they apply to rock music and, by extension, rock musicals. As rock 'n' roll developed into rock during the 1960s, it began to carry with it an air of imagined authenticity that has led many of its fans to distinguish the music from and hold it in higher esteem than more overtly commercialized and corporate-driven "pop." This perceived authenticity is bound up with the belief that despite its strong commercial moorings, rock is a transgressive, rebellious genre of music created and performed by uncompromising, soul-baring artists. Such notions about rock music are considered in this book in light of the fact that musical theater does not rely regularly on immediacy and is so strongly associated with older audiences that it cannot plausibly pose as a rebellious or transgressive art form.

Chapter 2 focuses on *Hair: The American Tribal Love-Rock Musical,* the first rock musical to have a successful run on a New York stage. The second interlude considers the history of audiences in the Western world, and examines the roles that audiences play in both rock and theater performances. Chapter 3 considers several "fragmented" rock musicals that were staged in the 1970s by producers eager to capitalize on the success of *Hair.* Most of these musicals, which emulated *Hair*'s free-form structure, were dismal failures, both critically and commercially. Their collective inability to win the favor of critics or audiences contributed to a rapid decline in enthusiasm for rock-influenced musicals among theater producers by the middle of the decade. The ways that "fragmented" rock musicals reflected current trends in rock music are exemplified in analyses of *Jesus Christ Superstar, Rainbow, Dude, Via Galactica, Godspell, Beatlemania,* and *Sgt. Pepper's Lonely Hearts Club Band on the Road.* Also in this chapter, the fragmentation—and segregation—of the rock market in the 1960s and early 1970s is discussed in relation to the so-called black musical renaissance in general, and to Melvin van Peebles's *Ain't Supposed to Die a Natural Death* in particular. The third interlude considers the rise of the megamusical in the early 1980s, its relationship to the rock musical, and its impact on the economics of theater production into the 1990s. Chapter 4 focuses on the increased reliance on visual spectacle and nostalgia in the 1980s; the musicals *Dreamgirls, Little Shop of Horrors,* and *Carrie* are detailed.

Interlude 4 considers the economic changes that have influenced American theater in general, and the Broadway musical in particular, beginning with the demise of the megamusical in the early 1990s. Since this time, rising costs and greater emphasis on the international marketing of entertainment properties have significantly changed the ways that musicals are developed, staged, and marketed. These changes have only accelerated since the mid-1990s, because of the renovation of the Times Square area and the increased presence of entertainment conglomerates as theater producers. The increasing "corporatization" of commercial theater in New York has led to the rise of ever more spectacular productions that structurally and stylistically reflect the influence of Andrew Lloyd Webber, and feature musical scores fashioned after middle-of-the-road pop music. Although such ventures prove popular with tourists, they also limit access by independent, original productions to Broadway theaters.

In chapter 5, the fates of several different rock-influenced musicals to open on or Off Broadway during the 1990s are examined, with emphasis on the difficulties that each production had in fusing such wildly divergent performing arts genres as rock and the musical theater. Shows discussed in this chapter include *The Who's Tommy, Rent, The Capeman, Hedwig and the Angry Inch,* and *Bright Lights Big City.* The fifth interlude considers the ways that various theater productions borrow from rock concert aesthetics to draw audiences. Finally, chapter 6 examines the state of the musical theater since the turn of the century, with emphasis on revivals of *Jesus Christ Superstar* and *The Rocky Horror Show,* the Off-Off-Broadway "happening" *The Donkey Show,* and the ABBA musical *Mamma Mia!*

I assumed, when I first began researching this topic, that I would be dealing with very few musicals, and that most of my attention would be focused on well-known shows like *Grease, Hair, Jesus Christ Superstar,* and *Rent.* I was even concerned, initially, that I would not find enough information to constitute an entire book. I was wrong in my assumptions, of course. Early forays into the topic, in fact, yielded such an overwhelming wealth of information that I developed a new appreciation for the cliché about how rock 'n' roll is here to stay: once it had been introduced into the American musical theater, rock 'n' roll simply refused to go away. Rather, its influences on the musical grew exponentially as the twentieth century wore on. So many musicals that have been staged since the mid-1950s reflect at least some influence by the burgeoning popular music style that space and time prohibit exhaustive discussion. In researching, organizing, and writing this project, I tried to include, in as much detail as I could, discussions of as many shows as possible. But, of course, there are many that have been excluded.

In the interest of shedding as much light as possible on a subject that has been virtually ignored until now, I chose not to focus on the compositional attributes of specific songs, but instead to concentrate on broader dimensions of the topic. This book is thus a social history, not a book of music analysis. Readers who are primarily interested in close readings of specific rock songs on the one hand, or musical theater numbers on the other, might do well to look at works by, for example, Walter Everett, David Brackett, Richard Middleton, Larry Stempel, Gerald Mast, and Stephen Banfield.[12]

In researching this project, I have interviewed many individuals who are or have been active in New York's professional theater circles, including actors, directors, producers, musicians, administrators, conductors, vocal coaches, press agents, critics, and theater historians. I have also interviewed performers and critics of rock music. Most of these interviews were conducted by telephone or in person. Most were scheduled in advance at the convenience of the interviewee, with the exception of audience members at specific productions, all of whom were approached at random. With the exception of one or two that were conducted via email, all interviews were tape-recorded with the consent of the interviewee and were later transcribed in full.

I also attended numerous musical theater productions, as well as several rock concerts. In almost all cases, field notes were recorded within forty-eight hours of the production in question. Finally, I attended twenty hours of rehearsals and a number of performances of the New York Theatre Workshop's premiere of Paul Scott Goodman's *Bright Lights Big City* in January, February, and March 1999, which greatly aided my understanding of the way a major musical production develops from first read-through to opening night.

My reliance on interviews and participant observation makes my work qualitative, not quantitative, and thus not scientific by any means. Nevertheless, in the five years that I worked on this project, I found that the insights of my informants helped to shed light on the subject in ways that no written source possibly could have. My forays into "the field"—New York City's many commercial and not-for-profit theaters—have also allowed me to gain deeper insights into the tastes and preferences of popular music audiences on the one hand, and musical theatergoers on the other.

This said, I have also gathered a great deal of information from periodicals, scholarly studies, sound recordings, program and liner notes, documentaries, scripts, and critic's reviews. The Billy Rose Theatre Collection at the New York Public Library for the Performing Arts houses a veritable treasure of old newspaper clippings, programs, production notes, photographs, and rare recordings, which I spent many hours sifting through. These holdings were particularly helpful in researching musical flops, which, once panned by critics and rejected by theatergoers, tend to slip quietly and sadly out of theaters, and thus fade quickly from public memory.

1 🎸 The Birth of the Rock Musical in New York City

IN THE YEARS SINCE ITS BROADWAY PREMIERE at the Biltmore Theater on April 29, 1968, *Hair: The American Tribal Love-Rock Musical* has been awarded landmark status as the very first rock musical.[1] The musical's designation as a revolutionary piece of theater began almost immediately: although publicly derided by a handful of Broadway potentates and dealt a few scathing reviews, *Hair* was nevertheless ecstatically received by some of New York City's most influential theater critics—notably Clive Barnes and Brooks Atkinson of the *New York Times*. Audiences also embraced *Hair*. The original Broadway production outlasted the youth movement it depicted, running for 1,750 performances and spawning several international touring companies and productions across North America, Asia, and Europe before closing on July 1, 1972.

Hair's milestone designation results not only from the experimental qualities of its conception and direction, but also from its effective blend of rock and Broadway musical styles, which had previously been regarded as mutually exclusive.[2] Without question, *Hair* was unique in a number of ways. It was the first Broadway musical devoted to the hippie culture of the 1960s; the first to feature nudity; the first critically and commercially successful Broadway musical to rely exclusively on rock instrumentation; and, as a result, the first to feature elements of rock music throughout its entire score. Despite its many accomplishments, however, *Hair* ultimately failed to spur the "revolution" in the American musical theater that many critics and historians predicted it would.[3]

Perhaps awarding any musical "revolutionary" status in the first place is unfair, especially since labels assigned with such fervor are often bound to be inaccurate. What tends to be ignored or forgotten in most musical theater histories is that *Hair* was by no means the first staged musical to feature rock music, nor was its composer, Galt MacDermot, the first to attempt to fuse two genres that had previously been considered mutually exclusive. In fact, Broadway and Off Broadway composers had been grappling with rock 'n' roll for at least a decade before *Hair* premiered at the Biltmore. Although these composers usually failed where MacDermot succeeded, their work sheds light on a fact that is often overlooked: *Hair* was less a revolutionary musical than an evolutionary one, whose creators managed to offer audiences a fusion that had been desired for years.

Early Attempts at Rock 'n' Roll on Broadway

The interest in adapting rock 'n' roll for use in the musical theater was at least initially born of a perceived necessity, not out of any affection on the part of Broadway composers for the new style. The popularity of Broadway music, which for decades had been synonymous with America's popular music, had begun to decline through the late 1950s and early 1960s, as reflected in several disappointing seasons dominated by unexceptional musicals (notable exceptions included *West Side Story* in 1957).[4] Concurrent with Broadway's decline in popularity was the emergence of rock 'n' roll, a popular music style that was closely linked to an increasingly powerful youth market.

Initially convinced that rock 'n' roll was a noisy, vulgar fad that would fade with time, Broadway's theater composers simply ignored the new musical genre. Yet by the end of the 1950s, rock 'n' roll was only continuing to gain momentum, while Tin Pan Alley fare was, without question, dying away. Of particular cause for concern among Broadway composers was the fact that while Tin Pan Alley had traditionally catered to audiences of all ages, rock 'n' roll was almost exclusively the domain of the young. On Broadway, the average age of audiences began to rise, and the American musical "became theater for a complacent, Eisenhower America."[5]

For some of the more traditional Tin Pan Alley composers, the advent of rock 'n' roll signified the abrupt end of long and lucrative careers. Even those composers who remained active gradually found that their newest songs were not selling as well or being broadcast on the radio as frequently as their older songs had been.[6] Broadway composers' ambivalence toward rock 'n' roll would only continue to plague them in ensuing years. Although most theater composers reacted negatively to rock 'n' roll, some nevertheless attempted to work elements of the style into a musical number or two, in hopes of appealing to young audiences. In these cases, however, a lack of appreciation for or understanding of the new genre was usually thuddingly obvious. That the creators of Broadway musicals were attempting to capitalize on a musical style with which they were largely unfamiliar and uncomfortable is clear upon examining some of the earliest attempts to bring rock 'n' roll to the Broadway stage.

In general, Broadway composers who experimented with rock 'n' roll during the middle and late 1950s did so by mocking the music, either through staging, dialogue, lyrics, or combinations thereof. This approach may be interpreted as an attempt to appeal to younger audiences while simultaneously insuring that the majority of Broadway theatergoers— historically white, middle-class, middle-aged adults—would not be alienated.[7] Such a tactic was perhaps necessary at first. In its early years, rock 'n' roll was poorly received by many such adults, who found it abrasive, incoherent, and linked to social problems like juvenile delinquency, racial strife, sexual permissiveness, and the widening generation gap.[8] Yet in trying to appeal across the generational divide, theater composers usually succeeded in simply mocking the growing youth culture for the benefit of adults.

Take, for example, the final edition of the Ziegfeld *Follies*, which opened at the Winter Garden Theater on March 1, 1957. The production, which commemorated the fiftieth anniversary of the *Follies*,[9] was a critical and commercial failure that closed after three months and 123 performances.[10] While the show's star, Beatrice Lillie, received strong reviews, many critics saw in this last edition a desperate attempt to recapture the past glories of a fading genre. "Perhaps the formula of the big, brassy Broadway revue is obsolete, quite apart from the 'Ziegfeld Follies,'" Brooks Atkinson argued in his review for the *New York Times*. "The energy is now going into other forms of entertainment."[11]

The production did, however, feature what is likely the very first musical number even approximating rock 'n' roll to grace a Broadway stage. The song "I Don't Wanna Rock," written by David Rogers and Colin Romoff, was performed by fifty-year-old Billy De Wolfe in the role of "The Juvenile Delinquent" and an ensemble chorus of "Tenth Street

Sheiks."[12] Unfortunately, the music used in this edition of the Ziegfeld *Follies* was never recorded and the notated music seems to have been lost; it is thus impossible to determine how, exactly, a brassy, old-fashioned musical revue negotiated a brand-new form of popular music.

The second Broadway show to experiment with rock 'n' roll was a revue entitled *The Girls Against the Boys,* with music by Richard Lewine and Albert Hague, and sketches and lyrics by Arnold B. Horwitt. Although this production, like the 1957 *Follies,* was never recorded, a piano score survives. *The Girls Against the Boys* featured Nancy Walker, Bert Lahr, Shelley Berman, and the up-and-coming Dick Van Dyke, among others, in a series of sketches and songs that explored the ups and downs of domesticity. Despite the efforts of what critics roundly praised as an admirable cast, *The Girls Against the Boys* was a flop; it opened at the Alvin Theatre on November 2, 1959, and closed after sixteen performances. One sketch from the show featured the thirty-seven-year-old Walker and the sixty-four-year-old Lahr as "a pair of rock and rollers, he in blue jeans, one of those crazy loafer jackets and a T-shirt of blue and white stripes, she in a pleated skirt and blue jacket."[13] During this sketch, the actors mocked the fashions and dances accompanying early rock 'n' roll with the song "Too Young to Live."

"Too Young to Live" features few elements that are truly reminiscent of 1950s rock 'n' roll. While most early rock 'n' roll songs, like their rhythm-and-blues predecessors, were built on successions of choruses adhering to the standard twelve-bar blues form, "Too Young to Live" is in a verse-chorus form that has always been typical of Tin Pan Alley fare. The song modulates between the verse and chorus—oddly, from G major to E-flat major—which is not reminiscent of the tonally simple language typical of early rock 'n' roll.

The one element that "Too Young to Live" clearly borrows from early rock 'n' roll is the syncopated bass line featured in its verse section, which emulates bass lines used in songs that accompanied the rock 'n' roll line dance known as the stroll. The bass line, however, disappears at the beginning of the chorus, as does any further indication that "Too Young to Live" is supposed to be a rock 'n' roll song.

Despite the composer's attempt to infuse elements of rock 'n' roll into "Too Young to Live," the song—as suggested by its facetious title—did more to mock the blossoming youth culture and the popular music associated with it than it did to attract young audiences:

Why can't we share the passion
That thrills us through and through,
Though we be adolescent
And adenoidal too?

They tell us we're too young to live.
But who are they to say?
When Saturday night in your daddy's Chevrolet
We found we're not too young to . . . live!

They tell us we're too young to live.
But we know more than they.
And when we come home with that tiny relative,
They'll know we're not too young to . . . live!

The subject matter of "Too Young to Live"—adolescent love and sexual longing—is certainly reminiscent of much early rock 'n' roll. Yet the lyrics, especially the punch line, depart egregiously from the music style in mocking teenagers from a decidedly parental perspective.

Bye Bye Birdie

On April 14, 1960, the first commercially successful Broadway musical to feature rock 'n' roll in its score premiered at the Martin Beck Theater. *Bye Bye Birdie*, with book by Michael Stewart and music and lyrics by Charles Strouse and Lee Adams, parodied Elvis Presley and his teen fans, but unlike the rock 'n' roll spoof in *The Girls Against the Boys*, the musical managed to steer clear of mean-spirited humor. A thinly veiled satire based loosely on Presley's 1958 induction into the U.S. Army, *Bye Bye Birdie* gently poked fun at teens and adults alike, and thus proved popular with audiences of all ages.

Bye Bye Birdie producer Edward Padula first thought to satirize the rock 'n' roll phenomenon in the mid-1950s; he nevertheless waited to execute his idea because he wanted to make sure that the resultant musical would be free of elitism or condescension.[14] Padula eventually hired Michael Stewart to develop his idea into a full-length book, and was pleased with the results: Stewart succeeded in realizing Padula's desire for a musical that refused to side with one generation over the other, but that instead parodied all of its characters equally, and with affection.

The lighthearted plot of *Bye Bye Birdie* centers around Conrad Birdie, a handsome but dim-witted rock 'n' roll sensation who has been drafted into the army. His call-up muddies the plans of his manager, Albert Peterson, whose intention to marry his longtime secretary and girlfriend, Rose Grant, requires Birdie's continued output as a recording artist. Eager to become Albert's wife and business partner, Rose devises a plan: in a publicity stunt to be aired nationally on *The Ed Sullivan Show*, Birdie will sing a new song, "One Last Kiss," to a carefully selected teen admirer; if the song is a hit, Albert and Rose will be able to live off the royalties until Birdie is discharged.

The teenager selected for the stunt is fifteen-year-old Kim MacAfee, from the small town of Sweet Apple, Ohio. In preparation for the television broadcast, Birdie and his entourage converge on the tiny town. Chaos ensues: Birdie, Albert, and Rose stay at the MacAfee household, to the dismay of Kim's father Harry, who embodies the older generation's befuddlement over the teen obsession with rock 'n' roll. Birdie's flirtatiousness drives a rift between Kim and her steady boyfriend, Hugo Peabody, while Albert's overbearing mother shows up to cause friction between Albert and Rose. Rose responds to her future mother-in-law's meddling by going on a bender, bursting into a local Shriners meeting, and breaking into a wild dance. Meanwhile, on the night of the telecast, Birdie is upstaged by the mugging, camera-happy Harry McAfee, and knocked over by the jealous Hugo before he can give Kim her kiss. Of course, everything works out in the end: Kim reconciles with Hugo, Birdie enlists, and Albert and Rose plan to marry.

While *Bye Bye Birdie* was something of an equal-opportunity satire, the musical nevertheless resorted to particularly exaggerated parodies of rock 'n' roll when it borrowed from the style at all. While most of the score from *Bye Bye Birdie*—which includes the standards "Put on a Happy Face" and "Kids"—does not reflect any rock 'n' roll influence, the two songs performed by Conrad Birdie are heavily influenced by the style, and are thus sharply distinguished from the rest of the score.

The first of these songs, "Honestly Sincere," is sung in act 1 when Birdie arrives in the town of Sweet Apple. The song does not resemble early rock 'n' roll in terms of form; its sophisticated harmonic progressions and lack of focus on the I, IV, and V chords keep it firmly in the realm of Tin Pan Alley fare. Yet "Honestly Sincere" borrows heavily from rock 'n' roll in other respects: it is scored for electric guitar, bass, drums, and a brass section; it features a syncopated walking bass line; and the melody is built largely of short, repeated melodic fragments in a narrow range.

The utterly ridiculous lyrics of "Honestly Sincere," however, cause the song to veer sharply from homage to parody. There is no attempt at rhyme or thematic development in the song. Rather, Birdie sings the following in the town square upon arrival in Sweet Apple, after finding himself surrounded by screaming local teens, one of whom has asked him to explain how he makes "that glorious sound":

> In everything I do
> My sincerity shows through
> I looked you in the eye
> Don't even have to try
> It's automatic! I'm sincere!
> When I sing about a tree
> I really feel that tree!
> When I sing about a girl
> I really feel that girl!
> I mean, I really feel sincere!

Of course, the joke is on rock 'n' roll and its fans: the claim of sincerity is made by an overamplified boob in a gold-lamé suit, who sings and gyrates madly while his impressionable audience swoons and sighs before him.

Birdie's second song, "One Last Kiss," borrows heavily from rock 'n' roll in its instrumentation, chordal framework, amplification, syncopation, and fragmented melody. Like "Honestly Sincere," this song is built of absurd, repetitive lyrics:

> Oh, gimme one last kiss!
> Oh, gimme one last kiss!
> It never felt like this!
> No, never felt like this!
> You know I need your love!
> Oh-oh-oh
> Gimme one last kiss!

Of course, these lyrics are no more or less inane than those found in many contemporaneous chart-toppers. Yet in *Bye Bye Birdie*, the lyrics are rendered by a character whom the audience has come to know as a self-absorbed dimwit; by the very nature of their context, then, the songs work more to spoof early rock 'n' roll's emphasis on emotionalism over lyricism than they do to accurately reflect rock 'n' roll hits of the time.

Only one song in *Bye Bye Birdie* reflects a true integration of traditional Broadway melody and early rock 'n' roll. Vibrant and imaginative, "The Telephone Hour," performed early in act 1, depicts small-town teenagers tying up their families' phone lines after school, as they buzz excitedly about the budding romance between Kim and Hugo. "The Telephone Hour" features rock 'n' roll's heavy syncopation, as well as its instrumentation and orchestration: the acoustic bass and saxophone double on the walking bass line; an electric guitar and snare drum alternately emphasize backbeats; and frequent triplets in the vocal lines contribute to the metric complexity. The song's lyrics emulate teen slang of the time ("What's the story, morning glory? What's the word, hummingbird?"; "It's crazy, man!"); and the intensity with which teens chat with one another on the phone is evoked by featuring a number of different conversations taking place at once, all of which fit into the overall harmonic framework.

In the original production and subsequent cast recording, the young voices used in "The Telephone Hour" sound comparatively raw, thus departing from the clear, vibrato-heavy, classically trained voices typical of musical theater at the time. Many of the lines are shouted excitedly, with more emphasis on emotion than vocal clarity. Original cast member Dean Stolber, in the part of the awkward Harvey Johnson—who calls house after house throughout the song in a desperate search for a prom date—sings in the unpredictable, cracking voice of a boy in early adolescence. Near the end of the song, doo-wop groups are emulated, as male and female characters punctuate one another's melodies with rhythmic glissandi sung to slangy lyrics like "Ooooh yeah!" and "Doo-oo-oo tell!"

"The Telephone Hour" mixes these rock 'n' roll elements with some that are more reminiscent of the Tin Pan Alley sound. In the first place, unlike the songs performed by Conrad Birdie, "The Telephone Hour" is not heavily amplified. Typically lush Broadway orchestrations fill out the accompaniment of the piece. Along with brass, bass, electric guitar and drums, the song is scored for flutes and strings. The many overlapping vocal parts are often more harmonically complex than they tend to be in early rock 'n' roll, and even in doo-wop, where, typically, a solo line would be backed by a small chorus.

While "The Telephone Hour" borrows further from early rock 'n' roll in focusing thematically on teen romance, it is nevertheless directly related to the plot of *Bye Bye Birdie;* thus, like a great deal of American theater music that has been written since the early twentieth century, its form follows its function. "The Telephone Hour" features a number of recurring, alternating, and eventually overlapping themes sung by male chorus, female chorus, and the character of Harvey Johnson. These themes either advance the action onstage, introduce characters and explain their relationships to one another, or set up the romance between Hugo and Kim, which will be challenged later in act 1 with the appearance of Conrad Birdie. The lyrics to "The Telephone Hour" are therefore too plot-specific for the song to be successfully detached from its setting.

While the critical reception of *Bye Bye Birdie* was largely positive, the musical's use of rock 'n' roll seemed to reinforce, at least for many critics, the idea that the new popular music style was easily dismissible as loud, ridiculous noise. Critical reviews for *Bye Bye Birdie* remain in keeping with the Broadway establishment's utter lack of respect for rock 'n' roll. As one of the few critics to give the show a negative review, Brooks Atkinson wrote in the *New York Times,* "Dick Gautier plays the primitive singer [Conrad Birdie] with pompadour, sideburns, gaudy costumes, a rugged voice, and a contemptuous vulgarity that are funny—a good, unsubtle cartoon of hideous reality."[15] Similarly, in an otherwise favorable review, Ernie Schier of the *Evening Bulletin* wrote that the musical's score "slyly demonstrates the difference between music and rock 'n' roll."[16]

Snide remarks from the critics aside, *Bye Bye Birdie* enjoyed a healthy run of 607 performances, and proved that Broadway audiences could tolerate, and perhaps even appreciate, the occasional nod at rock 'n' roll. For the time being, however, the critics got their way: after *Bye Bye Birdie* closed in October 1961, very few musicals featuring any rock 'n' roll influence whatsoever would grace Broadway stages for much of the rest of the decade.

After *Birdie*

There are a number of reasons why *Bye Bye Birdie* did not spawn many imitations. In the first place, the musical came along at a time when rock 'n' roll, still in its infancy, was commonly deemed not sophisticated enough to carry an entire musical, especially at the hands of theater composers who had little understanding of or respect for the burgeoning style. In the second place, rock 'n' roll influences notwithstanding, *Bye Bye Birdie* was by no means a bold departure from previous theatrical forms. On the contrary, in a period when dark, music-and-movement-laden musicals like *West Side Story* were becoming increasingly influential, *Bye Bye Birdie* was a throwback, offering cheery sentimentality, light humor, and the ages-old boy-meets-girl, boy-loses-girl, boy-wins-girl-back structure that Padula felt would be comforting to Broadway audiences.[17]

Padula's desire to appeal to audiences with gentle, inoffensive material points to yet another reason why rock 'n' roll disappeared from Broadway for much of the 1960s. Economically speaking, this decade was profoundly unpleasant for commercial theater in New York City. An Equity strike in 1960 resulted in a sharp increase in the cost of production. Tickets for Broadway shows subsequently skyrocketed, and, at the same time, producers often drastically reduced the size of choruses and cut corners on scenery and props, thereby offering much less for much more.[18] Financially strapped producers grew wary of anything but the most conservative "escapist fare aimed at middle-aged businessmen and theatre parties from the suburbs"; this, in turn, resulted in season after season of derivative, disappointing and forgettable shows. This vicious cycle continued to alienate young people and to perpetuate Broadway's reputation as increasingly irrelevant and out of touch.[19]

Despite the success of *Bye Bye Birdie*, then, most Broadway composers steered clear of rock 'n' roll in the years following its success. The style was featured in the occasional revue; but even then, anything approximating rock 'n' roll was reserved for parodies. The 1964 British import *The Cambridge Circus*, for example, featured a sketch entitled "I Wanna Hold Your Handel," in which three performers sang a Beatles version of the "Hallelujah" chorus from Handel's *Messiah* while a fourth flailed away at the drums.[20]

Occasionally during the 1960s, however, the odd Broadway composer would attempt to work a rock 'n' roll number or two into their musicals. Such attempts seem to reflect a desire to keep up with changing times, rather than any true interest in the musical style. In *Broadway Musicals*, the critic Martin Gottfried argues that such composers were merely "looking for hits by thinking new (rock) and old (ballads) at the same time. Inevitably, these were bastard songs, defeating a show's integration and making for isolated numbers."[21]

Indeed, composers who tossed elements of rock 'n' roll into a Broadway show simply for the sake of acknowledging the style learned of an insurmountable problem: while a musical like *Bye Bye Birdie* practically demanded some rock 'n' roll in its score, a vast majority of musicals had no compelling reason to feature it. A fitting example is Irving Berlin's last original Broadway musical, *Mr. President,* which opened at the St. James Theater in October 1962. Hardly Berlin's most memorable work, the musical was tepidly received and had an unexceptional run of 265 performances before closing in June 1963. "At best," the esteemed critic and editor Henry Hewes quipped, "*Mr. President* could be summed up as a series of mildly pleasant and disappointingly innocuous jokes about how being President of the United States or the First Lady can be a damn nuisance."[22]

In stark contrast with much of Berlin's previous work, none of the songs from *Mr. President* won wide public acceptance, despite (or perhaps because of) Berlin's obvious attempt to keep up with the changing times.[23] The score for *Mr. President* included a song called "The Washington Twist," which attempted to emulate the dance that was popular with teenagers at the time. "The Washington Twist" featured a full Broadway orchestra dutifully thumping out an insistent I-IV-V progression as a female soloist talk-sang the lyrics, which lamented the duplicitous nature of Washington society. The placement of the song—during a scene depicting a formal party at the White House—was downright bizarre: why, exactly, would characters in a political satire suddenly burst into the twist at a stuffy White House reception?

Flush with the success of *Bye Bye Birdie,* producer Edward Padula attempted to score again with a musical that reached beyond the Tin Pan Alley sound for inspiration. The country-and-western- and folk-inspired musical *A Joyful Noise,* which Padula wrote, directed, and produced, premiered at the Mark Hellinger Theatre on December 15, 1966. Based on the novel *The Insolent Breed* by Borden Deal, *A Joyful Noise* recounts the romance between small-time country-and-western singer Shade Motley and his sweetheart, Jenny Lee. When Shade is run out of Macedonia, Tennessee, by Jenny Lee's father, he takes up with a shady promoter and rises to fame as a singer at the Grand Ole Opry. Caught between the trappings of stardom and the desire for a quiet, simple life, Shade ultimately turns his back on fame, and returns to Macedonia to settle down with Jenny Lee.

Sadly, Shade Motley's rags-to-riches story failed to generate much interest on Broadway. *A Joyful Noise* received scathing reviews and closed after only twelve performances. Despite its brief run—and the fact that it featured minimal rock 'n' roll influence in its score—*A Joyful Noise* is noteworthy because it introduced a new approach to adapting popular music for Broadway: rather than hiring an old-school musical theater composer to adapt popular forms for the stage, Padula enlisted an outsider who was not terribly experienced with theater music, but who was very comfortable with folk and country music. The folk musician, satirist, and radio host Oscar Brand teamed with Broadway composer and lyricist Paul Nassau to write an original score for *A Joyful Noise*. The desired result was a score that would retain enough of a traditional Broadway sound to keep from alienating older audience members, but that would also have enough of a fresh, country and folk flavor to capitalize on the then-robust folk revival.

Unfortunately, the result failed to strike a proper balance. In the attempt to mix popular strains with Tin Pan Alley, most of the score was a muddy, confused mess. In his review, *Women's Wear Daily* critic Martin Gottfried argued that William Stegmeyer's lush orchestrations clashed with Brand's simple melodies. "There was a fine idea for a musical at the root of *A Joyful Noise*," he wrote, "and Oscar Brand was just the kind of guy to write its music, but Mr. Brand and his collaborator, Paul Nassau, got mixed up with people who demanded a 'Broadway' look, a 'Broadway' sound. As a result, still another chance for a fresh musical went down the drain, dragged most of the way by an interfering, irreverent injection of brassy nonsense, put together cheaply and ignorantly."[24] After the disappearance of *A Joyful Noise*, no further attempts were made to bring popular music to the Broadway stage until *Hair* arrived at the Biltmore Theater in the spring of 1968.

Interlude 1

Rock "Authenticity" and the Reception of the Staged Rock Musical

As 1950s ROCK 'N' ROLL DEVELOPED into the more sociopolitically aware rock music of the 1960s, an ideology of authenticity became increasingly central to its culture. Such an ideology implies that as artists who bare their souls in composition and performance, rock musicians somehow transcend the influences of the music industry. In keeping with this ideology, the music itself is regularly celebrated as a transgressive and rebellious genre, despite its obvious commercial moorings.

While many writers on rock music argue that this putative authenticity exists largely in the collective imagination, most argue further that such imagined authenticity is nevertheless powerfully influential.[1] Indeed, rock's associations with authenticity have led many fans, critics, and historians to set the music apart from and above "pop" music. While the line dividing rock and pop is impossibly blurred and regularly contested—especially since the terms *rock, pop,* and *popular* are often used interchangeably—pop is generally seen to be more overtly manufactured and commercialized than rock, and thus less representative of the true emotional state of the performer.

While many popular genres have lent themselves successfully to the musical theater, rock has always struggled in that realm due in large part to its relationship with authenticity. Rock's imagined authenticity has made the reception of rock musicals in the media, the industry, and among rock fans problematic. The means by which rock's imagined authenticity is perpetuated thus deserves examination, as does its relationship to staged rock musical reception.

Origins of the Authenticity Myth

Among the cultural claims made for rock music by the end of the 1960s were that it was the genuine reflection of the experience of some idealized, undefined youth community and that there was "no distinction of social experience between performers and audiences."[2] These ideologies link rock to a long line of vernacular genres that were similarly idealized. During the late nineteenth century, scholars in the UK and in North America drew sharp distinctions between "folk" and "popular" music by placing the artistic and social value of the former over that of the latter. They drew no distinctions between folk performers and audiences, thereby arguing that folk music was particularly representative of the rural communities from which it emanated.[3]

The notion of folk music as a unifying genre, or as a mouthpiece for the masses, was adopted by the American radical Left in the 1930s and 1940s.[4] Such a conception, of course, did not correspond to reality. During this period, most of the working class was much more likely listening on the radio to Benny Goodman, Glenn Miller, and Frank Sinatra than they were to protest songs of the Spanish Civil War or the Harlan County picket lines.[5] The "People's Music" movement was thus one in which the lives and experiences of the rural working class were selectively celebrated by urban radicals.

A similar, selective ideology infused the commercial folk music revival that took place in the United States during the late 1950s and 1960s. Although initially apolitical, this revival took on political undertones in its later years in response to the civil rights movement and the Vietnam War. Simon Frith writes that during the height of this revival, "there was, in theory, no separation of performer and listener," and that "the aesthetic emphasis was less on technique than on truth."[6] There were, however, a few important differences between this and earlier folk movements: by the mid-1960s, many performers who were active in the folk scene became increasingly interested in expressing personal sentiments, and thus shied away from their designated roles as civic representatives for their audiences or their generations. Although he rose to prominence as a performer of politically charged folk songs, for example, Bob Dylan turned his attention to songs that he composed and set to his own introspective, increasingly obscure lyrics.[7]

Yet associations with authenticity did not wane in the transition from folk to rock; they merely shifted. As Terry Bloomfield writes, "the authentic came to be seen not just as the genuine, that is some kind of 'real' 'folk' art, but also as raw, direct emotion that would somehow break through 'the trappings of showbiz.'" In the hands of the counterculture, authenticity "swelled up to embrace emotional honesty and sincerity, autobiographical truth and political correctness."[8] Paradoxically, then, late-1960s rock musicians' claims to represent a community were reinforced by how aggressively they expressed their individuality.

At least in theory, it was a rock musician's ability to display "real" emotion in composition and in performance that set him or her apart from pop performers. Simon Frith points out that prior to Bob Dylan, popular performers who wrote their own songs were not regarded as possessing "authentic" voices. "Paul Anka's 'Diana,' for example, had never been thought to express his own experience except in terms of clichés so general that they could be used by everyone." But when singer-songwriters began to emulate folk singers in writing and singing about political and personal issues, "faking an emotion . . . became an aesthetic crime," and rock musicians began to be judged not only for their ability to make music, but also "for their openness, their honesty, their sensitivity."[9]

While rock's connection to authenticity is perhaps most immediately perceptible in the performances of singer-songwriters, Dylan and his emulators influenced rock performance in general. By the late 1960s, many prominent rock musicians perfected the art of at least seeming to bare their souls while onstage in ever-larger concert venues. Frith argues that performers like Janis Joplin and Jimi Hendrix

> fed the rock audience's need for the emotional charge that confirmed they'd been at a "real" event. The questions they posed were central to rock: how to guarantee the emotional impact of their performances night after night . . . (the answer lay in technology, volume, a gradually evolved repertoire of rock signs of emotion); how to relegate public and private life when rock audiences expected no distinction (the answer was to ignore the audience, to deny that there was such a thing as a separate public persona—musicians soon found that they could make lots of money by apparently playing only to please themselves).[10]

While it borrowed heavily from folk ideology, then, rock ideology shifted in order to more comfortably embrace the star system that prevails in the world of popular music.

Rock ideology differed further from folk ideology in its comparative, if not entirely untroubled, acceptance of technology. Through the nineteenth and early twentieth centuries, the relative lack of technology, combined with the ideological bond between performer and audience, resulted in folk's emphasis on live dissemination via acoustic performance. In folk circles, technology was often seen to falsify or cheapen the music and its message. Rock, however, was dependent upon the very technology that was decried in folk circles. The increased use of amplification and electric instruments, first in rock and then in folk-rock, led to the rise of tensions both within folk circles and between folk and rock camps by the mid-1960s.[11] The attempt to rectify rock's imagined relationship to authenticity with its very real relationship to technology has since proven arduous for many rock fans. Many critics, too, have expressed difficulty in reconciling technology with authenticity,[12] hence a tendency in rock journalism to consistently herald new rock subgenres as more authentic and less laden with technological baggage than their predecessors.[13]

The friction between authenticity and technology was eased somewhat once a significant number of rock musicians learned to produce their own recordings. At roughly the same time that it became trendy among scholars and critics to equate rock lyrics with poetry,[14] technologically sophisticated albums like the Beatles' *Sgt. Pepper's Lonely Hearts Club Band* were being elevated to the status not of mere pop but of "art."[15] Through the 1970s, perceptions of the recording studio as a site for artistic creation, and of the rock musician as an *auteur,* helped reconcile the contradictory associations evoked by technology on the one hand and authenticity on the other.[16] Hence, to some extent, technology was circumscribed within rock's ideology of authenticity under the rubric that whether onstage or in the studio, "genuine" rock musicians remained in total control of their art.

The Role of Rock Criticism in
Perpetuating Rock "Authenticity"

Rock ideology is both influenced and perpetuated by rock criticism, which developed in the United States in the middle to late 1960s.[17] Especially in its formative years, rock criticism was largely dominated by men who tended to valorize rock—which was perceived as "serious," "authentic," and "masculine"—and to dismiss pop—which was perceived as "trivial," "prefabricated," and "feminine."[18] A handful of influential critics have challenged such perceptions; in his 1977 essay on the Clash, the distinctively obstinate and delightfully blunt Lester Bangs argued that "like Richard Hell says, rock'n'roll is an arena in which you recreate yourself, and all this blathering about authenticity is just a bunch of crap."[19] In recent years, especially since a growing number of women have joined the rock critic corps, some journalists have challenged ideological assumptions, especially those that link "trivial" popular music with femininity and "serious" popular music with masculinity. Nevertheless, as rock critic Evelyn McDonnell argues, the rock press remains "aggressively male—or passive-aggressively male! Everything has to be authentic, even though authenticity can also be constructed. Rock critics have a history of being hung up on the singer-songwriter, and Dylan being the godhead figure. So everybody has to be writing from this Dylanesque space."[20]

Not only do individual critics perpetuate such ideology; music periodicals do, too. *Rolling Stone,* one of the oldest, most widely circulated, and most influential American rock music magazines, is regularly criticized as a case in point. As David Sanjek argues, *Rolling Stone* founder and publisher Jann Wenner clearly "identified rock's authenticity with a specific set of figures who formed the publication's icons of the rock canon," including Dylan, the Beatles, and the Rolling Stones. The result is a magazine that takes an "essentially conservative, even mystical approach to music." Further, the community that *Rolling Stone* purports to represent is "always assumed, never assessed or theorized."[21]

Of course, the influence of rock critics and periodicals on fans is limited in many respects. In the first place, not everyone who listens to rock reads about it. In the second, publications in which rock criticism appears can be frustratingly discriminatory and even revisionist, often reflecting little more than the evolving taste preferences of their editorial staffs. *Rolling Stone,* in particular, has been criticized for either giving short shrift to or even completely ignoring important popular subgenres like punk, funk, and rap, simply because Wenner disliked them.[22]

Despite the shortcomings of rock criticism, it is nevertheless without question that critics can color public opinion. As Fred Goodman emphasizes in his portrait of the critic-turned-producer and manager John Landau in *The Mansion on the Hill: Dylan, Young, Geffen, Springsteen, and the Head-on Collision of Rock and Commerce,* rock journalists can exert tremendous influence on—and even become members of—the very music industry on which they report.[23] Further, while critical pans do not necessarily result in the commercial failure of a band or artist, a combination of commercial and critical failure can lead to a musical act being dropped by its label. On the other hand, if a new band generates support among critics, the buzz is typically used in record promotions, and to attract the attention of radio programmers and MTV executives.[24]

The Role of the Music Industry
in Perpetuating Rock "Authenticity"

Rock's popularity among American youth in the 1960s resonated with the New Left, many members of which heralded the music as a vehicle for massive sociopolitical change.[25] Yet for all its associations with authenticity and rebellion, rock was also proving a valuable commodity. The music thus found itself embraced at once by the radical Left and by multinational record companies. The latter quickly picked up on the language of the former for use in advertisements. For example, Columbia Records ran an ad in *Rolling Stone* in November 1968 that appropriated the slang of the counterculture in posing the rhetorical question, "If you won't listen to your parents, the Man or the Establishment, why should you listen to us?" The same company took out an ad in the December 21 issue that depicted a group of young people passing a joint: "Know Who Your Friends Are" read the ad copy. "And look and see and touch and be together. Then listen. We do."[26] Rock's ideology of authenticity was thus cultivated simultaneously by the New Left and the very "Establishment" they were working against.

This phenomenon resulted in tensions between the commercial and artistic aspects of rock, which continue to exist. Such tensions arose in part because the commodification of rock was not as obvious as that of previous popular forms. This was especially true once the music industry became populated with rock fans who might well have believed in rock's sociopolitical potential even as they exploited it for commercial gain. As Simon Frith points out, for example, some of the most influential people in the Bay Area music scene of the late 1960s were rock fans who also happened to be brilliant entrepreneurs. People like Jann Wenner and Bill

Graham thus "disguised the exploitation involved in the rock marketplace in the name of 'the rock community.'" This is significant not because rock was co-opted, but because "the terms of its cooptation were concealed. Pop commercialism was so blatant that pop fans could never forget their consumer status; rock fans, by contrast, could treat their record buying as an act of solidarity."[27]

One result of this overlap between fans, critics, and industry members is that decades after its inception, rock continues to be marketed, criticized, and consumed as a genre that defies even its most obvious commercial trappings. Despite their commodification, their interest in appealing to mass audiences, and their carefully cultivated images, rock musicians thus continue to be marketed as artists whose onstage personae are no different from their private ones, and who are somehow untouched by crass commercialism in a way that pop artists are not.

The Role of the Rock Audience in Perpetuating Rock "Authenticity"

Because the commercial and artistic aspects of rock have coexisted since the genre's inception, both have exerted powerful influence on rock's large and varied fan base. Marketing strategies aimed at romanticizing rock music's genuineness do not explain away the continued correlation by many fans of rock with authenticity, rebellion, and personal freedom, and yet the influence of corporations on the individual cannot be ignored. Many theories attempt to explain the reasons that rock remains associated with such qualities. David Scudder, for example, argues that although the association between rock and the New Left collapsed long ago, the movement nevertheless imprinted on rock its "temporary transcendent aesthetic quality," since an "aesthetic form cannot be divorced from the historical contexts . . . in which it had aesthetic meaning."[28]

Rock's commercial and artistic dichotomy is central to theories of Theodore Gracyk, who argues that tensions between these two aspects supply much of rock's power. Rock's commercialism, he writes, cannot smother its basis in Enlightenment assumptions about the self, which are empowering because they proclaim the individual as central to authenticity.[29] Despite insistences, by contemporaries like Lawrence Grossberg, that rock's connection to authenticity is waning,[30] Gracyk insists that the connection will never be completely severed since authenticity is so deeply ingrained in rock aesthetics.[31]

The equation of individuality with authenticity is also central to the work of Simon Frith, who argues that one's musical tastes aid in self-definition. Frith holds that popular music fans take particular pleasure in identifying with the music and the performers they like, and with fellow fans. According to Frith, then, popular music is read by its fans as something that can be possessed. Rock fans "own" their favorite music in ways that can be deeply personal and highly meaningful. "Obviously it is the commodity form of music which makes this sense of musical possession possible," Frith acknowledges, "but it is not just the record that people think they own: we feel that we also possess the song itself, the particular performance, and its performer."[32]

It might be suggested that, rather than simply swallowing media and industry insistences on the purported authenticity of a given rock musician, rock fans choose instead to accept performers who mean something special to them as authentic—or to pretend, even when faced with evidence to the contrary, that they are authentic—simply because such perceptions help legitimize the significant roles that they play in a fan's life. It is additionally possible that the association of rock with authenticity takes place on an emotional plane and not a logical one, not because fans are merely pawns of the music industry or the media, but because fans use music that is important to them to help define themselves and their social milieu.

Rock's Myth of Authenticity
and Its Conflicts with Musical Theater

Reception of even the most well-received rock musicals, both in the press and among actual and potential audiences, almost always reveals recurring imbalances: a successful staged production offering a blend of rock and musical theater aesthetics usually wins the favor of either the rock or the musical theater realm, but rarely of both camps at once. Despite the incorporation of props, costumes, scenery, characters, and choreography, for example, concerts staged by Alice Cooper have never been widely embraced in the musical theater world; nor have concerts by Frank

Zappa, despite the inclusion of humorous skits. On the other hand, while largely received as an excellent musical, *Rent* (1996) has failed to be embraced in the music press or among most rock fans as a production that offers any "real" rock in its score.

Further, when performers who are embraced by one camp tip the balance too far in the direction of the other, the results are usually commercially and critically disastrous. For example, all but the most established popular musicians shy away from revealing too much of an interest in the musical theater, since doing so is seen as potentially damaging to one's credibility and career.[33] While a flair for the theatrical is often deemed acceptable in the rock realm, then, many rock musicians will not appear in musical theater productions, record or perform Broadway show tunes, or otherwise show an interest in the genre.

There are a number of reasons for this, all of which add veracity to the notion that characteristics extant in the musical theater counteract those imagined qualities that are valued and perpetuated in the rock world. In the first place, unlike rock music, the musical theater does not have a profound relationship with notions of authenticity, per se. One might argue, in fact, that the opposite is the case: the American musical traditionally celebrates a self-conscious blending of high and low cultures, revels in artifice and kitsch, and, unlike rock music, has been overtly associated with the capitalist market system from its inception.[34]

Along with a comparative lack of emphasis on authenticity in the musical theater comes a less central role played by the composer. In contrast with the singer-songwriter-musician of the rock realm, the reputations of musical theater composers are almost always built exclusively on songwriting ability: like many pop songwriters, theater composers write music for other people to perform. As a result, they are often required to be more open to collaboration than their rock counterparts, since musical scores are regularly and sometimes drastically altered during the staging of a piece. Such compromises are not as acceptable in the rock sphere, where performers seen to maintain the most artistic control over their work are traditionally held in highest esteem.

The musical theater and rock realms differ further in their approaches to technology. While rock's myth of authenticity has managed to accept and even to encompass technological advances, musical theater has traditionally been resistant to them. In the theater, technology is largely viewed as a necessary evil that has worked to attract wider audiences, but has also made theater too much like cinema by placing undue emphasis on spectacle and driving a wedge between performers and audiences.

Finally, two very important differences between rock and musical theater are found in their particular performative approaches and in the behaviors of their audiences. While rock concerts and theatrical productions are both carefully rehearsed and staged, there is ultimately more need for accuracy and precision in the latter than in the former. As a result, rock concerts often seem more spontaneous and its performers more "genuine" when compared with staged rock musicals.

In the same light, although more young people are attending the theater in recent years, and rock music is now half a century old, the theater nevertheless remains associated with older people and more restrained behavior, while rock continues to be associated with younger people and more rebellious behavior. Rock critic Evelyn McDonnell suggests further that extant gender stereotypes play a role in influencing the rock world's often strongly negative view of the musical theater, in that the stereotypical association of rock with straight, idealized masculinity clashes with the stereotypical association of musical theater with gay men.[35]

These young/old, legitimate/artificial, and straight/gay associations are often evoked in the press, in marketing departments, and among rock fans and musical theater aficionados. McDonnell acknowledges that most rock journalists and industry members disregard rock musicals as "corny" and "inauthentic."[36] Indeed, Don Summa, press agent for *Rent,* notes that despite his best efforts and the monumental success of the show, he failed to stir interest among members of the music industry when he tried to shop the show's songs around to recording artists in hopes of promoting the musical via radio airplay. He was also unable to generate interest at *Rolling Stone.* Although the magazine ran a fashion spread featuring cast members of *Rent* early in its run, a ten-thousand-word feature about the musical was bumped to Wenner's general entertainment magazine, *Us Weekly,* after editors decided that there was "no room" for it in *Rolling Stone.*[37]

The notion that musical theater is not as "authentic" or as socially acceptable as rock is regularly echoed among fans of both genres. Some musical theater aficionados view a successful rock musical as lending legitimacy to their genre. Press agent Tom D'Ambrosio, for example, touches on the discomfort he felt as a self-described "musical theater queen" in explaining his appreciation for *Rent* and the Off Broadway production of *Hedwig and the Angry Inch* (1998):

Growing up, I thought I was the biggest musical theater queen there is. I come to New York and realize I'm the furthest thing from it—well not the furthest, but there are bigger queens than me. I completely flipped for *Rent*. I loved it. And *Hedwig* was a musical that I was not embarrassed about liking a lot. This gets into liking musicals. For me there's always been a little shame involved with it, you know what I mean? Buying a show-tune CD is like buying pornography. You go ahead and buy a Prince CD too, just so you can be like, "I'm kind of cool—and *that's* for my mother." There's a weird legitimizing feel with *Rent*. With *Rent* it was the same as with *Hedwig*—I was like, "You *have* to see it, it's *great!*" and I wasn't embarrassed to be like that, and I think partly it's because of the music. Because the music is—if I had a CD of *Hedwig* and I sent it to my brother, who doesn't go to the theater, he'd like it. So there's part of—"Oh, I can finally like rock music like I'm supposed to," for me at least.[38]

Such perceptions are rarely challenged. Rock musicians seldom involve themselves with musical theater projects, in large part because the risks far outweigh the benefits. Performing in a musical is certainly not economically advantageous for prominent rock musicians; as Pete Townshend has noted, "when it comes down to it, the prospect of going onto Broadway and being paid $50,000 a week to do eight shows is not a prospect that the modern wanky little pop star thinks he wants."[39] Rock musicians who do emerge as performers or collaborators in musical theater productions usually do so for one of two principal reasons: either their careers have slowed, as in the case of Joan Jett and Sebastian Bach, who appeared on Broadway in *Jekyll and Hyde* (1997) and *The Rocky Horror Show* (2000) respectively, and who both reached the heights of success as performers in the 1980s; or they are in the latter stages of long and fruitful careers, and are thus in little danger of harming their images by trying their hands at such projects, as in the cases of Pete Townshend, Paul Simon, Elton John, and Billy Joel.

The presence of such performers in the musical theater realm reinforces the idea of the musical theater as a site for older people, where popular musicians appear only after they age or see their recording careers falter. Producer Tom Viertel notes,

What we are seeing in the theater are some former pop writers who are flirting with or working on musicals. Barry Manilow has a musical,

Elton John has obviously written for the form, and Billy Joel . . . I consider all three of those guys past it in terms of what's on the playlist—
this is something that they turn to. And part of it is how old they are.
They are now the age at which people start to go to the musical theater.
And these guys are probably finding themselves at the musical theater
more often than they used to and thinking, well, gee, maybe there's
something for me in here. Paul Simon wrote *Capeman,* that kind of
thing. In terms of *today's* rock musicians writing for the theater, we
aren't seeing any of that, and I don't think the theater would know what
to make of it if they did.[40]

The association of musical theater with the middle-aged is reinforced in
comments like one made by Paul Stanley, singer and guitarist for the
group Kiss, who on the occasion of the band's retirement told *Us Weekly,*
"when this is over, I'll be doing Broadway."[41]

Of course, the notion that musical theater is somehow inherently less
fashionable a genre than rock is due in large part to exposure, economics,
and history. As genres more suitable to sound recording than musical theater, rock 'n' roll and its offshoots have proven internationally influential
since the 1950s, while the musical theater continues to be seen in many
circles as decidedly old hat. These lasting perceptions cause particular
difficulties for staged rock musicals. While the most successful ones are
lauded by theater critics, embraced by theatergoers, and celebrated by
members of the theater industry, they are just as often savaged or ignored
by the rock press, pigeonholed by the music industry, and mocked sight-
unseen by many rock fans.

In terms of reception, rock musicals are thus forced into a corner: they
are inevitably aimed at two different camps that do not share the same
aesthetic values and do not entirely understand one another. Making
matters worse is the fact that trends in rock and popular music tend to
elapse much faster than those in the musical theater. In discussing *Rent,*
for example, Clifford Lee Johnson III, director of the musical theater program at Manhattan Theatre Club, notes, "*Rent* came out in the mid-
nineties, and that music was already, like, ten years old, to tell you the
truth. It's funny, when they said, 'This is the rock musical for the kids,'
well, when I talk to 'the kids'—even *I* can tell that that music was ten years
old."[42] Indeed, it often takes so long to develop, workshop, and launch a
stage musical that relying too heavily on any specific popular music trend

can be disastrous, since, as Mark Steyn writes, "by the time you've got your grunge musical up on stage, grunge will be out and splurge will be in."[43]

Furthermore, while there is some overlap, audiences, journalists, and industry personnel affiliated with one camp do not regularly involve themselves with the other. When they do, they often lack the tools and expertise to properly convey what they are seeing. As Theodore Gracyk writes, "standards for evaluating rock will only have importance for those who have a personal investment in the continuation of that musical culture."[44] In this light, theater critics may not be adept at determining what is or is not a successful use of rock music on the stage, just as their rock counterparts are not ideal evaluators of the musical theater. Yet rock musicals are almost always assigned to theater critics, in part because the rock press continually shows little interest in them.

Michael Cerveris, who originated the title role in *The Who's Tommy* (1993) and replaced John Cameron Mitchell in the title role of *Hedwig and the Angry Inch*, argues that the hesitancy on the part of rock journalists is the result of their insistence on embracing and perpetuating rock's connection to authenticity.

The rock press are very slow to give the nod to any kind of rock musical, partly because they never would want to look like they were being establishment, or condoning the marketing of rock 'n' roll into old people's culture, which is how theater, wherever it is, is perceived. Maybe they just don't see it as legitimate and think it's something of a cop-out. I know that in the music business, *Tommy* was perceived as that. People would come see it and find that they actually enjoyed it, but they would go with a lot of skepticism. I loved when they came and walked away fans of it. I think they also came and walked away feeling confirmed in their suspicions, or they didn't show up at all, and those people did not seek me out to tell me how much they didn't like it—which I appreciated. Part of it is that rock 'n' roll pretends to be so much about authenticity. The rock press pretends that rock 'n' roll is about authenticity, and really *being* there, man. The truth of the matter is that it's all business. But the press has so much invested in pretending it's *not* a show that it's really hard for them to embrace something that *is* a show.[45]

Don Summa agrees. As a press agent in charge of a number of nontraditional musical theater pieces, he regularly finds himself in the unenviable position of "trying to get people to cover theater who don't go to the theater, and who don't know theater, and who don't have any sense of theater," which often proves a futile exercise.[46]

Such an exercise, however, is deemed necessary by those who hope to attract audiences beyond those who regularly follow theater reviews. Press agent Tom D'Ambrosio recalls working long hours trying to convince members of the rock press to review *Hedwig and the Angry Inch,* as well as to come up with new ways of attracting people who do not usually attend musicals but who might nevertheless enjoy *Hedwig.* According to D'Ambrosio, "So many music critics do not go to the theater. They live in New York City, and they've never been to the theater! They laugh at the theater. They don't care."[47] Up against surprising rigidity, D'Ambrosio learned that bridging the gap between camps is extraordinarily difficult.

Press agent James LL. Morrison, who supervised D'Ambrosio's work on *Hedwig,* adds that watching D'Ambrosio's struggles to build *Hedwig's* audiences helped him realize that at least in this respect, journalists are highly representative of the taste cultures they ostensibly epitomize. "We are discovering that there isn't a crossover, just as there isn't a crossover for us," he explains. "We're theater people. How often do we go to see dance? When is the last time I went to the symphony? To a gallery opening? If someone goes to hear bands and is really up on who plays where and when, *that's* the way they're spending their entertainment dollar."[48] D'Ambrosio and Morrison eventually found that at least during the early run of *Hedwig,* they could attract audiences by focusing less on trying to get coverage in the rock press and more on the illicit practice of "sniping," or handing out flyers at local clubs and spray-painting or stickering the show's logo on sidewalks, bathroom walls, the backseats of taxi cabs, and scaffolding facades in and around New York City.[49]

The few tidbits that do appear about rock musicals in the rock press are the result of a great deal of hard work, often mixed with sheer luck. Michael Cerveris explains, for example, that the interest *Rolling Stone* took in *Hedwig and the Angry Inch* was the result not only of persistence by publicists, but of Cerveris's friendship with Pete Townshend. In response to a question about a photograph that appeared in *Rolling Stone* of him and Townshend sitting together backstage at the Jane Street Theater, Cerveris says,

> That *Rolling Stone* thing, that "Random Notes" photo? There was nothing random about it. It was the result of a lot of hard work from the show's publicist, and a friend of mine who is also a publicist who has friends at *Rolling Stone* and who worked very hard to get them to come see the show. They were still sort of taking their time and dragging their heels until Pete was coming, and *then* suddenly it was something that was worth checking out. A couple nights later, Jann Wenner, the founder of *Rolling Stone,* came to see the show.[50]

At least in this case, attendance by a respected rock musician helped legitimize the production for the rock press.

In keeping with the notion that rock musicals are inauthentic and unworthy of a true rock fan's attentions, the coverage of rock musicals by rock and theater journalists alike is often notably defensive. Emphasis is almost always placed on convincing readers from both camps that the particular piece being discussed is worth seeing, even though all other representatives of the genre from which it emanates are not. Favorable comparisons of the rock musical with its predecessors are ubiquitous, as are proclamations like "Broadway finally got a rock musical right"[51] and "at long last the authentic rock musical that has eluded Broadway for two generations . . ."[52] The pieces about *Hedwig* that did appear in the rock press were no different. In *Billboard,* Jim Bessman proclaimed that *Hedwig* was the "rare rock musical that works,"[53] while David Fricke of *Rolling Stone* insisted, "In the whole, long, sorry history of rock musicals, *Hedwig and the Angry Inch* is the first one that truly *rocks,*" especially since it "was born a million miles away from the Broadway sugar of *Rent.*"[54] Andrew Dansby, also of *Rolling Stone,* took an even harsher potshot, calling *Hedwig* a "great white shark to *Rent*'s sickly guppie."[55] Finally, Zev Borow of *Spin* called *Hedwig* "glammy, rock-inspired theater for people who think glammy, rock-inspired theater sucks."[56]

The Theater Press and Industry Reacts to Rock

The defensiveness that is often detectable when members of the rock press discuss staged rock musicals is often matched by a palpable elitism from the theater press corps. While there exists a strong interest in attracting young, enthusiastic audiences to the mainstream theater, there exists simultaneously a significant amount of snobbery among members of the theater industry and press. Such snobbery implies that even decades since rock 'n' roll's inception, the popular music audience tends on the whole to be crass, stupid, or uneducated as to proper theater behavior.

The tradition, in the American popular press, of using condescension to educate potential audiences about proper behavior—thereby implying that theater audiences are divided between sophisticated "insiders" and boorish "outsiders" who should either learn proper behavior or stay home—predates rock 'n' roll by at least a century. Through the nineteenth century, for example, magazines and theater memoirs regularly featured "green'un" stories, which focused on unsophisticated theatergoers who reacted to the actions on stage as if they were real—thus for example shouting threats at the villain, or leaping to the stage to come to the aid of an imperiled heroine—much to the smug amusement of the rest of the audience.[57]

The underlying condescension of green'un stories is still perceptible in contemporary theater journalism. In 1991, for example, Alex Witchel of the *New York Times* was so appalled by the behavior of a talkative spectator during one performance at an Off Broadway house that she published an article listing rules of behavior for theater audiences. These included admonishments about chewing gum and wearing too much perfume, as well as a patronizing reminder to readers that the theater is not one's den at home, where, in front of one's own television, "you can say anything that comes into your head." Like the green'un stories, Witchel's underlying message was that "it is the height of disrespect to impose yourself on the show or anyone watching it."[58]

Witchel's lofty tone matches that of *New York Times* critic Ben Brantley, who, in a 1999 article about Broadway and London's West End, characterized contemporary theater audiences as stubbornly anaesthetized and unwilling to attend challenging theatrical productions.[59] The implication, here—that problems in the mainstream theater are largely the fault of its audience—is, in turn, also evident in a *New York Times* article in 2000 about new musicals, in which theater writer Ethan Mordden is quoted as calling current audiences "stupid," "lazy," and thus incapable of appreciating "sophisticated" musical theater scores.[60]

This inherent snobbery is especially noticeable when it comes to rock musicals, many of which are produced in the hopes of attracting broader audiences than those who typically attend the theater. While this new audience is strongly desired in theater circles, it is often simultaneously looked down upon by journalists and industry members alike. The treatment in the press of the audience at *The Who's Tommy* (1993) is a case in point.

Shortly after *The Who's Tommy* opened, gossip about the rowdy crowds flocking to the St. James Theater began to circulate among members of the press and theater industry. Within days of the musical's premiere, Margalit Fox of *Newsday* wrote:

> It was a quiet night Wednesday at "The Who's Tommy." Only a few people in the audience sang along. Nobody threw up. Visit the St. James Theater on a weekend, however, and it's a different story. Fridays and Saturdays, observers say, audience members at the new musical based on The Who's 1969 rock opera are apt to be more familiar with Madison Square Garden than the Great White Way. "You see guys with long hair and leather jackets and studs and you tend to think they're not your average Broadway audience," said Wendy Wright, one of the St. James ushers, who's seen it all since previews began March 29. "Some of them don't know how to act in a Broadway theater. Occasionally, they're a bit drunk and throw up. Some of them have to be restrained from singing along." Onstage and off, it is more than a little like going to a rock concert.[61]

Michael David of the production company Dodger Theatricals was quoted later in the article as saying, "what I think has happened is we have been able to introduce the nontraditional theatergoers into this new 'club' called Broadway," and thus to convince people "to come to an address they're not familiar with: 'There's this club on 44th street and you've gotta try it out.'"[62] The condescension inherent in the "insider" view of the very audience that *The Who's Tommy* was staged to attract is evident here. The producers seemed hopeful that the production would attract a large crossover audience, members of which were then scorned once they dared to act too much like actual fans of the music.

Unsurprisingly, rock composers and performers involved in musical theater productions often find themselves caught between two worlds, neither of which fully accepts them. Adam Pascal, an aspiring rock singer whose raw energy and vocal quality earned him the role of Roger in the original cast of *Rent,* had misgivings about taking the part, and such misgivings were warranted: although his work in *Rent* helped establish him as a successful musical theater performer, his appearance in the musical hurt his chances of winning the attentions of record executives. Despite the local success, post-*Rent,* of his rock band, Pascal found himself pigeonholed by the record industry. Although his band had earned a strong following and frequently appeared before large audiences in the New York area, "a lot of rock people, producers and managers, looked at me and said 'He's a theater guy.' We couldn't get them to come hear us."[63]

Indeed, simply being associated with the musical theater can be seen as potentially harmful to a rock musician's reputation as an uncompromising artist. Take, for example, the case of Joan Jett, who originated the role of Columbia in the 2000 Broadway revival of *The Rocky Horror Show,* but refused to take part in the cast album "when it became apparent that she would not have creative control over her performance on the record."[64] Evoking the image of the rock musician as ever-faithful to his or her artistic vision, Jett's manager, Kenny Laguna, told the press, "We had a deal, they chose not to live up to it, and they found out that real rock ['n'] roll doesn't work that way."[65]

2 ♣ HAIR and Its Imitators

HAIR WAS NOT BORN ON BROADWAY. Nurtured in the experimental realm of Off-Off-Broadway, the musical had an eight-week run as the inaugural production at the Public Theater, and then ran at a midtown discotheque before being retooled and reopened at the Biltmore on Broadway in 1968. Such a move is not atypical. In a strategy that continues to be popular among producers, shows that open Off Broadway to positive reviews and strong ticket sales are often hurried uptown and reopened on larger, more profitable stages. Yet the critical and commercial success of its first run notwithstanding, *Hair* very nearly never made it uptown at all.

An understanding of *Hair*'s development, and its transformation from the fringe to the mainstream, is contingent upon an understanding of the relationship between Off Broadway and Broadway at the time. New York City had been home to many theater companies that existed beyond the shimmer of Broadway since early twentieth century. But Off and Off-Off-Broadway theater companies began to exert their strongest influences, and to most directly challenge conventions imposed by the mainstream theater, in the decades immediately following World War II. The term *Off Broadway* was, in fact, not coined until the early 1950s, at a time when the power of fringe theater in New York City was about to peak.

The term has since been used to describe theaters and theater companies that are geographically removed from the commercial Broadway houses in Times Square, and that strive to offer productions that are both artistically riskier and less expensive to produce than their Broadway counterparts. The term *Off-Off-Broadway* was coined in the early 1960s. Off-Off-Broadway theaters and companies generally share geographical territory with Off Broadway houses, but are often even less commercial and more experimental. At both a physical and a philosophical distance from Times Square, Off and Off-Off-Broadway companies have devoted themselves to developing and performing innovative, experimental work in alternative spaces, including the black-box theaters, cafés, churches, parking lots, garages, lofts, and basements of lower Manhattan.[1]

The attempts, Off and Off-Off-Broadway, to challenge the commercial theater gained momentum through the late 1950s and early 1960s. In the 1960s, when Broadway was at a creative and economic standstill, the cheap performance spaces and lack of interest in star power proved highly beneficial for New York's alternative theater scene. Further, unlike the commercial theater, the fringe was invigorated by the antiwar movement and the influence of the counterculture. Various forms of "protest theater" proliferated in the 1960s and early 1970s, as members of the fringe pondered the role of theater in an increasingly tumultuous, divided nation.[2]

Many Off-Off-Broadway companies active at the time grew interested in making social and political statements. Several reflected the influence of directors like Jerzy Grotowski, whose works were designed to enhance the relationship between performer and spectator, and Julian Beck and Judith Malina, whose Living Theatre attempted to blend political and aesthetic radicalism.[3] The works of such directors and their followers included attempts at breaking the fourth wall (or imagined barrier between audience and performer), extending the realm of what the mainstream had deemed theatrical, and using theatrical events to comment on social and political issues. Because members of the New Left and the counterculture, with which rock music had become associated, were involved in the alternative theater scene in New York in the 1960s, it is no coincidence that the rock musical in general, and *Hair* in particular, would take root in this place and time.

Hair was written by two young New York–based actors: James Rado (b. 1932) and Gerome Ragni (1935–91). A Broadway veteran, Rado turned his back on the commercial theater in favor of more experimental projects in the mid-1960s. Ragni was similarly lured from the mainstream; he became actively involved with Joseph Chaikin's Open Theater—which took a nonhierarchical, communal approach to theatrical production—from its inception in 1963.[4] In fact, the Open Theater's 1966 production *Viet Rock*, developed by director Megan Terry and a group of actors that included Gerome Ragni, directly influenced *Hair*.

Viet Rock premiered at Café La MaMa on Armed Forces Day (May 21).[5] During weekly workshops in 1965 and 1966, the company performed improvisations based on newspaper, television, and firsthand accounts of war-related activities in the United States and Vietnam, and eventually built a full-length show around the resultant material.[6] When not in rehearsals for the piece, Gerome Ragni, along with James Rado, got into the habit of spending time with a group of Greenwich Village hippies. Borrowing techniques learned during Ragni's experiences with *Viet Rock,* Ragni and Rado recorded their observations and experiences in the Village, and used them as the raw material for *Hair.*[7]

The plot of *Viet Rock*—in which a group of young men are inducted into the army, sent to Vietnam, and killed—is similar to that of *Hair.*[8] Further, both pieces emphasized spirituality, which helped connect one scene to the next: *Viet Rock's* underlying narrative stresses the passage from birth to death and then to rebirth,[9] while production notes for *Hair* emphasize "the spiritual theme running through the play; outer space, astrology, the earth, the heavens, interplanetary travel, mysticism."[10]

While not technically a musical, *Viet Rock* featured six incidental songs that were clearly inspired by the socially conscious folk-rock popular at the time. The title song, for example, includes notes directing the actors to perform the song in a "Dylanesque drone-like" way.[11] Handwritten notes on the original transcriptions of the songs indicate that they were performed on electric or acoustic guitar, harmonica, snare drum, "Eastern percussions" and, in one case, "possibly a trumpet."[12] Many of the songs are blues-based, and almost all of them have stridently antiwar lyrics. Composed by Marianne de Pury, who attended the workshops during which *Viet Rock* was developed, the songs, like the show itself, were the result of a collaborative process.[13]

In spite of—or, perhaps, because of—their commitment to experimental theater in general, and their interest in collaborative theater in particular, Rado and Ragni had hoped from the outset that *Hair* would run on Broadway. "We wanted to make it as authentic as possible, and we were very aware that this was the audience we were going to reach," remembers Rado. "That's why the original impulse was to write it for Broadway. We didn't want to just preach to the colored folks, to the Off-Off-Broadway scene. We wanted to bring the whole message and the scene uptown to a wider audience."[14] This plan was initially quashed after Ragni and Rado shopped an early draft of *Hair* around to various Broadway producers, all of whom rejected it. Temporarily abandoning their plan for a Broadway run, Rado and Ragni approached the Off Broadway producer Joseph Papp, who was struck by the social relevance of their show. Papp selected the musical to be the inaugural production at his new not-for-profit Public Theater. His sole stipulation was that Ragni and Rado, who had written lyrics for the show but as yet no music, find a composer.[15]

Given the fact that theater composers had experienced more bad luck than good in adapting rock music for the stage, it is fitting that the first fully realized rock musical to make it on Broadway would be composed by an outsider. Galt MacDermot, whom Ragni and Rado hired to write the music for *Hair,* came upon the project coincidentally. "I met Ragni and Rado through a mutual friend—Nat Shapiro, who was a publisher and a publicist," MacDermot recalls. "I was strictly from jazz, and rock 'n' roll, and rhythm and blues. I was making a living at the time playing demo records and stuff in the city. I knew nothing about the theater. But I had been bugging Nat to get me some kind of a project. So he just put us together. It took him a long time, 'cause they were pretty far-out guys, and he didn't know how we'd get along. But we got along fine."[16]

Within two weeks of joining the project, MacDermot had written the score. With Papp's stipulation met, *Hair* was cast and staged by Gerald Freeman, the Public Theater's artistic director. The musical opened for a limited, eight-week engagement at the Public's three-hundred-seat Anspacher Theater on December 2, 1967.[17]

During this initial run, *Hair* captured the interest of Michael Butler, a young, Chicago-based liberal whose family had built a sizable fortune in paper mills and real estate in Illinois. Butler attended the first preview and was so impressed by what he saw that he secured the first-class rights to *Hair* once Papp let them expire.[18] Butler initially attempted to bring *Hair* to Broadway as soon as its run at the Public ended, but was unable to secure a theater. Not wanting the show to lose momentum, he moved the production to the Cheetah, a rundown discotheque at Forty-fifth Street and Broadway that was about to be torn down. *Hair* ran for forty-five performances at the Cheetah while Butler courted Broadway theater owners.

Butler's task was not an easy one. Most of the theater owners he approached were either unimpressed by the musical, or offended by its subject matter, or both. "Nobody wanted to have it in their theater," Galt MacDermot recalls. "The Shuberts wouldn't and the other ones wouldn't. We had to go to a guy, sort of a renegade guy, at Forty-seventh Street, who just owned that one theater."[19] The "renegade guy" in question was David

Cogan, who owned the Biltmore Theater on Forty-seventh Street between Broadway and Eighth Avenue. As luck would have it, Cogan was a close friend of Michael Butler's father, Paul, who convinced Cogan to open the Biltmore's doors to the homeless production.[20] Once the theater had been secured, a new director—Tom O'Horgan, long associated with Off-Off-Broadway's innovative Café La MaMa—was brought in to recast and retool *Hair* in preparation for its Broadway opening.

The musical's creative team struck a successful balance between the traditional and the experimental, in both theatrical and musical terms. Although vastly different musicals, *Hair* can be compared with *Bye Bye Birdie* in this respect. In *Bye Bye Birdie,* innovation—in the form of rock 'n' roll songs, however parodied—was offered in small, careful doses, and offset with comparatively traditional theater music, plot, and direction. While *Hair*'s subject matter, music, and structure were much riskier, it too offered a blend of inventiveness on one hand, and tradition on the other. *Hair*'s chief influences came from the experimental realm, but it was also influenced by past Broadway musicals.

In *The Age of "Hair": Evolution and Impact of Broadway's First Rock Musical,* Barbara Lee Horn argues that the de-emphasis on plot development and reliance on integrated song and dance bring *Hair* into the realm of what theater critic Martin Gottfried termed "concept musicals" and John Bush Jones has since renamed "fragmented musicals": sophisticated productions that de-emphasize the book, and rely instead on music and movement to tell a story or elaborate on a unifying theme.[21] The concept or fragmented musical would come to dominate the Broadway stage during the 1970s and early 1980s, especially following the critical adulation of Stephen Sondheim's *Company* in 1970 and Marvin Hamlisch's *A Chorus Line* in 1976.[22]

Hair, like these aforementioned works, was a musical in which the plot and characters tended to be "generated by attitudes and perceptions rather than the reverse."[23] Rado, who grew up with a passion for the musical theater, remembers that he and Ragni were more interested in depicting a specific group of people at a particular point in time than they were in creating a conventional musical:

We were trying to capture the essence of the movement. We really believed in it—we really loved what was happening. In the case of *Hair,* we were very aware of breaking the form of a musical. We were audacious because *Hair* was the first book show we had written. We proceeded to sort of demolish the book, or bring in twice or three times as much music and still maintain the characters. We were exploring, we were open to changing and rewriting and finding out what worked for us. There *was* a story line, even though some people thought there wasn't—and we just knew this was a new form of the musical.[24]

In comparison with more traditional musicals, the narrative of *Hair* was so loose, and the musical numbers—thirty-two in all—so abundant that many critics described *Hair* as devoid of story. For example, Clive Barnes of the *New York Times* wrote, "the authors of the dowdy book—and brilliant lyrics—have done a very brave thing. They have in fact done away with it altogether. *Hair* is now a musical with a theme, not with a story."[25]

It is certainly easy to mistake *Hair* for a musical with no cohesive story, since it consists largely of interrelated vignettes, during which the musical's many characters examine various countercultural concerns. Loosely connected songs and sketches explore drug and sexual experimentation, Eastern spiritual and religious practices, the civil rights movement, class issues, the generation gap, and the Vietnam War. Uniting these vignettes, however, is a cohesive, albeit somewhat skeletal, plot: Claude Hooper Bukowski, a young man who flees his parents' middle-class home in Queens for the hippie enclave of Greenwich Village, debates whether or not he should burn his draft card or go to Vietnam. He weighs this conundrum while spending time with his friends, fighting with his parents, and pining after Sheila, a politically active student at New York University. In the end, Claude goes to Vietnam, where he is killed. The musical ends as his friends gather to celebrate his life and mourn his untimely, senseless death. Thus, while *Hair* does have a cohesive plot, it nevertheless departs from the comparatively straightforward structure of the traditional musical. It departs further from convention in its reliance on techniques that came to fruition Off and Off-Off-Broadway during the 1950s and 1960s.

The general influence of Off-Off-Broadway theater, for example, is evidenced in the musical's regular negation of the fourth wall. Fourth-wall breaks had become characteristic of many fringe productions by 1968, but were still relatively unusual on Broadway, especially when it came to the musical theater. Upon entering the Biltmore Theater during the run of *Hair*, audiences were thus confronted by something rather novel: a bare stage, stripped to the wings, on which members of the company were dressing and putting on makeup in preparation for the performance.[26] Other cast members, already in character, were scattered throughout the house. "They were there, lying, sleeping in the aisles," Tom O'Horgan remembers with a chuckle. "You had to step over them. There were actors in people's seats—sometimes they would take somebody and put them in the wrong seat. And so you never quite knew when the show started, and that's what I wanted to happen. As if it were going on forever."[27] Original cast member Natalie Mosco adds that as a result of the fourth-wall breaks, *Hair* became "almost a show within a show, which gave us the license to perform and to acknowledge that we were performing."[28] As they were at many an Off-Off-Broadway production, audiences at *Hair* were thus encouraged to view the performers simultaneously as characters and as the actors embodying them.

Breaking the fourth wall, especially on Broadway, had great symbolic importance for Tom O'Horgan. "It's hard to understand now why it seemed so important then, but there was an incredible urge and need to do it," he remembers. "You would sit in the audience and you would just suffocate. The lights would go down, and you could feel yourself beginning to get nauseous. There was even one theater where they used to pump perfume into the audience. You felt you just had to break through that—it was an emotional reaction to something the body simply didn't want to do."[29]

O'Horgan's use of fourth-wall breaks in *Hair* certainly resonated with critics. Clive Barnes wrote in the *New York Times* that he was thrilled by O'Horgan's "irreverent, occasionally irrelevant staging."[30] On the other hand, John Chapman of the *New York Daily News* clearly would have preferred being sprayed with perfume: "The best title for the show would be 'The Dirty Foot-Follies,'" he wrote, "for hardly anybody in this twitchy, itchy extravaganza wears shoes and they all kept running up and down the center aisle waving their calluses at me."[31]

Perhaps *Hair*'s biggest debt to fringe theater lay in the decidedly unorthodox ways that its creative team cast and rehearsed the company. During the audition period, Ragni, Rado, MacDermot, and O'Horgan were less interested in professionalism than they were in finding actors who could interpret the material realistically. "We were looking for the real thing," O'Horgan says, "but the kids who did it at the Public were like glossy print kids—regular kids that they dressed up like hippies. It was pretty awful. But we finally got a cast together."[32] Much of the difficulty lay in finding actors who could sing rock music convincingly. A number of actors who appeared in *Hair* remember auditioning with rock songs, a practice that was unheard of on Broadway at the time. For example, original cast member Marjorie LiPari earned a role in the chorus (known as "the tribe") after performing a Beatles song at her audition;[33] Heather MacRae, who replaced original cast member Diane Keaton eight months into the run, is perhaps the first actor in history to audition for a Broadway show with Jefferson Airplane's 1967 hit "White Rabbit."[34]

Once the cast had been chosen, the creative staff watched the performers to make sure that they were bonding properly, and made adjustments when bonding did not occur. Natalie Mosco remembers,

> We had two people, a boy and a girl, who were in rehearsals on the first two or three days, and they were fired. And it was not because they were bad—it was just because they did not fit into the tribe. And I did not realize then, but obviously they had overcast and were planning to fire, just to see who meshed. And the guy, who was probably a terrific guy, had a slightly English accent, and he kept talking about Paul Scofield being a great actor. He obviously did not fit in. The girl later became very famous playing a cello naked. It was very interesting though—why did they keep me instead of someone else? I don't know. I do know that we did a lot of bonding exercises and a lot of tribal stuff.[35]

Many members of the Broadway company remember that rehearsals were more befitting an Off-Off-Broadway show than one typical of Broadway. Marjorie LiPari, who, like O'Horgan, had been affiliated with La MaMa before being cast in *Hair*, likens rehearsals to an exhilarating period of collaboration: "Tom [O'Horgan] had a strong vision of what he wanted, but he gave us a lot of permission to move and figure out ways that we would go. It was very freeing and challenging creatively. We were moving in a realm that was very different than what average theater was about."[36] Similarly, Mosco, who had trained as a ballet dancer and attended the American Academy of Dramatic Arts before being cast in *Hair*, remembers that the rehearsals for *Hair* were radically different from rehearsals for anything else she's been involved with, before or since:

> Maybe I was handed a script, but I don't think it mattered, since we didn't look at it. We did sensitivity exercises where we took people on

journeys. At one point, [fellow cast member] Paul Jabara was at Variety Arts Studios hanging out the window, and he opened his eyes and screamed. There were a lot of trust exercises, bonding exercises, relaxation exercises. I remember, once we stood around in a circle, and Tom wanted us to hang there, letting our jaws hang loose until we all drooled on the floor, because he didn't want that control. Other times we did—especially because it was the late sixties and a very important time for civil rights—a lot of black-and-white bonding. The show was totally integrated. It had to be.[37]

Rehearsals differed further from those for more traditional musicals due to an emphasis on improvisation, much of which was subsequently scripted and incorporated into the production.[38] The show's resultant loose, spontaneous feel not only encouraged continued bonding among cast members, it also had a strong impact on many audience members. For example, Tom O'Horgan remembers that during the run of *Hair* in London's West End, "people began to just come up onstage and start dancing with the cast at the end of the show. Nobody asked them to, they just did it. I thought that was amazing, so we put it into every production after that."[39]

While such alternative ways of creating theater were unique to the Broadway musical, it should be noted they were not entirely new to Broadway plays. Works by innovative playwrights like Pinter, Ionesco, and Beckett were appearing on Broadway as early as the middle to late 1950s, and experimental directors followed suit by the mid-1960s. As a result, while *Hair*'s staging was cited by many critics as particularly innovative, a greater number argued that *Hair*'s score was what made the musical especially groundbreaking.

During the 1960s, while Broadway composers were still struggling with the earliest forms of rock 'n' roll, the music began to evolve into what is known simply as "rock." This term refers to a much broader, often more musically sophisticated genre, which became linked with the social and political turmoil of the time. Rock departs from rock 'n' roll in many respects. More dependent on electronic sound generation, amplification, and distortion, the style moves beyond the twelve-bar-blues form, and borrows from a wider variety of forms and structures. Rock lyrics are more likely than rock 'n' roll lyrics to reflect social or political issues; also, they tend more often to deal with personal experiences, which are often described in intentionally introspective or obscure language. Although rock continues to rely, as rock 'n' roll did, primarily on guitars, bass guitars, and drums for its execution, its instrumentation is generally more varied; rock musicians are thus more likely than their rock 'n' roll forerunners to experiment with and incorporate folk, symphonic, or non-Western instruments into their work.[40]

By the time *Hair* reached Broadway, rock 'n' roll had developed into a more musically, lyrically, and structurally sophisticated genre. It is no wonder, then, that as the 1960s wore on, rock and theater had begun to reflect some mutual influences, which were especially apparent on the one hand in theatrical experiments known as "happenings,"[41] and on the other in rock concerts that began to make more conscious use of visual imagery. In New York City in 1966, for example, the experimental rock group Velvet Underground became the house band at Andy Warhol's Factory, as well as a key ingredient in his mixed-media happening, the Exploding Plastic Inevitable. On the West Coast at roughly the same time, the psychedelic bands popular in California's Bay Area were bringing a new theatrical flair to live performances by playing to the accompaniment of slide and film projections, and colored- or strobe-light displays. Although it continued to elude Broadway, then, rock music had found the fringe theater, and vice versa, by the middle of the decade.

In rehearsals for *Hair,* the creative team emphasized a collective approach to music making. In marked contrast to a traditional Broadway pit band—which is usually rehearsed separately and brought in to work with the company a week or two before the preview period begins—the band members joined the cast during the length of *Hair*'s rehearsal period. As Natalie Mosco remembers, the result was a production that *Hair* grew out of intense collaboration among musicians, actors, and the creative team:

> Galt [MacDermot] would just let everyone sing. And we were basically allowed to make up our own—and then if Galt liked what we made up, we kept it. Actors like Leata Galloway had five octaves. So Galt would turn around and say, "Leata, can you give it one of your dog notes, one of your freak notes?" Or, "Could you give me a wail, Melba [Moore]?" and that would be it. Throw something out and let people do it. Then he would give the rest of us, after we had experimented, a more solid foundation. In rehearsal, Steve [Gillette, the lead guitarist] would jam

and we would all dance. And the choreographer would go around and say, "Let's do a Marjorie LiPari step!" and we would put that into the show. I had one that was my step, which was a kick thing. And we had another one which was somebody else's. And she would grab what we were doing individually and we would all do it as a group. *Hair* came out of free-form rock, theater, and dance.[42]

The connection established between actors and musicians remained strong during the run of the musical, in large part because the musicians were never relegated to the orchestra pit beneath the stage. Instead, the band, which for the first few months was led by Galt MacDermot on keyboards, was set onstage, further intensifying the bonds between musicians, actors, and the composer. "All the musicians sat in a open pickup truck," Mosco recalls. "Steve Gillette was outside the door with his foot on the stage, leaning against that truck, playing the guitar. So he was as much a part of us as he was a part of the band. He bridged that gap."[43]

Hair reflects the fact that rock music had matured significantly, both musically and lyrically, in its first decade of existence. A rich array of maturing popular American musical styles are woven into the musical's score, from the funky, soul-infused "Aquarius," to the Motown-inspired "Black Boys/White Boys," to the free-form jam of "Walking in Space," to the psychedelia-tinged "Donna" and "Be-In." MacDermot's use of a variety of styles distinguishes his score from previous composers' attempts at bringing rock music to the Broadway stage by simply featuring recurring bass-lines or repetitive lyrics that parodied rock 'n' roll.

Many of the songs in *Hair* had lyrics that commented on topical political and social issues including the Vietnam War ("Three-Five-Zero-Zero"), drug use ("Hashish," "Walking in Space"), free love ("Black Boys/White Boys," "Sodomy"), and the generation gap ("Hair"). The score featured a number of introspective, confessional songs that have less to do with plot development than with the emotional state of the characters ("Easy to Be Hard"; "Where Do I Go"); other song lyrics are densely poetic and ambiguous ("The Flesh Failures"), or even playfully incoherent ("Good Morning Starshine").

What is most striking about MacDermot's score is how evenly most of the numbers blend forms that are common to Tin Pan Alley with the straightforward harmonic language and electrified instrumentation of rock. Most of the songs in the score are structured in thirty-two-bar form, which has been a mainstay on Broadway for decades. There's no conflict here: By the time *Hair* made it to the Biltmore, this form—which had been utilized by rock 'n' roll pioneers like Buddy Holly—was becoming increasingly important to rock's expanding musical vocabulary. Hence, while a quiet ballad like "Frank Mills" borrows its thirty-two-bar structure from Tin Pan Alley, its simple keyboard and guitar accompaniment, bluesy chord progressions, and confessional lyrics all reflect rock's influence.

MacDermot was praised up and down the Great White Way for doing what many had deemed impossible: capturing the sounds of current rock music while simultaneously remaining within the boundaries of what was deemed acceptable on a Broadway stage. "This is a happy show musically," Clive Barnes raved in his review of *Hair* for the *New York Times.* "Galt MacDermot's music is merely pop-rock, with strong soothing overtones of Broadway melody, but it precisely serves its purpose, and its noisy and cheerful conservatism is just right for an audience that might wince at 'Sergeant Pepper's Lonely Hearts Club Band,' while the Stones would certainly gather no pop moss. Yet . . . the show is the first Broadway musical in some time to have the authentic voice of today rather than the day before yesterday."[44]

Many of the songs from *Hair* resonated with popular music audiences as well. *Hair* remains one of the few Broadway musicals to achieve chart status in the years since the rise of rock 'n' roll. In November 1968, the original Broadway cast recording became the first to rise to number 1 on the *Billboard* album chart since *Hello, Dolly!* in 1964. Further, many of the songs from *Hair* became Top 40 hits. By 1969, radio stations across the country were airing the 5th Dimension's medley "Aquarius/Let the Sunshine In (The Flesh Failures)," Three Dog Night's "Easy to Be Hard," the Cowsills' "Hair," and Oliver's "Good Morning Starshine."[45] While the musical itself has aged poorly, many of its songs, which remain pop standards, have not.

MacDermot had been schooled in a variety of music styles, and thus differed from many Broadway composers who, firmly rooted in Tin Pan Alley, were attempting to imitate a popular style that they did not fully understand or respect. MacDermot, who studied all kinds of music during his youth in Montreal and Capetown, South Africa, rejected rigid boundaries when composing the *Hair* score, and instead drew on all of his influences. "I am not sure what rock 'n' roll really is, and I don't care," he asserts. "The important things is that no two songs in *Hair* are exactly the same. I don't feel like a rock 'n' roll composer. I studied music in Africa, so I consider myself an African composer and a West Indian composer. But I would not know how to describe my style, and I'm not interested in categories."[46]

If the score is so diverse, then, why does *Hair* hold the distinction of being the very first Broadway show to be billed as a "rock musical"? According to MacDermot, the phrase was unintentionally coined by Ragni and Rado, who subtitled their work *The American Tribal Love-Rock Musical*, with the intention of spoofing the growing trend of subcategorizing popular music styles. "In those days," MacDermot explains, "there was folk-rock, and this kind of rock, and that kind of rock. So they were making a joke about that" by coming up with the phrase "love-rock."[47] "Love-rock" never caught on in quite the way that descriptors like *folk-rock, acid rock,* and *pop rock* did, but critics picked up on the term *rock musical,* which would theretofore be applied to any show that featured even the scantest trace of popular music influence.[48]

Ragni and Rado's jokes aside, there is one rather important element of rock music performance that likely contributed to the designation of *Hair* as a rock musical: it was a lot louder than the average Broadway production, and necessarily so. Because the band members were onstage playing electrically amplified instruments, the actors needed to sing into microphones in order to be heard. Although body mikes were available by 1968, O'Horgan chose to use standard hand mikes, which were shared by the cast members.[49] Rare on Broadway stages at the time, this element of popular music performance would subsequently become commonplace, much to the chagrin of traditionalists.[50]

Because of its youthful orientation, its topical themes, its eclectic score, and its young, interracial cast, *Hair* attracted a significant number of young people, and a greater proportion of African Americans than attended most Broadway shows. According to Barbara Lee Horn,

A little more than four months after opening night at the Biltmore, *New York* magazine's George Nash conducted an informal sampling of *Hair*'s patrons. Forty-six percent were under thirty, only 13 percent were fifty or over, and 7 percent were black, all of them under thirty. The trend toward youthful audiences continued. Following the Nash survey, the *Wall Street Journal* reported the outcome of a similar head count taken in June 1969. The *Journal*'s tally revealed that one half of *Hair*'s audience was between the ages of eighteen and twenty-five, as compared to 3 percent for other Broadway productions.[51]

Hair's appeal to young, diverse audiences should not be underestimated. Almost thirty years after *Hair*'s Biltmore debut, a survey of Broadway audiences sponsored by the Theatre Development Fund found the average Broadway audience to be merely 3.7 percent African American, and predominantly middle-aged.[52]

For all of its appeal, *Hair* saw its share of controversy, especially as a result of its act 1 finale, which featured the cast reenacting a be-in and—in very dim light—stripping naked before the abrupt blackout. As a result of the much-talked-about nude scene, *Hair* had its fair share of legal scuffles. Several touring companies were picketed in Washington, D.C., and unsuccessfully targeted by concerned citizens in St. Paul, Minnesota. The Boston company faced criminal charges of obscenity after District Attorney Garrett Byrne saw a preview at the Wilbur Theatre in 1970; in 1971, the production was forced to sue for permission to stage *Hair* in a municipally owned facility in Chattanooga, Tennessee. Both the Boston and Chattanooga cases reached the U.S. Supreme Court, where the production prevailed.[53]

Although the Biltmore production of *Hair* was never the target of full-scale protests, it was frequently criticized as subversive propaganda by supporters of the war in Vietnam. One scene in particular tended to sit poorly with self-appointed flag-wavers.[54] During this scene, three characters fold an American flag military-style while singing its praises with the song "Don't Put It Down." One of the characters, stoned and mesmerized by the flag's colors, shouts, "I'm falling through a hole in the flag," and collapses. He is caught by the other two characters, who swing him in the flag as if it were hammock.

In June 1970, *Variety* reported that the Apollo 13 astronauts James A. Lovell Jr. and John L. Swigert Jr. stormed out of a performance of *Hair* before the first-act intermission, having taken offense at the scene in question.[55] While Horn has since suggested that the incident was merely a publicity stunt, actor Joseph Campbell Butler remembers that during his stint with the Biltmore company, the "Don't Put It Down" number was interrupted at least twice by infuriated patrons who interpreted the number as disrespectful to the American flag.[56]

Original cast member Marjorie LiPari remembers that regardless of whether or not the astronaut incident was genuine or not, strong reactions to the decidedly nontraditional musical were hardly out of the ordinary. "The show had an impact that was palpable," she remembers. "I always waited for someone to go 'Hmph!' and walk out. And to me that was a successful show. It happened frequently. It was not like fifteen people got up [at each performance], but maybe two."[57]

While some audience members perceived the musical as going too far, just as many seem to have felt that *Hair* did not go far enough. According to James Rado, "the intellectual side of the counterculture did not really respond well to *Hair*, which was compared to Archie comics. They thought *Hair* was too pandering or simple, or didn't express the Left's sentiments in exactly the right way."[58] Such dissent from the Left was particularly evident during a Central Park concert sponsored by Michael Butler in the spring of 1970, in celebration of the Biltmore production's second anniversary. During the event, a group of disgruntled leftists handed out leaflets "branding 'Hair' as a culture ripoff and inviting followers to the cast's own private party at the Four Seasons afterwards. 'With all the green power "Hair" promoters have taken in, has any of it come back to the people?' the leaflets asked."[59] Similar comments are occasionally found in the extensive press that covered the Broadway run of *Hair*. For example, at the end of an otherwise positive review in the *New Yorker,* one journalist wrote, "Sometimes *Hair* is disturbingly commercial—the hippie turned into just another marketable product. (For example, Wig City, in conjunction with the show, already has produced an instant male-hippie kit, complete with wig, beads, bells, incense, etc., for $29.95)."[60]

Such concerns notwithstanding, *Hair* was generally embraced as laudable at best, and harmless at least. Bill Compton, an actor and antiwar activist who lived and performed in New York during the 1960s acknowledges, "I guess *Hair* is a little sugary. But I don't think *Hair* was written for us. *Hair* was written to educate the masses *about* us."[61] Indeed, as Gerald Bordman writes, "for many staid, older playgoers in the audience, *Hair* allowed a brief, vicarious participation in the protest movements of the sixties."[62]

Hair's position in time helps explain its broad appeal. By the close of the decade, the youth culture that the musical represented had been active and growing in size for some time. Thus, a Broadway musical about hippies would likely not have been particularly shocking to the average spectator in 1968, even despite the fleeting glimpse of male and female nudity that audiences were granted at the end of the first act. Further, the show's political and social agenda was no different than that espoused by the actual New Left. Thus, audience members who attended *Hair* would certainly have been familiar with the musical's messages by 1968, regardless of whether or not they agreed with them. As one anonymous journalist, writing about various theatrical depictions of youth culture in New York City at the time, quipped, "Even hawks, let alone parrots, have learned to deplore Viet Nam by now, so this particular arsenal of invective doesn't stir up . . . [the] audience as visibly as it once did. Time was when playgoers would weep on their armrests at the old 'We won't go' non-fight pep talk."[63]

Perhaps most important to *Hair*'s success was the simple fact that it was the first musical of its kind. Because it was unique, and because it opened at a point when youth culture had not yet become quite as commodified as it soon would, *Hair* seems to have been more regularly lauded for its crossover appeal than it was criticized for "selling out."

For much of the company, the commercial aspects of *Hair* did not conflict with its messages. The original company members who were interviewed for this project were all quick to acknowledge that *Hair* was as commercial as any Broadway musical. They argued, nevertheless, that the musical carried important social and political messages that were well worth conveying to audiences. These messages worked to reaffirm, or even to significantly strengthen, the ideals of many of the cast members.

James Rado notes that although the alternative casting employed by *Hair*'s creative team yielded a diverse company that varied widely in terms of professional experience and lifestyle, many cast members nevertheless came to believe firmly in what they were depicting. "I think the immediacy of the material—that it was about the present youth movement— made it very easy for them to identify with," he says. "I found the actors coming to believe—and the audience came to believe—that what they were seeing onstage were actual hippies. They were not, necessarily. But they became that. I think it was easy for them to identify with the causes."[64]

Natalie Mosco agrees, adding that integrating the personal and the political was especially easy since *Hair* touched on so many issues and featured such a diverse cast. "We were a cross-section of what was out there in New York, probably in the country, probably in the world—politically and emotionally of that generation," she recalls. "The way each one of us thought reflected somebody, somewhere. We were almost prototypes of what was going on."[65]

An actor who was particularly affected by his work in *Hair* was Walter Michael Harris who, at sixteen, was one of the youngest members of the original cast. He remembers that although he "approached *Hair* initially from a 'commercial,' career point-of-view," he became "utterly, completely transformed" by his experience: "With *Hair* I developed a sense of mission about my life which never left. I reached the point where I could no longer justify playing a hippie on stage—I had to go out and try to live the life."[66] After eleven months as a tribe member, Harris left the show and moved from New York City to San Francisco. "I went into *Hair* an actor and came out a hippie!"[67] he exclaims.

Similarly, Heather MacRae acknowledges that being in the show had a profound impact on her personal ideology:

> I became very idealistic about the war, and what [parts] I chose to do. I would not go out for jobs that I couldn't believe in. I turned down *Promises, Promises*. They asked me to do it in San Francisco and I went to see it, and I was like, "ick." I was very naive—I was young and impressionable, and I thought, "I don't want to do a show where she's in love with a married man." I became really idealistic. I think it was to my detriment because I could have probably done some wonderful roles and maybe learned from them. But I was trying to live a particular type of lifestyle, and I could not in good conscience do things that I did not really believe in.[68]

It is because of this ideology that MacRae cites *Hair* and *Falsettos*—the William Finn musical about homosexuality, AIDS, and the concept of family—as two of the musicals she has most enjoyed working on during the course of her career.

On the other hand, MacRae argues that *Hair*'s impact on its cast had some negative ramifications, as well:

> There were people who took drugs backstage. I never did. I had to have my wits about me. But there were people that would drop acid and go onstage. Very scary. But that was definitely part of the culture. Some of

the actors were very undisciplined, and were like, "Hey, man, I'm living this lifestyle and now you're telling me I have to do *this*?" That created some problems. There was lots of stuff going on backstage. There was a person we called the Phantom who would slash people's clothes. It was a very volatile kind of thing. They never found who it was. And there were some bizarre things that went on—people having sex in dressing room 1, which was the big hangout. I remember when I first joined the cast, I walked into dressing room 1 to hang out with everybody, and I saw somebody shooting up, and I asked what it was and they said, "vitamins." A lot of cast members got hooked on these vitamin B-12 shots that had speed in them. When they were in their preview period, because they were so tired, they had this Dr. Mitchum come in. So in addition to the wonderful love-peace-hippie thing, there was also a more sinister side.[69]

In short, as a microcosm of the actual youth movement, the Broadway company of *Hair* experienced many of the same inconsistencies that plagued the counterculture and hippie movements by the end of the decade. Tribe member Marjorie LiPari remembers that for all the ups and downs that various other members of the company might have experienced, she "went in the way I went in and came out the same way. *Hair* did not alter me as much as it fortified my ideology. Which was very much about being who you naturally are. Which is what the show was about."[70]

After *Hair:* The Birth (and Death) of a Trend

Because of its extraordinary commercial success, both at the Public Theater in 1967 and at the Biltmore in 1968, *Hair* generated a spate of imitations, billed as rock musicals, which cropped up on, Off, and Off-Off-Broadway well into the mid-1970s. The first to follow on *Hair*'s heels was Hal Hester and Danny Apolinar's *Your Own Thing*. Billed as "a new rock musical," *Your Own Thing* opened Off Broadway at the Orpheum Theater on January 13, 1968, while *Hair* was still running at the Cheetah.[71]

Like *Hair*, *Your Own Thing* was very much a product of its time. As Scott Warfield writes, "the cast's psychedelic costumes and the dialogue's youthful slang date the production almost to the year."[72] The musical, which remained Off Broadway for its entire 933-show run, was a critical and commercial smash, which won the New York Drama Critics Circle Award for Best Musical in 1968 and spawned multiple touring companies and a London production. As in *Hair, Your Own Thing* replaced the traditional theater orchestra with a rock band, which was placed on the stage instead of in the orchestra pit.

Your Own Thing differed markedly from *Hair,* however, in that it was not nearly as experimental or as risky a venture. In contrast with MacDermot's eclectic score for *Hair,* Hester and Apolinar's music took fewer chances, and thus proved far less memorable. Whereas MacDermot's score offered an ever-changing variety of rhythms, tonalities, and contemporary styles, almost all of the songs featured in *Your Own Thing* were composed in major keys, with bright, busy orchestrations and rapid tempos. As a result, the score is most reminiscent of the bouncy sound that music producer Don Kirschner and songwriters Tommy Boyce and Bobby Hart cultivated for the Monkees, a bubblegum-pop group that was formed in 1966 for an NBC television show based loosely on the Beatles' *A Hard Day's Night.* As *Stagebill* editor Robert Sandla writes in the liner notes of the original cast recording for *Your Own Thing,* "the show spoke for what it was pleased to call 'the Now Generation,' but there was nothing in it to scare Grandma."

Sandla's comments apply not only to the score of *Your Own Thing,* but also to its plot. Loosely based on Shakespeare's *Twelfth Night,* it involves the antics of the twin-brother-and-sister rock duo Viola and Sebastian. When their boat sinks early in act 1, they are separated, but both land in Illyria (in this case, modern-day New York City). Viola, mistaken for a boy, meets Orson, the manager of a shaggy-haired rock group called the Apocalypse, which features four musicians who perform under the aliases Death, War, Famine, and Disease. Because Disease has been drafted, Orson hires Viola as his replacement. When Viola and Orson develop romantic feelings for one another, Orson is thrown into a state of sexual confusion, which increases when he meets Sebastian (since the boat wreck, mistaken for a girl), and confuses him with Viola. Eventually, all is resolved and the characters live happily ever after.

Despite infrequent mention of the war and a few lighthearted topical references, *Your Own Thing* steered clear of the many sociopolitical issues that were confronted in *Hair* (although it did reflect some fairly open views about sexuality in general and homosexuality in particular). Instead, the show focused on the more freewheeling, whimsical aspects of the 1960s. The musical was also much more conventionally plotted: for all of its gender-crossing and sexual confusion, this was ultimately just another traditional boy-meets-girl, boy-loses-girl, boy-wins-girl-back musical comedy. *Your Own Thing* was also directed more conservatively than *Hair,* with, for example, few if any breaks to the fourth wall and an emphasis on the mistaken identity and wacky, fast-paced antics that one would expect of a French farce. It is perhaps due to its utter lack of originality that in spite of the commercial and critical success it enjoyed during its run, *Your Own Thing* dropped quickly from public memory once it closed.

Although *Your Own Thing* was the first show billed as a rock musical to follow *Hair,* it remained distinct enough that the two were never compared terribly closely. In this respect, *Your Own Thing* is wholly unique among rock musicals that opened in New York around the turn of the decade. By 1969, in a mad scramble to reap the rewards that *Hair* brought its financial backers, many theater producers threw their weight and money behind shows that closely emulated or even directly referenced *Hair*'s experimental direction, rock instrumentation, disregard of concise narrative, emphasis on the social mores of the counterculture, or use of nudity—whether justified or not.

In 1969, in an editorial strongly supporting the use of rock music on the theatrical stage, John Lahr forecast that "the commercial success of the rock musical is assurance that there will be more of them. But formula imitations will bring a quick death for an explosive new dimension on the musical stage."[73] Lahr turned out to be correct. While a few of the rock musicals offered in the years after *Hair* opened at the Biltmore were successful—*Godspell* (1971), for example, and the "new '50s rock'n'roll musical" *Grease* (1972)—most were critical and commercial disasters.

Before the close of the decade, a rock musical backlash brewed slowly in the New York press; this would grow increasingly strong—and would be echoed by the ticket-buying public—well into the 1970s. That critics and audiences alike would quickly grow tired of *Hair* imitations is no wonder, considering how many appeared in New York at the turn of the decade. One, a revue called *Salvation,* pitted the social mores of the counterculture against those of older generations. Another, *Stomp,* was billed as a "multimedia protest rock musical," and opened the 1969–70 season in limited run at Joseph Papp's Public Theater. Although the commercial success of both productions indicates that the public did not initially agree with the reviews, many critics began to show signs that their patience for *Hair* imitations was rapidly wearing thin.

Peter Link and C. C. Courtney's *Salvation*, which was part rock concert and part revival meeting, opened at the Village Gate before moving to the Jan Hus Theater on East Seventy-fourth Street in September 1969. The show was well received by a handful of critics, but was often compared unfavorably to *Hair*. Clive Barnes, who liked both productions, nevertheless wrote in his review, "Here there is also a non-book, a popularized pop-rock score and a theme that doodles around young, almost-hippie people, with their sex, their drugs, and their longings to be touched. *Salvation* does challenge comparison with *Hair*, and from that comparison it emerges a clear second best.[74]

While *Hair* had managed to escape being labeled too commercial by most journalists, *Salvation* seemed to strike a number of critics as superficial. Robert Sealy, writing for The *Episcopal New Yorker*, was unbothered by the strongly anti-Christian sentiments expressed in *Salvation*, but was clearly infuriated by what he saw as the producers' attempt to package the show for a self-congratulating, mainstream, middle-class audience. Noting that "everything in this sad show—including the indignation—is borrowed," he writes,

The audience at "Salvation" . . . were rich; they were middle-aged; they were uneasy; and they were gulled. Certainly these were not despicable people; they had standards, the imbecilities and indignities they witnessed and suffered through could by no possible casuistry be thought applicable or deserved. Yet they sat there, reacting like drugged rats to a buzzer: Vietnam, H. L. Hunt, President Nixon, the Pope, the popular words for fornication, sodomy, fellatio, etc. In their heart of hearts, they must have felt ashamed and queasy, but this was the rhythm of the day, this was being with it, grooving, swinging, doncha-know. Being with it! They should live so long! Seven dollars a ticket . . . to crowd into an Off Broadway basement . . . for barely eighty minutes of show time during which not one second is anything more than stale, factitious routine. And they emerge, faintly smiling, thinking they have walked that last mile over the bridge of the "generation gap." "I am cleansed, I am pure, I am young again. This is what they want. This is what our children want." Horsefeathers.[75]

The mixed reviews they earned for *Salvation* were ultimately the strongest that C. C. Courtney and Peter Link would get. Their next—and final— rock musical offering, *Earl of Ruston,* was billed as a "country rock musi- cal" that told the story of Earl Woods, a lunatic who lived in Ruston, Louisiana. *Earl of Ruston* opened on Broadway in May 1971 and was roundly criticized as being even weaker than *Salvation.* The musical folded after just five performances.[76]

If Courtney and Link's *Salvation* was, in the eyes of most critics, the derivative son of *Hair,* then *Stomp*—which opened at the Public Theater in November 1969—was its even-more-hackneyed grandchild. *Stomp* was developed by a group of young graduates and dropouts from the Univer- sity of Texas who called themselves the Combine. A great deal of public- ity was generated by the fact that the Combine lived communally at the Public Theater in the weeks before and during the run of the show.[77]

Like *Hair, Stomp* incorporated a number of experimental influences. In a nod to environmental theater—in which the fourth wall is ignored and the audience is placed in the center of the action—spectators were seated in bleachers or on the floor in a big circle surrounding the actors, who often interacted with them during the performance. The plotless show, more performance art than musical theater, featured film clips and a light show. At the end of the performance, a huge piece of translucent plastic that symbolized pure, flowing water was dappled with lights and pulled over the entire audience.

Stomp emulated *Hair* in its attempt to cover a wide variety of current events; unlike *Hair,* however, the show struck many critics as repetitive and uninspired. In his pan of the show for the *Village Voice,* John Lahr wrote, "Protest is much more dangerous and complicated than holding placards which read 'Fuck the Establishment.' 'Stomp's' homespun earnestness never convinces us of its liberation."[78]

Just as it likely contributed to the success of *Hair,* timing very possibly hindered the success of *Stomp.* While rock's connection to social protest was an important underlying feature of *Hair,* the turn of the decade saw youth culture and its accompanying music becoming increasingly main- streamed and commercialized. Further, the social upheavals of the 1960s were followed by a series of ugly events in the early 1970s—the United States' secret invasion of Cambodia, the subsequent Kent State and Jack- son State shootings, the Watergate scandal, the seemingly endless war in

Vietnam—that added to a feeling of deep disillusionment in this country. As the 1960s drew to a close, the rock lyric was being heralded in theater circles as a highly effective new "vehicle for emotional expression, philosophical debate, political activism—you name it, the rock lyric can and does express it daily from audio sources and from the stage."[79] But by the early 1970s, it seems that mainstream audiences had joined critics in tiring of theatrical productions that functioned as agents for sociopolitical change.

It is also possible, Galt MacDermot cynically suggests, that political theater was never anything but a fad, especially on Broadway, where most "people go to theater to have their values reinforced." In his eyes, *Hair* was a fluke; a commercial success despite and not because of its subject matter. MacDermot acknowledges, however, that rock musicals most likely fell out of vogue by the early 1970s because too many producers grew more interested in rushing new rock musicals to the stage than they were in offering strong, interesting work. "When you lose a couple of million bucks on Broadway," he concludes, "you are not asked back fast, if at all."[80]

Interlude 2

Audiences

As historian Elizabeth Burns writes in *Theatricality*, an audience has the power of "making or breaking a play by attendance or abstention, and has always been ultimately responsible for sustaining the performance."[1] Because audience behavior exerts tremendous influence on the outcome of any live performance, the function of the audience is of particular interest here. When it comes to rock and musical theater performances, accepted modes of behavior among respective audiences have always differed widely in a number of ways. Thus, attempts to appeal simultaneously to members of both audiences are as, if not more, challenging than combining the aesthetics of these two divergent performing arts genres themselves.

For all its importance, the audience has long been avoided as a topic of study for obvious reasons: how, exactly, does one characterize an audience of hundreds, or thousands, or hundreds of thousands of people without resorting to generalizations?[2] It should thus come as no surprise that a majority of writers on popular culture do exactly this when it comes to tackling discussions about audiences. For example, although they had different reasons for arguing as they did, cultural critics as diverse as the arch-conservative T. S. Eliot and the neo-Marxist Theodor Adorno were both highly negative in assessing popular culture and, by extension, its audience. Eliot saw popular culture as a manifestation of the authority of the unrefined masses, who threatened to overwhelm a precious high culture that was being conscientiously preserved by a privileged minority of elite aesthetes. On the other hand, Adorno saw popular culture as a form of domination from above, which alienated, manipulated, and confounded the collective class-consciousness of a working class that was otherwise potentially highly progressive.[3] Adorno felt that popular music, in particular, was a synthetic, homogenous form of entertainment that placated, instead of challenging, its audience. In Adorno's eyes, all consumers of popular music were anesthetized by hackneyed music that failed to challenge the intellect.[4]

More recent cultural critics have formed theories in attempts to explain what they have perceived as the passive behavior of Western audiences. Elias Canetti, for example, posits that most Western theater and art music audiences have been culturally conditioned to restrain from any freedom of the body, and as a result, suffer from collective stagnation of the mind.[5] Building on Canetti's work, Robert Baker-White argues that the abolition of physical restraint was thus a central innovation of the rock concert.[6]

Of course, any sweeping generalization about audiences is bound to be problematic. Eliot's and Adorno's blanket statements about the anesthetized mass audiences of popular culture fail to acknowledge ways that popular entertainment can fuel audiences to dispute sociopolitical structures. The theories posed by Canetti and Baker-White are similarly thorny; as scholars like James O. Young and Stephen Davies have effectively argued, the fact that some audiences are more or less subdued than others does not imply that they are thus more or less engaged.[7]

In recent years, an increased number of works dedicated to the study of different types of audiences has begun to appear, due in large part to the sophistication of research techniques.[8] Many of these studies focus specifically on American theater audiences. For example, the landmark study *The Audience for New York Theatre*—sponsored by the Theatre Development Fund and the League of American Theatres and Producers, and prepared by Audience Research and Analysis in 1997—examines audiences on and Off Broadway in both for- and not-for-profit realms during a single season, and is the first study to relate current findings to long-term trends.

Such analysis allows for new insights into the backgrounds and tastes of theater audiences. As a result, according to Billy Zavelson, account executive of the marketing company The Karpel Group, new techniques geared at understanding and tapping into potential theater audiences have been welcomed with open arms by the theater industry, especially since the late 1990s.[9] Indeed, *Rent* press agent Don Summa credits that musical's hit status in large part to savvy marketing, which allowed for the unprecedented targeting of potential audiences. "The audience breakdown they can give you from credit cards is amazing," Summa marvels.

"They can give you a zip-code breakdown of where your credit card purchases are coming from, and each zip-code has a personality."[10]

Innovations in audience research thus allow for a clearer picture of contemporary performing arts audiences than those of even the very recent past. Critics point out, however, that at its most sophisticated, market research nevertheless sheds little light on individual interests or tastes; reducing people to zip codes and spending patterns simply results in different types of generalizations.[11] As illuminating as they can be, statistics used to characterize an audience can sometimes be misleading, especially when they are used carelessly to back, rather than to delve deeper into, the same oversimplifications that have been perpetuated for decades.

Rock and the musical theater have both been documented enough that relatively clear pictures of their audiences have emerged. Yet these pictures remain general, despite the recent advances in audience studies. Despite even the most sophisticated market research, audiences, as collectives of individuals with myriad opinions and perceptions among them, remain nearly impossible to characterize.

Western Theater Audiences

There is a consensus among Western theater historians that audiences were once more inclusive than they tend to be at present. During antiquity, for example, Greek theater was inseparable from the social, political, and economic organization of Athens. The very size of most ancient auditoriums, which were often designed to hold tens of thousands of spectators at a time, implies that theater audiences comprised a majority of the population, rather than the elite segments that have become associated with the Western theater more recently.[12]

Although slightly less democratic than thought to have been in antiquity, Western theater audiences continued to be considerably socially inclusive through the seventeenth century.[13] During this century, however, private theaters—with higher admission prices—were established. The result was a more selective audience that enforced new codes of behavior; as audiences became increasingly bourgeois, they also became increasingly passive. An exception lay in what is now known as the orchestra pit, which was often reserved for a relatively rowdy working-class audience. Yet after 1850, the pits were replaced by stalls that were more physically confining, and thus also more encouraging of sedate behavior.[14]

In the United States, even audiences at the rowdiest popular entertainments followed the same gradual course, from raucous to comparatively subdued, through the eighteenth and nineteenth centuries. This is especially the case during the 1880s, when variety shows made a general shift from the saloon to the vaudeville theater. With this shift came a dramatic change in the physical structure of most performance spaces: balconies, galleries, and rows of seats likely encouraged more genteel behavior than that tolerated in saloons. The advent of electric light at the end of the century, which led to the tradition of slowly dimming the houselights to signal the onset of a performance, helped to further suppress the audience.

At around the same time, entrepreneurs grew interested in improving the reputation of variety theater by offering "family-oriented" entertainments that would appeal not only to middle-class men, but also to their wives and children.[15] To this end, vaudeville theater owners like Benjamin Franklin Keith, Edward F. Albee, and Frederick Freeman Proctor built theater chains across the country, which were monitored by a single, centrally located manager. By early in the twentieth century, the two largest chains were the United Booking Office, which controlled four hundred theaters across the eastern and midwestern United States, and the Orpheum Circuit, which oversaw theaters from Chicago to the West Coast.

These structural changes in the theater industry resulted in a shift in control from audiences and performers to producers and managers, who made newly concerted efforts both to define vaudeville and to orient audiences accordingly. Theater entrepreneur Benjamin Franklin Keith, for example, banned words that were "unfit for the ears of ladies and children" from his stages and his auditoriums, prohibited spectators from "smoking, spitting, whistling, stamping feet, crunching peanuts, and wearing hats," and was known to lecture audiences on proper theater behavior during intermission.[16]

Over many centuries, then, Western theater audiences on both sides of the Atlantic have been culturally conditioned to behave in specific ways: to sit quietly in seats and to refrain from disturbing actors or one another during performances. What with modern precurtain announcements advising audiences to unwrap candies, turn off cell phones, and refrain from taking photographs during performances, it is clear that what has been deemed proper theater behavior continues to be built upon to date.

The Theater Takes Note of
Popular Music Audiences

Rock 'n' roll, on the other hand, was associated from its inception in the 1950s with rebellion, sexual desire, physical and emotional empowerment, and the celebration of youth.[17] Shortened to "rock" in the 1960s, the music became closely linked with a youth culture interested in challenging extant social and political conventions.[18] While rock's connection with the counterculture has long since died away, popular music's associations with youthful abandon remain important aspects of its overall aesthetic.

The transformation of rock 'n' roll into rock occurred at around the same time that alternatives to the mainstream theater were being explored, especially Off and Off-Off-Broadway. Through the 1960s and early 1970s, members of the fringe theater observed, often with great interest and not a little jealousy, the excitement generated among audiences at live rock shows. In discussing the 1969–70 Off-Off-Broadway theater season, for example, Robert Schroeder wrote enviously of crowds flocking to the Fillmore East:

> In all of New York during 1969–70, there was only one theater that had to ask police to fend off the crowds. That theater housed none of the serious or camped revivals that clung to the one edge of off off Broadway's spectrum, nor did it contain any of the elitist fantasies that touched at the other. . . . The only theater in New York that needed help in handling its crowds was hosting The Who and the like. It housed theater that people—actual great masses of actual people—were breaking down the doors to experience. The Fillmore East in lower Manhattan, the theater about which I am speaking . . . is filled the year round with that great new audience the theater's professionals all talk about . . . Bill Graham sees that the Fillmore East's stage speaks to his audience's life-concerns, and that's how Fillmore East gets filled. Using the same tools that David Merrick uses—words, music, motion, lights, sound, projected live from a stage to a living audience—Graham proves that even today, even among the "alienated," living theater is desperately needed, and urgently sought.[19]

The desire to capture the excitement obvious at rock concerts helped fuel explorations into different kinds of theater, as well as into potential new roles for the theater audience.

The Influence of the Rock Concert: The Performer-Audience Relationship

Because they were born as one result of this desire, staged rock musicals have always reflected an interest in finding ways to connect with audiences that are not typical of mainstream theater productions. One of the most notable aspects of *Hair*, for example, was the relationship cultivated between cast and audience from the moment that spectators walked into the theater to encounter members of the cast wandering around the stage, through the aisles, and into the rows of seats. Breaks to the fourth wall were consistent throughout the production: cast members talked directly to the audience before and during the show and, after the final curtain, invited spectators up onto the stage to mingle and dance.

Hair's indifference to the fourth wall is reminiscent of live rock performance, which has always served as an important site for bonding, both between audience and performers, and among fans. Rock concerts allow fans to immerse themselves temporarily into a community that has a shared sense of purpose; many musicians play off this sense of community by, for example, engaging in banter with fans; stage-diving into the waiting crowd; leaning down to shake the hands or slap the palms of spectators standing at the edge of the stage; selecting audience members to bring up onto the stage; asking fans to sing, shout, or dance along to songs; or all of the above.[20]

It is thus no wonder that the sense of bonding cultivated in rock concerts, and emulated to such noteworthy effect in *Hair*, has been so often attempted in rock musicals. A significant number of rock musicals include specific songs or scenes during which performers work to engage with the audience. As in *Hair*, for example, *Rent* features several scenes, including the very first, in which characters break the fourth wall to address the audience directly. Near the end of the first act, one character—Maureen Johnson, a kooky performance artist—plays directly to the audience during her performance-art protest-piece, "Over the Moon," about a cow trapped in Cyberland. In a nod both to 1960s happenings and to audience participation segments at live rock shows, Maureen ends her over-the-top performance by good-naturedly encouraging the audience to moo with her. *Rent* features a much subtler and less rehearsed moment before each performance officially begins, when performers and audience members acknowledge a special connection.

When *Rent* moved uptown, from the cozy New York Theatre Workshop in the East Village to the much larger Nederlander Theater on West Forty-first Street, its producers developed a policy of reserving thirty-four front-row seats, to be made available for twenty dollars each, at every performance. These tickets, which are assigned via lottery a half-hour before each performance, have proven remarkably popular with young *Rent* fans, many of whom have returned for repeated viewings of the show. Before a performance begins, as the cast and band members walk onto the stage to take their places, members of the company nod at or wave to the people seated in the twenty-dollar seats, who respond by whistling, cheering, and breaking into energetic applause. Actor Carla Bianco, who has appeared in both the Los Angeles and New York productions of *Rent*, notes that this warm, enthusiastic response from the audience helps to galvanize the cast even before the show has begun:

> They get more involved, as if you were in a rock concert, where people stand up and scream and have their lighters—there is more of a sense of that than in other musicals. If they could, if we asked them to and that fourth wall was broken more, I think they would even stand up and start screaming in the middle of numbers. That makes it really exciting. With traditional musicals, I think that fourth wall is really up and they are just watching the piece and they tend to be more quiet. Not as free to laugh as loud, depending on the size of the house. I think there's a heightened energy that just gets them psyched. Especially the young people who come to *Rent*. Forget about it, they're not going to be quiet, they're screaming as soon as we walk out—we haven't even said, "Hi."[21]

While the lottery system is unique to *Rent*, a similar phenomenon typically occurred before the beginning of *Hedwig and the Angry Inch*, when the members of the Angry Inch band sauntered onto the stage for a quick tuneup before the houselights were dimmed and the Hedwig character entered. In both cases, this momentary disregard of the fourth wall before the onset of the performance allowed for a small but profound connection between audience and performer that is rare in more traditional musicals.

In many cases, the connection between performers and audience members is heightened at the very end of the performance, during which the cast sings a rousing, anthemic number directly to the audience. These anthems tend to feature strongly upbeat refrains that are sung repeatedly and with rising emotion by the cast; the repetition and fervent delivery both encourage the audience to sing and sometimes to dance along. Like countless rock ballads, these numbers are often about finding connections to other people in the face of alienation or adversity, and are thus meant to celebrate both the musicals' characters and the audience themselves. Such numbers include *Hair*'s "The Flesh Failures (Let the Sunshine In)," during which the cast mourns the death in Vietnam of the Claude Hooper Bukowski character before breaking into the ecstatic refrain, "Let the sun shine in"; *Godspell*'s reprise of the rousing, repetitive "Day By Day" after Jesus is crucified and his followers resolve to follow his teachings; the reprise of the gospel-tinged "No Day But Today" at the end of *Rent*, which is sung by the entire cast as it stands downstage center facing the audience; and the finale of *Hedwig*, "Midnight Radio," an anthem about emotional wholeness and the strength of a loving community that ends as the cast sings repeatedly and with increasing urgency for the audience to "lift up your hands" in solidarity with the Hedwig character. These anthemic finales not only encourage bonds between audiences and performers; they also pay direct homage to rock concerts, many of which conclude in much the same way.

Musicals that borrow from rock and popular music aesthetics must take into consideration not only the sounds that they are trying to imitate, but the audiences they are trying to win over. While finding the right blend of popular music and musical theater aesthetics proves extraordinarily challenging, successful rock musicals can succeed, with a little creativity, in bringing the raw energy that members of the Off and Off-Off-Broadway community envied in first observing crowds flocking to the Fillmore East in the 1960s.

Fifty-year-old Billy De Wolfe as "The Juvenile Delinquent" in the Ziegfeld *Follies,* 1957. ©Friedman-Abeles. (Billy Rose Theatre Collection, The New York Public Library for the Performing Arts, Astor, Lenox and Tilden Foundations.)

Bert Lahr and Nancy Walker in "Too Young To Live," *The Girls Against the Boys,* 1959. Photographer unknown. (Billy Rose Theatre Collection, The New York Public Library for the Performing Arts, Astor, Lenox and Tilden Foundations.)

PLAYBILL

a weekly magazine for theatregoers

THE GIRLS AGAINST THE BOYS

The band jams above the cast in the Off Broadway production of *Hair* in 1967. The band would be moved to the stage when the musical premiered on Broadway a year later. ©George Joseph. (Billy Rose Theatre Collection, The New York Public Library for the Performing Arts, Astor, Lenox and Tilden Foundations.)

(upper right) Leland Palmer (Viola) and Rusty Thacker (Sebastian) with the Apocalypse (Michael Valenti, John Kuhner, and Danny Apolinar) in *Your Own Thing*, 1968. ©Bert Andrews. (Billy Rose Theatre Collection, The New York Public Library for the Performing Arts, Astor, Lenox and Tilden Foundations.)

(lower right) Zero (James Patrick Farrell III, on the ground) and 33 (Allan Nicholls, above) wrestling on the dirt floor for the soul of Dude (Nat Morris) in *Dude: The Highway Life*, 1972. ©Dagmar.

Herod (Paul Ainsley) and friends mocking Jesus (Jeff Fenholt) in the original Broadway production of *Jesus Christ Superstar* (1972). ©Friedman-Abeles. (Billy Rose Theatre Collection, The New York Public Library for the Performing Arts, Astor, Lenox and Tilden Foundations.)

Minnie Gentry and the cast of *Ain't Supposed to Die a Natural Death* confronting the audience during the climactic number, "Put a Curse on You," in 1972. ©Bert Andrews. (Billy Rose Theatre Collection, The New York Public Library for the Performing Arts, Astor, Lenox and Tilden Foundations.)

Cast members from *Dreamgirls* invoking doo-wop and girl groups. *From left to right:* Loretta Devine, Jennifer Holliday, Sheryl Lee Ralph, and Cleavant Derricks, backed by the chorus. Photographer unknown. (Billy Rose Theatre Collection, The New York Public Library for the Performing Arts, Astor, Lenox and Tilden Foundations.)

Alphabet City on Broadway: The cast of *Rent* in 1996. ©Joan Marcus.

Hedwig (John Cameron Mitchell) fronts the Angry Inch (*left to right,* Stephen Trask, David McKinley, Chris Weilding, Scott Bilbrey, and Miriam Shor) at the Jane Street Theater in 1998. ©Carol Rosegg.

3 🎸 Rock Concept Albums and the Fragmented Musical of the 1970s

IN HIS BOOK *Our Musicals Ourselves: A Social History of the American Musical Theatre,* John Bush Jones takes issue with the term *concept musical.* This term began to appear in writings about the musical theater in the late 1960s, and was being bandied about with increasing regularity by the end of the 1970s. Although no one is sure who coined the term, it was eventually defined by—and is thus often credited to—the theater critic Martin Gottfried. According to Gottfried, a concept musical is "based on a stage idea, not a story, but a look, a tone—what the show will be like as a stage animal. The music, the dances, the story, the sets and the style of performance are all dictated by that production concept. . . .[T]his conceptual approach to musicals is theatrical and pictorial rather than intellectual."[1]

Jones argues, however, that the term as Gottfried defines it remains frustratingly vague: "By that definition, all of the *Ziegfeld Follies* were concept musicals, which is preposterous. And if the concept musical is 'theatrical and pictorial rather than intellectual,' why are Stephen Sondheim's most cerebral shows, such as *Pacific Overtures* and *Sunday in the Park with George,* often called concept musicals?"[2] In place of the offending term, then, Jones offers a new one: "fragmented musical."

Fragmented musicals, which were particularly fashionable throughout the 1970s, reflected both in form and in substance the fragmentation of American society that began as the 1960s drew to a close, the New Left and hippie cultures disintegrated, and the Vietnam war limped to its sad conclusion. As the "can-do" 1960s gave way to the "me decade," the collective mood of the nation shifted from enthusiasm over sociopolitical causes toward weary, disillusioned introspection. Many musicals that appeared during the 1970s reflected this cultural shift, from outward to inward; from hopeful to cynical. Those that most reflected the times—Jones's "fragmented musicals"—differ from traditional musicals in that they are more idea- or character-driven than they are plot-driven. In these musicals—for example, Sondheim's *Company,* or the long-running *A Chorus Line*—linear narrative is replaced by a more disjointed series of scenes and musical numbers, all of which contribute to the musical's main themes or the development of its characters.[3]

Because of their de-emphasis on traditional plot structures, some fragmented musicals were labeled "revues" by theater critics. Jones acknowledges that revues, like fragmented musicals, often feature segments that are linked by a common theme; they nevertheless do not feature the careful attention to character development that is typical of a fragmented musical. Perhaps unsurprisingly, Jones identifies the very first fragmented musical as one that was regularly mistaken for a revue due to its focus on character and collective mood at the expense of traditional plotting: *Hair.*[4]

In the years following *Hair*'s 1968 Broadway debut, staged rock musicals that appeared on, Off, and Off-Off-Broadway developed in two different directions. The more successful but decidedly less innovative were structurally traditional plot-based musicals that reflected more influence from the lighthearted throwback *Bye Bye Birdie* than from *Hair*. Examples include *Your Own Thing,* as well as the nostalgic *Grease,* which affectionately recalled the innocence of the 1950s with the kind of rock 'n' roll score that Broadway composers had deemed impossible during the 1950s themselves. *Grease* opened Off Broadway in 1972 and ran at the Eden Theater for 128 performances before moving to Broadway's Broadhurst for a whopping 3,388 performances and becoming what was then the longest-running show in Broadway history.[5]

Structurally traditional rock musicals that cropped up in the 1970s generally fared better than the second type, which were essentially fragmented musicals with scores that were heavily influenced by contemporary popular music. A vast majority of fragmented rock musicals to open during the early 1970s failed to win the favor of critics or audiences. In fact, the staggering number of fragmented rock musicals that met untimely—and very expensive—ends contributed to a rapid demise in enthusiasm among theater producers for anything termed a "rock musical" by the mid-1970s.

There are several related reasons for both the glut of fragmented rock musicals during the early 1970s and their recurring inability to connect with theater critics or audiences. The simplest explanation for their preponderance on and Off Broadway was that *Hair*'s enormous success implied to many theater producers that musicals with erratic narratives, hip young casts, and pit bands chock full of electric instruments represented the wave of the future. A second, more complicated reason has to do with the fact that several contemporary trends in rock music—even those that would seem to lend themselves easily to theatrical adaptation—failed to translate effectively to the musical stage. Between the mid-1960s and early 1970s, technological advances allowed for both the development of the concept album and for increasingly spectacular rock concerts. These developments influenced many of the fragmented rock musicals staged in New York City, while simultaneously contributing to their commercial or critical downfalls.

By the mid-1960s, in both the United States and England, many rock performers began to devote less time to giving live performances and more to mastering rapidly developing studio technology, in the interest of making increasingly sophisticated sound recordings. In 1966, for instance, the Beach Boys released the commercially disappointing but highly innovative album *Pet Sounds,* which had apparently been inspired by the Beatles' 1965 effort, *Rubber Soul.*[6] Also in 1966, the Beatles, who had retreated to the studio after tiring of playing to audiences who were screaming too loudly to hear them, released their own highly sophisticated album, *Revolver.* Their landmark *Sgt. Pepper's Lonely Hearts Club Band* would be released a year later.

These recordings, among others that would soon follow, were indicative of the fact that rock music was being taken in new directions by musicians who were attaining greater artistic control over their work. The increased time spent in recording studios indeed spurred an unprecedented period of artistic control for rock musicians. Whereas many rock musicians had already been composing and arranging their own music, the added experience in recording studios allowed them to be less willing to acquiesce to the tastes and suggestions of record producers, and more inclined to take full responsibility for their finished sound recordings.[7]

A familiarity with the workings of the recording studio, combined with advances in recording technology and greater artistic control, allowed rock musicians to move beyond the perceived limitations of the popular sound recording. From its inception, rock music had been oriented around the 45-rpm single record, with the LP typically viewed as a collection of distinct songs that are included either because they are likely to be commercially successful or because they comprise the entire current repertoire of the recording artist in question.[8] By the mid-1960s, however, many rock musicians began to turn their attention away from singles, and toward the LP as a whole. By the latter part of the decade, the LP was transformed from merely a medium upon which a number of independently conceived songs could be arranged to a potentially fully integrated work on which all the songs could be conceptually or thematically related.

The resultant efforts are commonly known as concept albums, the birth of which is traced to the mid-1960s. The question as to who was responsible for the first concept album is a matter for some debate among rock historians and aficionados, but the Beatles' *Sgt. Pepper's Lonely Hearts Club Band* is often cited as one of the earliest and most influential. Within a year of its release—June 1967 in both the United States and the UK—concept albums began to appear on both sides of the Atlantic with increasing regularity. They developed in various directions, as different groups explored the potential for large-scale structure. British art-rock bands like Procol Harum, Yes, and the Moody Blues exhibited a common interest in creating multimovement, instrumental soundscapes intended to evoke specific moods.[9] Other musicians focused on thematic connections. Marvin Gaye's 1971 *What's Going On* was a complex meditation on topical social issues, especially as related to black America; Pink Floyd's 1973 *Dark Side of the Moon* explored physical and emotional weaknesses— depravity, corruption, decrepitude, and madness. Still other bands attempted to develop characters, and to follow those characters through specific story lines in their concept albums. These attempts became known as "rock operas" by the late 1960s.

This term is elusive, for although rock operas usually share with traditional operas some attempt at character depiction and a coherent—if often very thin—story line, they tend, nevertheless, to be creations of the studio, not of the concert hall. This makes most rock operas more closely related to the concept albums from which they developed than to the traditional Western opera. Some of the most compelling examples of rock operas were never intended for live performance; still others were developed for the stage only after they had found success as LPs.[10]

As with the term *concept album,* there is some question as to exactly when the term *rock opera* was first coined, and by whom. The Who's LP *Tommy,* released in 1969, is often cited as the first, and it has certainly become one of the most well known; the term is often credited to Pete Townshend, the Who's lead guitarist, who conceived of the *Tommy* project and wrote most of the songs on the album. Yet critic John Rockwell argues that the term was coined by the little-known British band Nirvana, who applied it to their 1967 album *The Story of Simon Simopath: A Science Fiction Pantomime.*[11] Still others—including surviving members of the band itself—insist that the British group the Pretty Things invented the rock opera with the release of their 1968 LP *S. F. Sorrow.*[12]

Adding to the confusion over the term is the fact that, like the term *rock musical,* it is often applied so loosely that it serves to confuse as often as it clarifies. David Bowie's 1972 album *The Rise and Fall of Ziggy Stardust and the Spiders from Mars,* for example, traces the rise and fall of Bowie's alien rock-superstar alter ego when he lands on an Earth that is doomed to end five years in the future. This recording is most often referred to as a concept album, since its songs are thematically related and there is no real semblance of plot. But since it is also features a title character and the trace of a storyline, it is also occasionally referred to as a "rock opera."[13] The question as to what distinguishes a concept album from a rock opera—aside from the often strong opinions of people who follow and engage in such arguments—thus remains unanswered.

Whatever their designation, the increased interest in and development of album-length works, coupled with advances in technology, contributed to new trends in live performance, as rock musicians worked to match their grandiose studio efforts with increasingly large, spectacular, and, some would argue, pretentious concerts. Through the early 1970s, bands and solo artists like David Bowie, Alice Cooper, and Pink Floyd developed various stage personae, elaborate lighting, scenery, prop displays, and even staged skits or bits of dialogue for use during performances in ever-larger venues. In short, at the same time that the musical theater world was experimenting with less narrative, the rock world was experimenting with more.

These trends would seem to have lent themselves to more successful adaptations of rock music for use on the musical stage, especially since, coupled with the success of *Hair,* they rendered invalid the argument that rock music was too simplistic to carry a full-length musical. Even further, the early 1970s marked the beginning of an era in which experimentation with fragmentation on the one hand and narrative flow on the other, combined with a great many technological advances in both camps, brought musicals and rock concerts a few steps closer to one another. Coinciding with the arrival on Broadway of rock-influenced works by Andrew Lloyd Webber and Tim Rice, the approach to spectacle in the commercial theater began a significant transformation that would only intensify in the following decade.

The increased use of new technologies in the commercial theater led to a redefinition of spectacle. The word had previously connoted elaborate sets, huge casts, ornate costumes, or throngs of beautiful, scantily clad, high-kicking chorus girls. By the 1970s, "spectacles were architecturally and electronically conceived, relying on movable towers and bridges, frequently loaded with electric lights and other apparatus, and on what Hollywood terms 'special effects.'"[14] Just as increasingly theatrical and technologically challenging concerts proved both attractive and potentially lucrative to rock musicians, the chance to bring similar productions— and, thus, enthusiastic crowds—to the Broadway stage tempted theater personnel.

Many of the staged rock musicals developed through the early 1970s were fragmented, in that they de-emphasized traditional plot structures. But whereas many successful fragmented musicals simply downplayed the plot, the creators of fragmented rock musicals seem to have become too interested in simultaneously reflecting contemporary trends in rock performance. As a result, not only was plot development lost in many fragmented rock musicals, but characters, too, were trumped by an interest in visual spectacle at the expense of everything else. Many staged rock musicals to appear on or Off Broadway in the early 1970s were so fragile beneath the glitter that they failed to hold together at all.

Dude, Via Galactica, and *Rainbow*

Flush with the success of *Hair* and newly embroiled in a personal feud that put a temporary end to their collaboration, James Rado and Gerome

Ragni set about developing separate projects in the early 1970s. Ragni reunited with Galt MacDermot and got to work on the musical *Dude: The Highway Life*. At the same time, MacDermot joined the creative team of *Via Galactica*, a new musical that had been conceived and was to be directed by Sir Peter Hall. Meanwhile, Rado teamed with his brother Ted to write the book, music, and lyrics for his new musical, *Rainbow*.

Although they were no longer working together, neither Ragni nor Rado had lost sight of their desire to bring Off-Off-Broadway messages to Broadway audiences, thereby challenging from within the many conventions imposed by the commercial theater. The early 1970s saw the continuation, particularly Off Broadway, of the struggle for socially meaningful theater characterized by close collaboration, nonindividualized performances, and an avoidance of linear plot development. The last, of course, made the trendy fragmented musical particularly attractive to *Hair*'s dispersed creative team. While their work on *Hair* had implied that such challenges could be sustained, however, the post-*Hair* musicals became victims of the very system Rado and Ragni were attempting to reform. The result, MacDermot remembers, was a greedy scramble to repeat the success of *Hair,* during which much in the way of professionalism was lost.[15]

Dude and *Via Galactica* were both enormously expensive productions that reflected more of an interest in spectacle than in character, thematic development, or, ultimately, in making any sense. The reception of both of these shows was chilly, to say the least: theater historian Ken Mandelbaum writes that the "back-to-back awfulness" of these shows helped put an end to the theory that rock could somehow save the Broadway musical, and proved instead that audiences would not flock to see overproduced claptrap just because it had a beat.[16]

Dude began, like *Hair* had, as a series of ideas and observations that Gerome Ragni scribbled into the notebooks he habitually carried around with him. Between 1968 and 1971, Ragni amassed some two thousand pages of notes for the musical, from which he fashioned lyrics for fifty songs that were then set by Galt MacDermot. In 1971, the producers Adela and Peter Holzer agreed to finance *Dude*, provided that Ragni pare his notes into a workable script.[17]

Although no one involved with the production seemed clear, during its development, as to what *Dude* was actually about, the Holzers remained convinced that they had a big hit on their hands, and thus set about fulfilling Ragni's many outlandish, expensive demands. Although they rejected his request for the release of hundreds of live butterflies each night during performances, they did secure a theater that could be significantly redesigned to fit the needs of the production, with the stipulation that they pay to restore it to its original condition after *Dude* closed. The interior of the art-deco Broadway Theater on Broadway at Fifty-third Street was thus gutted and refurbished for the then-exorbitant fee of $110,000.[18]

Designing the set for the production proved particularly challenging. The orchestra seats were torn out, and the house was converted into a theater-in-the-round. A maze of runways leading from the stage into the seating area was constructed, and cables were suspended from the ceiling so that *Dude*'s "symbolic characters could descend on wires from symbolic heaven or roam all over the symbolic earth in search of truth, climbing a 'mountain' in the balcony aisles or wandering the deep 'forest' of the orchestra pit area."[19] The complicated set was made even more cluttered by the sound system, which consisted of a mess of microphones, "many hanging over the scene like shiny tears, others hand-held with long chords trickling down the aisles and still others planted in aisle railings."[20]

In hopes of invoking a forest, Ragni had requested that the set be adorned with live plants and inhabited by live animals. The flora and fauna were deemed impossible to acquire, let alone maintain, by the producers. By way of a compromise, paper flowers were brought in to decorate the interior of the theater, and the floor was covered with two tons of topsoil and peat moss. During rehearsals and early previews, the topsoil dirtied the costumes and constricted the throats of the actors, many of whom were regularly required to roll around on the stage floor immediately prior to singing musical numbers. Making matters worse was the fact that all the rolling around on the topsoil generated a thick layer of dust, which rose in great clouds from the stage floor and wafted up into the audience, where it covered patrons, caused a great deal of sneezing and coughing, and occluded the view of the stage. In an attempt to lessen the dust, stagehands experimented with watering the soil, which, of course, resulted in puddles of mud that covered the actors, making them long for the days when all they had to contend with was dust. When the aggravated, filthy cast finally threatened to complain to Actors' Equity, the soil was replaced, first with felt, and finally with shredded army blankets.[21]

As if clouds of dust and puddles of mud were not enough to worry about, a contrived seating system was devised for the production. In keeping with the environmental concept of *Dude,* the best seats in the house (seven dollars) became known as "foothills," while seats further from the stage were divided into sections labeled "trees," "mountains," and "valleys."[22] This system was created to help audience members feel as if they were an important part of *Dude,* but box office customers and patrons searching for their seats in the theater were often baffled by the gimmick.[23]

Even more problematic than its overly complex set, mountains of dirt, and bizarre seating system was its plot. By all accounts, *Dude* did not have one. During the early preview period, many of the audience members were infuriated by the aimlessness of the musical. Reports of early performances note that those spectators who did not choose to simply walk out of *Dude* in midperformance lingered so that they could boo, hiss, and shout things like "Ripoff!" at the stage.[24] After the third calamitous preview, the producers finally took notice of the fact that the director, Rocco Bufano, had no prior directing experience. The production was halted, Bufano was fired, and Tom O'Horgan was called in for an emergency stint during which, it was hoped, he could somehow rescue the production. "The audience thirsts for a story in *Dude . . .* For one tiny thread to connect your gorgeous songs," O'Horgan told the discouraged cast.[25] For three intense weeks, he and the company struggled to make sense of the production, while Ragni went back to work on the script.

Attempts to save *Dude* were futile. In his history of Broadway musical flops, Ken Mandelbaum calls *Dude,* which finally opened on October 9, 1972, "perhaps the most incomprehensible show ever presented on a Broadway stage."[26] This seems to be the sentiment of many people involved in or witness to the production. Galt MacDermot confides, "There was no book to *Dude.* I never knew what it was about. It was supposed to be about a guy traveling around America. But there was no semblance of traveling, just a lot of sand on the ground. Gerry was a brilliant guy, but on *Dude* he lost his way."[27]

Despite the lack of direction, MacDermot managed to write a score for *Dude* that is as stylistically eclectic as his score for *Hair* was. Several songs feature notably strong syncopation and a brass rhythm section, and are thus reminiscent of 1970s funk and soul. Others feature swing eighths rooted in a simple I-IV-V harmonic progression, played on acoustic guitar, Jew's harp, and harmonica; these songs exhibit a strong folk-rock or country-rock sensibility. Although stylistically varied, the songs function together in much the way those on a concept album would. Framed at the beginning and end by two instrumental pieces ("The Highway Life: Going" and "The Highway Life: Coming"), most of the songs are related by common themes: coming of age, good versus evil, and physical or spiritual travel.

The songs from *Dude* might have made for enjoyable listening, but the lack of narrative connecting them frustrated critics, for whom a bunch of loosely thematically connected, overamplified songs was simply not enough to support a million-dollar musical. As Mandelbaum argues, while attractive in their own right, the songs from *Dude* fail to function properly as theater music, since they "could have been sung in any order or by any 'character' with the same result."[28] Indeed, while some critics voiced an appreciation for MacDermot's songs, a majority were clearly flummoxed by *Dude*'s incoherent plot, as evidenced by the fact that almost all of them describe it differently, from an Adam and Eve–like parable, to an allegory about adolescence, to a battle between good and evil for the soul of Everyman.

Dude's lack of cohesiveness, coupled with what was perceived to be a tremendous waste of money spent to make a mess of a perfectly functional Broadway theater, prompted New York's theater critics to rip into *Dude* with the nastiest of notices. Richard Watts of the *Post* echoed a number of his colleagues in registering disappointment over the fact that MacDermot's score was almost impossible to hear clearly, due to both the overamplified sound system and Ragni's insistence on breaking up the orchestra and placing different sections of it in various parts of the theater. In *Women's Wear Daily*, Martin Gottfried wrote that *Dude* was "incoherent, childish, and boring" and "very noisy about it,"[29] while Jack Kroll of *Newsweek* wrote that the musical was "a stupid mess" and "a fake, 'multi-media' idiocy," adding, "It's the first time I ever felt sorry for a theater."[30] Apparently, audiences felt the same way. *Dude* closed after sixteen performances at a loss of eight hundred thousand dollars, making it one of the most costly flops in Broadway history.

Quick on the heels of *Dude* was *Via Galactica,* a futuristic rock musical conceived and directed by Peter Hall, with lyrics by Christopher Gore and Judith Ross, and a score by Galt MacDermot. *Via Galactica* served as the inaugural production of the Uris Theatre; unfortunately for those associated with the production, the new one-thousand-seat Broadway house was praised far more lavishly than the musical itself. Like *Dude*, *Via Galactica* was ripped to shreds by critics when it opened on November 28, 1972.

By most accounts, *Via Galactica* was slightly more coherent than *Dude*, but otherwise suffered from almost all the same problems: a contrived concept, a sound system that could not handle the amplified instrumentation, too much emphasis on elaborate staging and special effects, and not enough emphasis on plot. *Via Galactica* depicted a band of rebels living on an asteroid in the year 2972. The production was certainly spectacular: the stage was outfitted with huge trampolines on which members of the company bounced to simulate weightlessness; lighting gimmicks allowed "laser beams" to shoot across the stage and into the theater; and the elaborate set included a giant spaceship.

According to Mandelbaum, however, "The complexities of the production, not helped by the fact that *Via Galactica* was the first show booked into the new Uris Theatre, were so enormous that the show's textual problems took a back seat. (The show's original title, *Up!*, had to be abandoned when the producers realized that the marquee would contain an unwanted pun if it read "*Up! Uris.*")."[31] Late in the rehearsal period, Hall wrote in his diary that the technical aspects of *Via Galactica* were rapidly improving, but that the overall production was becoming "thinner and less worthwhile" by the day, due in part to a script that "was never right and still isn't."[32] To make matters worse, the amplification problems that plagued *Dude* took their toll on this production as well. Otis L. Guernsey, Jr., editor of the *Best Plays* series, wrote that at the performance he attended, the orchestra was playing so loudly that "it was hard to hear what was being sung. People in the balcony began shouting to the orchestra to tone down so they could hear the words."[33]

While little could be done about the sound, an attempt was made to clarify the plot of *Via Galactica:* synopses were printed and inserted into the programs during the preview period.[34] These plot summaries did not save *Via Galactica* from the critics. In his review for the *New York Times,* Walter Kerr quipped, "I would call the text childish but children are clearer."[35] For the same newspaper, Clive Barnes wrote that for all of its spectacle, *Via Galactica* featured an "appallingly weak" plot. "Presumably everyone thought that with a truly sumptuous and adventurous staging," he observed, "Mr. MacDermot's music would do the trick. This was a miscalculation." He continued:

The well-publicized use of trampolines, to suggest weightlessness, suggests nothing more than people pointlessly bouncing up and down on
trampolines. The mechanical space garbage cart (looking not at all
futuristic incidentally) is all too clearly chained to the stage, and the
attacking space ship from earth looks like a displaced lighting fitting.
. . . The trampolines should have gone, but with the trampolines would
also have gone the show's one small claim to innovation.[36]

Via Galactica closed after seven performances, losing nine hundred thousand dollars in the process.[37]

Ken Mandelbaum, who saw both musicals, remembers that *Via Galactica* was slightly more appealing than *Dude,* due to clearer direction, clever
special effects, and a score that seemed occasionally catchy, despite the
blaring sound system. Nevertheless, he argues, for all their gimmickry,
neither show had any "narrative or emotional content whatsoever that
could pull an audience in. And no musical can succeed without that."[38]

By this point, several poorly conceived rock musicals had already
opened on—and been quickly driven off—Broadway stages. The string of
disappointments included Joseph Kookolis, Scott Fagan, and Martin
Duberman's *Soon* (January 1971; three performances); C. C. Courtney and
Peter Link's *Earl of Ruston* (May 1971; five performances); and Tom Mar-
tel's *Hard Job Being God* (May 1972; six performances). By the time *Dude*
and *Via Galactica* arrived on Broadway, the patience for shows billed as
rock musicals had begun to wear thin among critics and audiences alike.

Compared with *Dude* and *Via Galactica, Rainbow* was a small and
inexpensive affair, which also happened to be the most critically successful of the three. This isn't saying much: *Rainbow* merely escaped the vindictive pans that critics lobbed at the other two musicals. Although *Rainbow* was originally intended for Broadway, financial problems brought
the production Off Broadway instead. It opened at the Orpheum Theater
on December 18, 1972.

Like *Hair, Rainbow* was a fragmented musical that, due to its forty-two
musical numbers and diffuse plot, was regularly misinterpreted by critics
as a revue. While even those critics who panned the musical acknowledged that they found the score enjoyable, most critics were not as kind in
forgiving what they perceived as a woefully convoluted plot. Even Clive
Barnes, who gave *Rainbow* one of its strongest reviews, was clearly
bemused by the story line:

[S]omeone called simply Man has been killed in Vietnam, and comes over the other side into Rainbow land. . . . There is a Mother, and a Father, and Jesus, and Buddha, a Stripper, a Wizard, a Girl, her Lesbian twin, a President and a First Lady. . . . The Man, accompanied by his Rainbow Room of cronies, goes to Washington and there sees the President. "Why was I killed in Vietnam, Mr. President," he asks plaintively. Mr. President, a good guy at heart, replies, "If it was my fault, forgive me." Yes, well.[39]

Confused plot notwithstanding, there is some indication that poor timing was what caused *Rainbow*'s rapid demise. In his pan of the musical for the *New York Times,* Walter Kerr acknowledged that he enjoyed much of act 1, but became "seriously uncomfortable" during act 2, wherein Man and his friends successfully beg the President to end the war. It's not terribly surprising that the second act didn't sit well with Kerr; *Rainbow*'s opening night coincided with the resumption of bombing in North Vietnam after the breaking off of peace talks.[40] It is certainly possible that many theatergoers, frustrated by the war in general and the most recent wave of violence in particular, shared Kerr's sentiments. For whatever reason, *Rainbow* did not connect with audiences. It closed on January 28, 1973 after forty-eight performances.[41]

Off and Off-Off-Broadway

Because *Rainbow* was staged in a small Off Broadway theater on a relatively modest budget, it did not get the same amount of press attention that *Dude* and *Via Galactica* got late in 1972. This turned out to be to its advantage, in the end, considering the fact that the press turned so viciously on both of the larger, more commercial shows after they opened. *Rainbow* was not unique in this respect. Through the 1970s, amid the many big-budget rock musicals that were opening on Broadway only to fall prey to annoyed critics and disappointed audiences, there were countless small, inexpensive rock-influenced musicals that were mounted Off and Off-Off-Broadway, at a relatively safe remove from the glaring eyes of the demanding press.

At worst, these shows, like their Broadway counterparts, were critical and commercial failures that closed quickly. For example, *The House of*

Leather, which matched an amplified, electric score with a plot about the inhabitants of a Civil War–era New Orleans whorehouse, opened at Café La MaMa in March 1970 and closed on the same evening.[42] A similar fate befell Theatre Four's *The Ballad of Johnny Pot* in 1971. This musical, the score of which was performed by a rock band called Bandana, envisioned Johnny Appleseed as a marijuana seed-sprinkling hippie who wanted to share his passion for reefer with all the people of the world. Despite its producers' attempts to boost a slumping post-review box office by offering a free performance, few spectators were interested in actually purchasing tickets to this musical, which folded within two weeks.[43] As with *Rainbow,* these smaller, Off and Off-Off-Broadway shows were not as expensive to produce, or as brashly spectacular as their Broadway counterparts; they thus tended to escape the critics' most vindictive notices. In general, the worst that happened to these low-budget flops is that they closed quickly, quietly, and at a relatively small loss to their investors.

And of course, amid the failures was a handful of Off and Off-Off-Broadway musicals with rock-influenced scores that never became as well known as *Hair,* but that nevertheless enjoyed modest commercial success and critical admiration. These include Gretchen Ford and Nancy Cryer's *The Last Sweet Days of Isaac* (1970), a two-character musical comprising two vignettes that explored the relationship of mass media and reality, which ran at the East Side Playhouse for 485 performances;[44] Gary William Friedman and Will Holt's *The Me Nobody Knows,* a musical about the lives of underprivileged urban children that opened at the Orpheum Theater in May 1970 and moved uptown to the Helen Hayes Theater for a modest run eight months later;[45] Elizabeth Swados's *Runaways,* a collage of monologues, songs, and sketches about teen runaways, which sold well enough at the Public Theater in 1978 to justify a move to Broadway for an additional eight months;[46] and Ford and Cryer's *I'm Getting My Act Together and Taking It on the Road,* also at the Public in 1978, which examined the impact of women's liberation on a middle-aged female pop singer preparing a comeback tour with her band.[47] Amid this string of modest successes, there was a show that was intimate, largely free of spectacle, cheap to produce, and greeted with indifference by critics, only to become one of the most successful rock musicals of its time.

Godspell

Through the late 1960s and early 1970s, many young Americans retreated from the increasingly volatile realm of left-wing politics toward a cultivation of the self in communes, cults, or various "new age" explorations.[48] A new interest in the therapeutic power of spirituality led to a fascination with Eastern religions on one hand, and evangelical Christianity on the other. Despite widely diverse approaches and agendas, the rise in interest among American youth in evangelical Christianity became known as the "Jesus revolution," or more commonly the "Jesus movement," and its adherents as "Jesus freaks." The Jesus movement was both reflected in and influenced by 1970s youth culture.[49] Jesus' wave of mainstream popularity was evident on the radio airwaves, where numerous Top 40 hits—including Ocean's "Put Your Hand in the Hand," the Doobie Brothers' "Jesus Is Just Alright," the Five Man Electrical Band's "Signs," and Norman Greenbaum's "Spirit in the Sky"—featured lyrics with overtly Christian themes.

The Christian revival was also reflected on the theatrical stage. On May 17, 1971, Godspell opened at the Cherry Lane Theater after a three-month run at Off-Off-Broadway's Café La MaMa. This musical, which had a score by Stephen Schwartz and a book by John-Michael Tebelak, featured a cast of ten actors accompanied by a small ensemble consisting of keyboards, guitars, bass guitar, and percussion.

Another fragmented musical that is often mistaken for a revue, Godspell was a celebratory, childlike retelling of parables taken from Matthew and Luke in the New Testament.[50] Its score was reflective of Stephen Schwartz's admiration for singer-songwriters like Joni Mitchell, Laura Nyro, James Taylor, Paul Simon, and Cat Stevens, especially in its largely acoustic instrumentation and its many spiritually introspective lyric passages.[51] Unlike other contemporary musicals to tackle religious themes— Hair, Salvation, and Stomp, for example—Godspell took an innocent, highly positive approach to Christianity, which has surely contributed to its staying power.

In keeping with the Christian revivalism of the time, the Jesus featured in the original production of Godspell was decidedly contemporary. Part hippie and part ragged clown, he wore a big red nose, suspenders, clown makeup complete with a red heart painted on one cheek, and a Superman T-shirt.[52] Sweet, approachable, and loving, the Godspell Jesus is less a God than a cherished friend. Summoned early in act 1 by a similarly ragtag John the Baptist—who functions here as Jesus' good buddy and trusty assistant—Jesus appears in an urban playground to an ensemble of lost souls who are in desperate need of spiritual direction.

Godspell makes no attempt to recount Jesus' life, although the Crucifixion serves as the climax to the piece. Instead, the parables are enacted in a series of humorous, energetic, topical skits, each of which is punctuated by a song. Despite the Crucifixion scene, *Godspell* concludes on a resoundingly positive note; saddened by the loss of their beloved friend and teacher, the ensemble is nevertheless rejuvenated. Joyously repeating the sung line "Long live God" before reprising the number "Day by Day," they are caught up in a joyous, infectious dance; it is clear by the curtain call that they have all resolved to live by Jesus' teachings.

Despite its use of standard rock instrumentation, a score clearly influenced by the burgeoning singer-songwriter movement, and the songs' reliance on call-and-response patterns, lyric repetition, and motivic fragments, *Godspell* was never explicitly promoted as a rock musical.[53] This is telling: since so many shows that *were* being promoted as rock musicals were opening to poor notices and indifferent audiences by the early 1970s, it is not surprising that those to connect most solidly with audiences would avoid any use of the term in appealing to the public.

While many critics found *Godspell* to be too syrupy for their tastes, the musical was widely embraced by audiences. It remained at the Cherry Lane for 2,124 performances before moving uptown to Broadway's Broadhurst Theater for another 567.[54] It also spawned a hit single in the song "Day by Day," which reached number 13 on the Billboard Top 40 in 1972 and attracted a broader national audience to the show.[55] Due to its simple setting and structure, its unflinching and uncomplicated embrace of Christianity, and the fact that its many topical references are easily updated, *Godspell* is still regularly revived across the country by amateur and professional theater companies, and, of course, countless church groups.

Adapting Concept Albums for the Stage

While fragmented rock musicals that are conceived for the stage can sometimes prove too abstract for their own good, those adapted from concept albums can be just as problematic. Imposing structure on a piece of art that is not meant to have any is, of course, just as awkward as staging a musical with no structure at all, if not more so. Tom O'Horgan notes that although such adaptations are risky, the logic behind them is simple: basing a theater piece on a well-known concept album will draw young people to the theater. Even further, the logic goes, the fact that the music has already proven commercially viable can only add to a musical's potential for success.[56] Yet such logic has proven faulty over and over again. While the practice of adapting literary works and popular films for the musical stage is common and has yielded many successful productions, the practice of adapting concept albums has proven especially challenging, in terms of both execution and reception.

A chief problem encountered in the adaptation of rock recordings for the stage lies in the fact that in the musical theater realm, sound recordings function very differently than they do in the rock realm. While rock recordings have proven hugely successful since the inception of the genre, original cast recordings of Broadway and Off Broadway musicals have almost always been viewed by the American music industry as risky ventures, especially since they preserve only one aspect of a multifaceted production. As early as the 1930s, and despite the commercial success of many staged musicals, "record companies weren't convinced that people who flocked to see a Broadway musical would be interested in having an aural record of its music and songs."[57] Although this attitude changed briefly during the 1940s, especially after the success of Rodgers and Hammerstein's *Oklahoma!* in 1943, original cast recordings have almost always been viewed as "specialty" items consumed by small markets.[58] Because musical theater productions are usually not mass-mediated, and only rarely become well-known enough to penetrate international or even national markets, cast recordings are often made more out of an interest in preserving theater music than they are for financial gain.[59] In contrast, rock recordings can and do function as ends in themselves. In his book *Rhythm and Noise: An Aesthetics of Rock*, Theodore Gracyk argues that although many critics and historians treat rock performance and rock recording interchangeably, or emphasize the importance of the former over the latter, it is ultimately recording technology that is of fundamental importance to rock's history and development.[60]

Whereas the American musical theater flourished long before the advent of sound-recording technology, and continues to function independently of this technology, it is impossible to conceive of rock music without it. Gracyk's argument certainly applies to concept albums. While some are conceivably performed live, as has been demonstrated by groups like the Who and Pink Floyd, concept albums are for the most part studio creations intended for private, repeated listening.

A related problem encountered in the adaptation of concept albums for the musical stage lies in the fact that while repeated listening might allow such recordings to become familiar, it also allows for, and even encourages, personal interpretation. The success of many concept albums is largely due to their lack of linearity and their polysemic nature. A studio effort by a well-known rock group may become the favorite of millions of people, yet its lack of narrative simultaneously allows listeners to form highly personal interpretations.

The stage adaptations of *Jesus Christ Superstar* and *Sgt. Pepper's Lonely Hearts Club Band* are cases in point. These musicals were expected to succeed in large part because the sound recordings they were based on were so enormously successful. What their creators did not anticipate, however, was the fact that by imposing their own visions on a popular concept album, they were simultaneously denying myriad other interpretations on one hand, while failing to attain narrative clarity on the other. Although the stage adaptations of *Jesus Christ Superstar* and *Sgt. Pepper's Lonely Hearts Club Band* had slightly different receptions—with the first a middling commercial hit and a critical disappointment, and the second a critical and commercial flop—neither production was as successful as had been anticipated because neither could transcend its own status as a sound recording.

Jesus Christ Superstar

The first Broadway rock musical to be adapted from a popular concept album was the greatly hyped, highly controversial rock opera *Jesus Christ Superstar,* which opened at the Mark Hellinger Theater on October 12, 1971. Dubbed by *Variety* "the biggest all-media parlay in show business history"[61] at the time of its Broadway premiere, the Andrew Lloyd Webber and Tim Rice collaboration recounted the last week in the life of Jesus Christ. One of the more thematically straightforward concept albums to emerge at the time, *Jesus Christ Superstar* tackled subject matter that was both compelling and familiar to much of the Western world. While theatrical stagings of *Jesus Christ Superstar* have regularly proven more challenging than successful, the concept album was wildly popular upon its 1970 release, and remains internationally known.

Lloyd Webber and Rice began their collaboration in 1965 with a musical based on the life of the Victorian doctor and philanthropist Thomas John Bernardo. When this project failed to garner the interest of producers, the two went to work on a rock cantata for children as a favor for a schoolteacher friend. The result, *Joseph and the Amazing Technicolor Dreamcoat*, became popular in England, and was soon being presented by children in schools around the country.[62] *Joseph*'s success earned Lloyd Webber and Rice a publishing contract and an agent, and thus the opportunity to develop more projects.[63]

After attempts to write a musical based on the life of Richard the Lionhearted proved fruitless, Lloyd Webber and Rice revisited a suggestion, made years prior to Lloyd Webber by an Anglican minister, for a musical about the life of Jesus that "modern youth could identify with."[64] The two decided that instead of simply setting the Gospels to music, they would attempt to explore the humanity of Jesus and his followers. Their piece, set to a modern score, would emphasize Jesus' relationship with Judas.

Although interested in developing their idea for the stage, they quickly abandoned hope of finding a producer who would finance such a project. According to Lloyd Webber, "nobody would put it on stage. I mean, every single producer in London said, 'You have to be joking. This is the worst idea in history.'"[65] Their plans for a stage musical quashed, Rice and Lloyd Webber began instead to court the music industry in hopes of making *Jesus Christ Superstar* into a concept album. Armed with a recording of "Superstar," the only song yet written for the project, they were rejected by a variety of record executives before garnering interest among employees at MCA-Decca.

At the time, MCA-Decca was a catalog company specializing in the repackaging of former releases. It represented only one well-known rock group—the Who. The commercial success of the Who's recent rock opera, *Tommy,* had made executives eager to develop similar projects, thereby strengthening the company's standing in the rock market. Members of the company's English and Australian offices had been scouting for rock musicians who might succeed in the United States. In November 1969, while in England, one of MCA-Decca's vice presidents took interest in "Superstar" and brought a copy back to New York, where executives agreed to back the as-yet unwritten rock opera, contingent upon the advance release of "Superstar" as a single. A successful single, it was hoped, would generate interest in the concept album once it was complete.[66]

"Superstar," recorded by the Scottish singer and actor Murray Head, along with a backup group called the Trinidad Singers, was released internationally in December 1969.[67] Although "Superstar" sold well in South America and the predominantly Catholic countries of Western Europe, it was banned by the BBC, and thus performed poorly in the UK. The song was also largely ignored in the States: it crept onto the *Billboard* Hot-100 charts at 99 in January 1970, and remained on the charts for four weeks, peaking only at 74.[68] Although disappointed with the outcome, MCA-Decca executives decided to take a risk and record the entire album.

Rumors and press reports about the development of this concept album listed celebrities like Marianne Faithfull, John Lennon, and Yoko Ono as potential leads. While Rice and Lloyd Webber were reportedly interested in casting Lennon as Jesus, executives at MCA-Decca insisted that Lennon's own star status would detract from the part.[69] Ultimately, actors and musicians with lower profiles were enlisted to sing the lead roles. Ian Gillan, who had recently replaced Rod Evans as lead singer for the British rock group Deep Purple, was cast as Jesus; Murray Head was retained as Judas; and Yvonne Elliman, a nightclub singer discovered by Lloyd Webber, was cast as Mary Magdalene.[70]

The resultant album reflects Lloyd Webber's eclecticism as a composer while consistently remaining true to a strong rock sensibility. *Jesus Christ Superstar* is scored largely for rock ensemble—electric and acoustic guitars, drums, electric bass, and keyboards—which provides riff-based accompaniment beneath the singers. Busy thumping bass-lines, repetitive electric guitar licks, brushy acoustic guitar chords, and syncopated backbeats on the drums propel most of the musical numbers. Lloyd Webber's interest in the contemporary art rock movement is revealed through the frequent use of Moog synthesizer (played on the album by Lloyd Webber himself) and the use of irregular meters ("Everything's Alright" is in 5/4, for example; "The Temple" is in 7/8). A small orchestra contributes to the incidental music between songs through act 1 and most of act 2. Honking woodwinds, trembling strings, and pealing brass join with the rock ensemble to add texture and dynamic range beneath the voices late in act

2, making Jesus' trial and crucifixion evocative of Romantic compositions by the likes of Berlioz and Wagner. Over the instrumentation, recitatives and songs—performed by singers whose croons and whispers frequently give way to shrieks and moans of concern, frustration, ecstasy, and despair—recount the final days of Jesus' life.

While the single "Superstar" failed to garner much attention in the States, *Jesus Christ Superstar* was a thundering success. The album was previewed for the American press on October 1970 at St. Peter's Lutheran Church in New York City, following an aggressive promotional campaign; two weeks earlier, executives from MCA-Decca invited personnel from three FM radio stations in New York to preview the record, in hopes that cuts from the album would receive ample airplay.[71]

Their efforts proved worthwhile. *Jesus Christ Superstar* was almost unanimously praised by critics, and connected solidly with a large listening audience. The album quickly went gold, and spent sixty-five weeks on the *Billboard* album charts, including three weeks at number 1.[72] Disc jockeys gave the album plenty of airtime, which yielded two hit singles: "I Don't Know How to Love Him" and the rereleased "Superstar."[73] By mid-May 1971, two different versions of "I Don't Know How to Love Him"—Yvonne Elliman's original, and one by Helen Reddy—had entered the Top 40. Elliman's recording peaked at number 28, and Reddy's made it up to number 9.

The overwhelming commercial success of *Jesus Christ Superstar* captured the interest of Robert Stigwood, the young rock impresario and future producer of blockbuster musical films like *Saturday Night Fever* and *Grease,* who had originally turned down the property. An innovator in the technique of cross-promotion—in which music is used to sell a movie, musical, or television show, and vice versa—Stigwood had a knack for taking a musical vehicle and building on it "by promoting the music so that it got better known than the play or movie."[74] Taking note of the fact that MCA owned the recorded version of *Jesus Christ Superstar* but had failed to secure the performing rights, Stigwood waited until Rice and Lloyd Webber's contracts were up for renegotiation, and then courted the two by promising to finance a staged version of the rock opera.[75]

Rice and Lloyd Webber accepted the offer, and Stigwood poured millions into the property in preparation for a Broadway premiere. He hired director Frank Corsaro to adapt the rock opera for the stage. When Corsaro was injured in an automobile accident shortly after casting had begun, Stigwood promptly replaced him with Tom O'Horgan. Opening night for *Superstar* was set for October 27, 1971, a year from the date that the album had been released in the United States.[76]

Exceedingly confident in his property, Stigwood estimated in interviews that the Broadway version of *Superstar* would enjoy the unusually long run of five or more years.[77] While enthusiastic assertions are expected of producers who discusses their own properties, there was certainly ample reason to believe that *Jesus Christ Superstar* would surpass *Hair* as the most commercially successful rock musical ever staged in New York City. The concept album had become so popular that within half a year of its initial release, unofficial concert versions had begun to crop up all over the country in churches, arenas, and school auditoriums.[78] Hoping to maintain control over the property, Stigwood sued many of these companies, and launched two "official" concert versions of the opera, tickets to which sold like hotcakes and grossed upwards of $3.5 million by October 1971.[79]

The success of both the album and concert versions helped generate a great deal of advance publicity for the Broadway adaptation. As a result, despite little in the way of advertising, *Jesus Christ Superstar* enjoyed an unprecedented advance in ticket sales. By the time it entered its preview period, the show, which cost a reported $700,000 to stage, had already sold $1.2 million worth of tickets, making the Broadway version of *Superstar* a commercial success even before it officially opened.[80]

For all of its hype, its unprecedented advance in ticket sales, and the fact that it, like *Godspell,* was opening at a time when Christian revivalism had entered popular culture and made Jesus newly cool, *Superstar* never became the long-running commercial success that Stigwood anticipated. It was tepidly received by critics, whose mixed-to-poor reviews clearly hurt the production. *Jesus Christ Superstar* ran to full houses for the first eight months as a result of its huge advance, but tickets sales plummeted once the reviews came out.[81] The show closed within two years; a majority of the 711 performances offered a large number of discounted tickets.[82]

There are a number of reasons for *Superstar*'s disappointing Broadway run. One was that because the rock opera was conceived as a sound recording, Rice and Lloyd Webber were not required to rely upon the narrative devices required of musical theater. Rice remembers that because they developed the rock opera as a record, they could not rely on any visual stimuli whatsoever to catch the interest of an audience. Rice adds that because *Jesus Christ Superstar* was originally a concept album, he and Lloyd Webber put no effort at all into developing a traditional book, or musical script. This, he believes, was at least initially to their advantage:

> I think if we'd had the show staged in the theater straight away . . . we'd have put in a long, boring book and there would have been scenes— you know, Jesus saying, "Hello, Judas, good to see you, sit down here." It would've been awful, and the music would not have been as dynamic and contemporary . . . [But] we never gave a thought to things like motivation, characterization, or even plausibility of staging it.[83]

In writing *Superstar,* Rice and Lloyd Webber were much more interested in asking questions than in providing answers. They thus took a great many liberties with their subject matter; the result was a rock opera that fictionalized the thoughts, motivations, and actions of a group of prominent historical characters. Like the creators of *Godspell,* Rice and Lloyd Webber took a modern approach in developing the character of Jesus, whose lyrics in the rock opera suggest not divinity but a slew of human characteristics, including fear, doubt, irritability, and, very possibly, a strong libido. Similarly, the Judas in *Superstar* is a deeply conflicted, ultimately sympathetic figure, whose betrayal is compelled by the fear that Jesus and the apostles are going too far. Mary Magdalene, not mentioned by name in the New Testament until the day of resurrection, is combined, in the rock opera, with the unnamed woman who anoints Jesus' feet to the chagrin of Simon in Luke 7:36–50. Herod, barely mentioned in the Bible, is given a private meeting with Jesus in *Superstar.* Pontius Pilate's wife Procula, who in Matthew 28:19 has a prophetic dream and warns her husband to treat Jesus kindly, is not mentioned at all in the rock opera; her dream, as well as the song describing it, are instead given to Pilate. Perhaps the most controversial liberty that Lloyd Webber and Rice take is in depicting the relationship between Mary Magdalene and Jesus as emotionally tangled and very possibly sexual.

Rice explains that he and Lloyd Webber had been "well-coached in the mechanics of Christianity and its legends and beliefs" as schoolchildren, but that taking such an approach to these familiar biblical characters struck both of them as unsatisfying. "I find Jesus as portrayed in the

Gospels as a God as a very unrealistic figure," Rice argues. "The same is true . . . for Judas, who is portrayed just as a sort of cardboard cut-out figure of evil."[84] Rice and Lloyd Webber realized that they were both more interested in trying to depict these biblical figures as human beings. Rather than simply recounting the last days of Jesus' life, the duo tried to examine "why it was that Judas betrayed somebody he clearly loved," as well as to shed light on Jesus's reactions to circumstances that had "arguably spun out of his own control."[85]

The result is a rock opera that places more emphasis on the possible thoughts and motivations of its characters than on their actions as conveyed in the scriptures. To this end, the opera is not paced adequately for easy translation to the stage, and the musical numbers fail to build appropriately toward the climactic final scene. The conflicts between Judas and Jesus, for example, are revisited again and again, but each clash seems no more or less intense than the one before it; the depths of Jesus and Mary Magdalene's relationship are suggested early on in "Everything's Alright" and "I Don't Know How to Love Him," and then never revisited; and Judas's concern over Jesus' growing influence is expressed in the very first number with the same panicked shrieks that the character emits as he betrays Jesus, and again near the end, just before he hangs himself.

The musical numbers on the sound recording are certainly energetically performed, and thus consistently exciting to listen to. Yet a song cycle describing little more than characters' states of mind, however hotly emotional, can ultimately make for a staged version of *Jesus Christ Superstar* that seems more two-dimensional than the sound recording.

Tom O'Horgan argues that while *Jesus Christ Superstar* had a theatrical concept, "it just was not very theatrically constructed." This led to problems in adapting the album for the stage. "When I first attacked the piece with Andrew [Lloyd Webber]," O'Horgan remembers, "he said he would write some other numbers that would help make it flow a little better. But he didn't. So we just had to create visual things that would work with the music and make it understandable."[86] Because *Jesus Christ Superstar* offers little in the way of dramatic progress, O'Horgan felt limited in potential approaches to staging the piece. He decided to compensate for the rock opera's dramaturgical shortcomings and lack of narrative flow by creating a production that was as visually spectacular as he could make it. Convinced that there was "nothing in Rice and [Lloyd] Webber's highly romantic score that would support an even slightly realistic presentation," and hoping that the success of the album would "bring people into the theater who would never, under any circumstances, consider entering one," O'Horgan decided to take a "mystic, metaphysical approach." He thus developed a grandiose concept comprised of spectacular scenery, special effects, and costumes.[87] "I had gone to the Museum of Natural History, and there was a whole thing about insects when I was in the process of putting [*Superstar*] together," he remembers. "So I thought, maybe I would do this piece as if a further civilization of evolved insects looked back at this primitive society's myth and decided to make a version of it. I don't think anybody ever got that. But if you look at the costumes, for instance, Judas is resurrected as a butterfly, and Christ comes up out of the ground in a chrysalis, and it breaks open and becomes a great moth."[88]

While the insect theme was lost on most spectators by the time *Superstar* entered its preview period, there is no question that O'Horgan had come up with a show that was visually dazzling from the moment the audience entered the theater and encountered a huge wall, hinged at the bottom, that was covering the proscenium. As the show began, the wall slowly began to fall. As it lowered, cast members leapt onto it and scuttled, insect-like, over the top. Once the wall had lowered to a safe enough angle, the cast ran down the slope toward the audience. As the cast reached the front of the stage, the wall touched the ground; it served as the stage floor for the duration of the performance.

In "The Theatrical Style of Tom O'Horgan," Bill Simmer writes that the opening sequence set the tone for the entire production. During the rest of the show, characters made entrances in the most dramatic of possible ways. Caiaphas and the priests were lowered to the stage from the catwalk on a large bridge made of bleached bones. Jesus rose from beneath the stage in a huge chalice wearing an enormous, golden robe. Scenery and props were similarly visually impressive; the production made ample use of smoke, laser beams, and wind machines."[89]

O'Horgan's attempt to dazzle his audience for fear that the story itself would put them to sleep backfired. Critics attacked his production. Many agreed that the opera was dramaturgically slim, but simultaneously opposed what they saw as the director's heavy-handed method of compensating for this fact. Walter Kerr wrote in the *New York Times* that the worst aspects of the production lay in "the unbelievable vulgarity of Mr.

O'Horgan's imagination,"[90] and the radio critic Richard J. Scholem argued that the outrageous visual effects worked not to help but instead to swallow up what little dramatic conflict the musical was able to generate. "There are spectacular songs and scenes that are moving," he concluded, "but as a totality, this offering failed to sweep up an audience or at times even to involve it.[91]

While the Broadway version *Jesus Christ Superstar* might well have failed to engage many spectators, it succeeded in infuriating a host of religious groups, many of whom were less offended by the concept album than they were by the perceived vulgarity of the staging and the visual depictions of the characters. This reaction was unique to the Broadway version: a smattering of clergy members had condemned the hit single "Superstar" when it debuted in the United States in 1969, but the concept album was never the subject of any organized protest, much to the surprise of MCA-Decca's public relations director.[92] In fact, the album was embraced by many Christian leaders, who reasoned that any record about Jesus that was being marketed to young people should be accepted and encouraged.[93]

While the Broadway version of *Superstar* was lyrically identical to the concept album, it nevertheless became the subject of organized protest. From the time of its premiere, picketers representing several different religious groups gathered outside of the Mark Hellinger Theater with signs protesting the depictions of various characters. The American Jewish Committee and the Anti-Defamation League expressed concern over what they saw as stereotypical depictions of the Jewish high priests as "Christ killers,"[94] while Catholic and Baptist groups protested the sympathetic depiction of Judas and what they perceived as a denial of Jesus' divinity.

O'Horgan reasons that a staged musical, unlike a record, exists in a specific location, and that his production was thus more easily targeted than the sound recording. "A lot of people who wouldn't even look at or come to see *Jesus Christ Superstar* were offended that it existed," he said. "So there was always somebody picketing in front of the theater. On the other hand, people who bought records *wanted* to buy the records, but it wasn't being foisted off on anybody."[95]

While O'Horgan may be correct, another likely possibility is that the album's lack of visual stimulus allowed aspects of the story to remain open to interpretation, while the visual aspects employed in the stage version offended the sensibilities of more people. In "*Jesus Christ Superstar*—Popular Art and Unpopular Criticism," James R. Huffman argues that the success of the concept album was largely due to its ambiguousness. "Works like *Jesus Christ Superstar,* which 'ask the right questions' but allow each individual to provide his own answers, will be appropriated by nearly all—the atheist, the agnostic, and the believer," he writes. "Since *Superstar* is basically neutral, it can profit from nearly everyone's inertia."[96]

O'Horgan's adaptation, on the other hand, combined evocative music with a stage production that struck many people as too heavy-handed. "*Superstar*'s vulgarity is less in the realm of religious than of theatrical taste," wrote critic Bill Bender of *Time* magazine. "Fans, in fact, may well be advised to open a new chapter in the age of McLuhan by turning down a chance at the show 'because I loved the record.' On LP, *Superstar* is abstract intimate, capable of subtly engaging the mind and the imagination. Director O'Horgan's frenetic Broadway incarnation is rarely any of those things."[97]

Malcolm Boyd, an Episcopal priest and author of *Human Like Me, Jesus,* took exception not to the score of *Superstar,* but to the onstage depictions of its characters. He found the interpretation of Jesus and Mary Magdalene's relationship especially crass:

> The sexuality of Jesus will undoubtedly comprise the Exhibit A controversy about the show. He and Mary Magdalene fondle and kiss each other; I felt an implicit acceptance of the fact that they have enjoyed intercourse. The exposure of this side of Jesus' humanity drew cheers from the audience, perhaps in reaction against the celibate Jesus . . . who has been used as a major argument against sex outside of (and before) wedlock as well as against homosexuality. Jesus as a human being . . . may be far overdue in our puritanical, sexually hypocritical society. Yet I feel that his sexuality was not handled with sensitivity or with taste in this gaudily inhuman parody.[98]

Contributing to what was perceived as a problematic staging of *Jesus Christ Superstar* were inevitable comparisons with the original recording, the pristine quality of which proved impossible to replicate in a live theater. Problems with sound quality—or lack thereof—plagued O'Horgan's production.

Superstar is orchestrated for electric instruments, which tend to overpower singing voices. This imbalance is easily rectified in a recording studio, but not in the Mark Hellinger Theater, which was built in 1930 and thus not designed for amplified sound. During rehearsals for *Superstar,* O'Horgan tried everything he could think of to balance the sound in the old theater. First, he attempted to cover the orchestra: "The conductor had a plastic bowl over him—the idea was to enclose the orchestra and make the pit into a recording studio. But everybody hated it, so they ripped it open before we opened." O'Horgan then appealed to producer Robert Stigwood for help. Stigwood designed a top-notch state-of-the-art sound system that O'Horgan remembers was impressive—but still unsatisfactory. "What it did was take out notes that were overamplified," he says. "As a consequence, we ended up with a bland, nothing sound. That went on for two or three weeks of previews. Eventually we all threw up our hands and got *another* sound guy to put in *another* system. Which worked better but was still not right."[99]

A related problem was how to amplify the actors so that they might be heard over the accompaniment. "Back when I was doing *Superstar* and *Hair,* wireless mikes were almost unknown," O'Horgan says. "We might have used one or two, but everybody else had hand mikes with long chords. As a consequence, my choreography had to be done very carefully. Otherwise, you would weave a basket, which was often the case."[100]

Handheld microphones had been put to good use in *Hair,* which had a contemporary setting. The use of handheld mikes, however, made a lot less sense in a musical set during biblical times. O'Horgan attempted to disguise all of the microphones, but the casts' reliance on them did not go over well with critics. John Kane, who covered the New York production for London's *Sunday Times,* wrote:

> Someone connected with *Jesus Christ Superstar* . . . decided that hand mikes would be incongruous in AD 33, so they are disguised as hand-mirrors, sceptres, fans . . . Judas has his disguised as a length of rope, and for the first half of the show I looked forward to the moment in the second half when, I hoped, Judas would hang himself with his own mike cord. It was not to be. . . . Barry Dennen . . . obviously felt the need of both hands in the role of Pontius Pilate; so his mike is grafted on to an ornamental breastplate and gilded in an attempt to camouflage it as a decoration. The ungainly result resembles a misplaced phallus with the unfortunate habit of waggling erratically whenever Mr. Dennen

gets excited, so that only one in every three words is delivered squarely into the mike. With so many characters carrying their own amplification while nimbly dodging and manipulating the cables that snake off into the wings, the dramatic mystery of Christ's last seven days is quite submerged in the more immediate suspense of who is going to come to grief first.[101]

Theatrical sound design has improved markedly over the past thirty years, but it nevertheless remains a challenge for many productions, especially those staged in cavernous theaters built long before the age of amplified sound. Problems tend to plague rock musicals in particular, since sound systems are expected to support both the loud volumes typical of rock performance and the clarity of voice that is deemed necessary in the musical theater.

While problems with amplification apply to rock musicals in general, those based on popular sound recordings face an additional problem: they are almost always compared unfavorably with the original. As John Kane wisely noted in his *Sunday Times* review of the O'Horgan production, "*Jesus Christ Superstar* has acquainted its audience with every number it has, making it one of the few Broadway shows where the audience comes into the theater humming the tunes."[102] While the lure of familiarity is surely appealing to producers, it inadvertently raises the stakes. If a Broadway adaptation takes any serious departures from the beloved sound recording on which it is based, the result is guaranteed to disappoint at least some of the audience. In the case of the original Broadway production of *Superstar,* not only was it impossible to bring studio-recording-quality sound design to the Mark Hellinger Theater in 1971, it was also impossible for the stage actors to emulate the singers on the original album.

The sound recording of *Superstar* features singers whose wide-ranging voices reflect the raw, gritty vocal quality expected of hard rock and heavy metal. Because the sound recording was created in sixty sessions over a six-month period, singers involved with the project had ample time to rest their voices between takes.[103] Actors performing live several times a week, however, do not enjoy similar luxuries, and usually cannot force their voices in the same ways over long periods of time. Those in more demanding roles are particularly susceptible to vocal injury: Jeff Fenholt, who created the role of Jesus on Broadway and years later served as the sixth of nine lead singers for the age-old heavy metal group Black Sabbath, was unable to sustain the vocal power that Ian Gillan demonstrated in the same role on the sound recording. Early in the rehearsal period, Fenholt strained his voice, broke a blood vessel, and was temporarily hospitalized.[104]

In order to protect their voices, actors in the stage adaptation of *Jesus Christ Superstar* had to take a more careful, subdued approach to the songs they performed. Yet while a muted approach can keep from shredding vocal cords, it can also disappoint spectators who appreciate the raw vocal power exhibited on the album. *New York Times* critic Clive Barnes wrote of the original Broadway production that the company was strong, but that the actors nevertheless "played second fiddle to the memories of the record album."[105]

While the original Broadway staging of *Jesus Christ Superstar* failed to generate the excitement that surrounded the concept album, the rock opera's reception was, in many respects, reversed in Great Britain. In England, the concept album failed to garner much interest; by late 1971, fewer than three hundred thousand copies had sold there. While the popularity of the concept album in the United States ultimately seems to have hurt the Broadway run, Jim Sharman's slightly less flamboyant London production, which opened in 1972, proved enormously successful, despite mixed reviews.[106] While the London production will not be discussed in detail here, it is worth noting that the stage version enjoyed more commercial success in a country whose population was less familiar with the original sound recording.

Evita

While his over-the-top staging of *Jesus Christ Superstar* would ultimately hurt Tom O'Horgan's career, the reputations of Tim Rice and, especially, of Andrew Lloyd Webber would be built on such spectacle during the 1980s. In this respect, *Evita*, even more so than *Jesus Christ Superstar*, helped establish Rice and Lloyd Webber as a musical theater team to be reckoned with.

After *Superstar*, the duo returned to their first collaboration, the children's oratorio *Joseph and the Amazing Technicolor Dreamcoat*, which they developed into a full-scale production for the Edinburgh Festival in

1972, and brought to New York in 1976 for a limited run at the Brooklyn Academy of Music. Rice and Lloyd Webber teamed again with *Superstar* producer Robert Stigwood to collaborate on *Evita* late in the decade. This production, which originated in London before opening in New York, catalyzed a wave of British musicals that would dominate Broadway through the 1980s and 1990s, and exert a multifaceted influence there.

Evita was loosely based on the meteoric rise and untimely death of Eva Perón, wife of the Argentine dictator Juan Perón. As with *Jesus Christ Superstar*, Rice and Lloyd Webber took some wild liberties with their subject matter: the actions of the title character—depicted as a cold, power-hungry opportunist who slept her way out of the slums of Buenos Aires and into the upper echelons of Argentine society—were regularly commented upon by the musical's narrator, a young revolutionary not so coincidentally named Che. As they had with their first rock opera, Rice and Lloyd Webber released *Evita* as a sound recording before adapting it for the stage. First made available in the UK in 1976, the recorded version of *Evita* circulated for two years before the stage version premiered in London's West End.

Evita was not nearly as rock-influenced as its predecessor; the musical borrowed instead from a wide variety of genres including the waltz, tango, and military march. The recorded version of *Evita* nevertheless featured a number of elements that reflected Lloyd Webber's interest in popular genres, including the electric guitar- and bass-driven introduction, the rhythm-and-blues-based "The Lady's Got Potential," and the synthesizer-driven, disco-influenced "Buenos Aires." On the sound recording, the role of Evita was sung by pop singer Julie Covington, and Che was originated by Colm Wilkinson, former singer for the Northern Irish rhythm-and-blues band the Witnesses, who would later star as Jean Valjean in Alain Boublil and Claude-Michel Schönberg's musical *Les Misérables*.[107]

While Covington's version of "Don't Cry for Me Argentina" was a number 1 hit in the UK in 1977, the studio recording of *Evita* never became as successful as that of *Jesus Christ Superstar*.[108] In fact, whereas *Superstar* remains most successful as a sound recording, *Evita* transcended its initial status to become internationally known as a stage musical. Director Harold Prince's celebrated adaptation of *Evita* opened at London's Prince Edward Theatre in 1978 and ran for nearly eight years; the New York production, which opened at the Broadway Theater in September 1979, defied mixed reviews and ran for nearly four years.[109] Subsequent productions opened in major cities across the globe; the musical has since enjoyed several international revivals.[110]

There are a number of reasons for the fact that *Evita* functioned more successfully as a stage musical than as a sound recording, while the reverse is true of *Superstar*. First, although Lloyd Webber and Rice were alternately accused of depicting Eva Perón too sympathetically on the one hand and too harshly on the other, the subject matter of this musical was nowhere near as controversial as that of its predecessor.[111] Second, as both a sound recording and a stage production, *Evita* featured a much clearer narrative. Whereas *Superstar* emphasized the inner lives of characters, and thus was comparatively dramaturgically limited, *Evita*, for all its historical flights of fancy, employed a narrator who not only commented regularly upon Eva Perón's actions, but also helped keep focus on the events depicted during the musical.

Finally, by the time it reached the stage, *Evita* featured little in the way of rock influence and was thus likely more accessible to a broader number of theatergoers than *Superstar*. In the process of adapting *Evita* for the stage, Lloyd Webber teamed with Hershy Kay to reorchestrate the musical, and consequently most of the rock elements were excised.[112] The stage version offered horns and bowed string instruments in place of the squealing electric guitars and the synthesizer formerly featured in the introduction and "Buenos Aires," respectively, and the thumping disco beat used in the latter song was relaxed; rapidly strummed acoustic guitars were featured more prominently than electric ones in an attempt to evoke a more Latin flavor; and the rhythm-and-blues-based "The Lady's Got Potential" was cut from the show.

Even further, the use of popular singers in prominent roles was downplayed somewhat in London and entirely in New York. In the former production, the only popular singer featured in a leading role was David Essex as Che; actress Elaine Paige played Eva, and Joss Ackland played Perón. In the latter production, the music theater denizens Patti LuPone, Bob Gunton, and Mandy Patinkin originated the roles of Eva, Perón, and Che, respectively.

What most distinguishes *Evita* from *Jesus Christ Superstar*, however, is the fact that the former was one of the first to be franchised. After Tom O'Horgan's adaptation of *Jesus Christ Superstar* failed to match the blockbuster success of the sound recording, Andrew Lloyd Webber vowed to maintain much more control over all future productions. Thus, since *Superstar*, he—and not the director—has had the last word on the way his musicals are to be realized for the stage. As a result, "no matter where in the world it is playing, each production of a Lloyd Webber show looks exactly the same as its Broadway or West End incarnation. What you saw before is what you get again."[113] It is *Evita*, then, and not *Jesus Christ Superstar*, that established Andrew Lloyd Webber as one of the most powerful composers in the commercial theater industry.

Evita, however, marked only the first stage of Lloyd Webber's profound influence on the postwar musical theater. This musical's impact paled in comparison with that of Lloyd Webber's next project, his first without Tim Rice. *Cats* would become the first in a long line of what have since become described alternately as "through-composed popular operas" or "poperas" and, much more often, as "megamusicals."[114] The megamusical explosion is discussed in the interlude following this chapter.

Sgt. Pepper's Lonely Hearts Club Band on the Road

Although Rice and Lloyd Webber were present at many rehearsals for the Broadway production of *Superstar*, the negative reviews and controversy surrounding the production compelled them to issue a statement shortly after it opened saying that they were deeply unsatisfied with Tom O'Horgan's realization of their concept album.[115] This exercise in self-protection, compounded by O'Horgan's association with the failed *Dude* a year later, contributed to the director's rapidly declining popularity among Broadway producers by the mid-1970s.[116] Unfortunately, his next project, *Sgt. Pepper's Lonely Hearts Club Band on the Road: A Rock Spectacle*, which opened in 1974, did little to help the director clear his name.

Sgt. Pepper's Lonely Hearts Club Band on the Road was developed in collaboration with Robin Wagner, who had previously worked with O'Horgan as the set designer for *Hair* and *Jesus Christ Superstar*. Interested, as always, in bringing more young people to the theater, O'Horgan set out to build a Broadway musical from songs by the Beatles. Convinced, especially after his experience with *Dude*, that musical theater could not function without the presence of at least some narrative, O'Horgan crafted a loose plot around songs featured on *Sgt. Pepper's Lonely Hearts Club Band* and *Abbey Road*, as well as a handful of B-sides and songs from other Beatles albums. "We put them together like a Tinkertoy set and made sense of it in our own way," O'Horgan explains. "We made a script of the songs, and we didn't add additional dialogue or change any lyrics. Maybe we changed genders or something, but basically it was the songs with the original orchestrations. We were just trying to use this music in a different way."[117]

The plot of *Sgt. Pepper's Lonely Hearts Club Band on the Road* revolves around the hero, Billy Shears, whose nickname is "Mr. Nowhere Man." A disagreeable bunch of ruffians known as Maxwell's Hammermen attempt to trick Billy into signing a mysterious contract after convincing him to wear a pair of magic spectacles. He puts the spectacles on and sees Lucy in the Sky with Diamonds. Although he quite enjoys meeting her, Billy refuses to sign the contract, so the Hammermen take the glasses away, and Lucy disappears. Billy turns his attentions to Rita, the Meter Maid, but their romance is foiled when Billy discovers that Rita is a man. Billy finally signs the contract, which appeases Maxwell's Hammermen for about thirty seconds. But soon all hell breaks loose and the Hammermen go on a killing spree. At the end, a statue of Sgt. Pepper, standing atop the set, comes to life and tells everyone to "Get Back," thereby restoring order.[118]

Sgt. Pepper's Lonely Hearts Club Band on the Road featured a cast of thirty-two actors performing twenty-nine Beatles songs before the elaborate scenery, dazzling special effects, and colorful costumes that had by this point become typical of O'Horgan's productions. This self-described "rock spectacle" opened Off Broadway on November 17, 1974, at the Beacon Theater, a concert venue on the Upper West Side. Like the vast majority of fragmented rock musicals that had come before it, *Sgt. Pepper's* was promptly and rather cruelly trounced by critics. The production ran for sixty-six performances before closing on January 5, 1975. A national tour that had been planned was subsequently canceled due to lack of commercial interest.[119]

O'Horgan acknowledges that adapting Beatles' songs for the stage proved especially problematic for the same reason that the songs were tempting to adapt in the first place: they were adored the world over. This conundrum was not lost on members of the press. During *Sgt. Pepper's* preview period, journalist Patrick Pacheco acknowledged in *After Dark* magazine that the Beatles had become deeply entrenched in the social consciousness of much of the Western world: "Memories of lovers, experiences, and drug induced 'trips' are closely aligned with these songs,"

Pacheco wrote. "Indeed, so intensely has this music touched us, so phenomenally has it affected our mores and attitudes and shaped a contemporary awareness, that for anyone to attempt to impose a dramatic coherency on these musical classics either borders on boldness or folly."[120]

O'Horgan remembers that he and Wagner had intended not to imitate the Beatles, but rather to offer new interpretations of their songs.[121] Yet critics and audiences alike had great difficulty with the fact that he and Wagner had reordered songs from the original *Sgt. Pepper's Lonely Hearts Club Band,* and had intermingled them with cuts from other albums. "I think that what we did offended Beatles fans," he acknowledges, "because we didn't follow the record. Whatever that record was about—we took some songs out and put other ones in, and—'how dare you!' It was like messing with Bach or something."[122]

In rearranging the order of songs on *Sgt. Pepper's,* O'Horgan and Wagner inadvertently eliminated the concept album's many unifying structures, which are part of what makes the album so innovative in the first place. Conceived as a unified entity, *Sgt. Pepper's Lonely Hearts Club Band* lacks traditional divisions between its thirteen songs, each of which segues smoothly into the next, and all of which are loosely linked by the reprise of the title song near the end of the album, as well as by a number of imaginative studio effects. Widely interpreted as an homage to psychedelia, the album features recurring themes including role-playing (the title song); the generation gap ("She's Leaving Home"); and both the creative freedom and excessiveness of the late-1960s youth culture ("Lucy in the Sky with Diamonds"; "Within You Without You"; "A Day in the Life"). These unifying themes are implied not only in the album's songs, but in its packaging: *Sgt. Pepper's* now-famous cover features the colorfully costumed Beatles posing in front of a collage of images of well-known public figures that the group members had listed as people they would most like to have in the audience at their fictional band's imaginary concert.[123] In altering the order of the songs on the album, imposing their own vision upon that of the band, and mixing songs from the album with unrelated others, O'Horgan and Wagner usurped the efforts of the band to which they were trying to pay homage.

Furthermore, like *Jesus Christ Superstar, Sgt. Pepper's Lonely Hearts Club Band on the Road* suffered from its inability to emulate the pristine quality of well-known sound recordings. A 1928 vaudeville theater–turned–movie house–turned–concert hall, the Beacon was only slightly less acoustically temperamental than the Broadway houses O'Horgan had previously struggled to amplify. This, combined with the fact that the sound recordings the musical was based upon were held in extraordinarily high esteem, led to problems. In his review for the *New York Post,* Martin Gottfried wrote, "However marvelous a sound system one can devise—and O'Horgan put together a fabulous one at the Beacon Theater—what can match "Sergeant Pepper" at full blast on headphones? . . . Musically, the show may well be a tremendous accomplishment in theatrical sound reproduction but it sounds like a floor-shaking performance of Beatles classics by the Doc Severinson band."[124] In the end, Gottfried was easier on the sound system than he was on the show, which he declared "a cheapskate circus" that had the feel of "a clumsy concert with dance movement and Thanksgiving parade props."[125]

Perhaps the perceived "cheapness" of this production was due in part to the fact that while Lennon and McCartney apparently granted permission for O'Horgan and Wagner to use their songs (George Harrison did not),[126] the songwriters actually had no say in the matter, since their songs belonged to the publishers.[127] As it would arguably contribute to the commercial and critical failure of Stigwood's 1978 all-star film adaptation of *Sgt. Pepper's Lonely Hearts Club Band*—which was also trounced by critics as cheap, silly, and, in the words of *Newsweek* critic David Ansen, bearing "a dangerous resemblance to wallpaper"[128]—a lack of involvement on the part of the Beatles seems to have hurt O'Horgan's production, which was seen by many critics as a crass attempt at profiting from someone else's creativity. The utter contempt that T. E. Kalem of *Time* has for O'Horgan on this front, for example, is palpable here:

If a medical dictionary of the theater should ever appear, one entry would be a grotesque disease known as O'Horganitis. Its chief aspect is the metastasis of spectacle over substance. Its subsymptoms are bloat, inanity, hallucination, sexual kinkiness and contagious vulgarity . . . if one wishes to be mortally infected, the place to go is Manhattan's Beacon Theater where *Sgt. Pepper's Lonely Hearts Club Band on the Road* is on germy display. Exploitation is at the core of this show. The idea was to cash in on the popularity of the Beatles. Their songs are probably as original and innocently evocative of the flower-child world of the '60s as they ever were, but here they are trampled under the dreck of Tom O'Horgan's grimagination.[129]

For all the bile projected upon it by critics, *Sgt. Pepper's Lonely Hearts Club Band on the Road* was ultimately no more ridiculous, plot-wise, than the far more successful animated feature film *Yellow Submarine,* with which the Beatles were directly involved and to which *Sgt. Pepper's Lonely Hearts Club Band on the Road* was regularly compared.[130] What the stage production lacked, however, aside from wide-screen distribution, was any direct involvement by the band.

Rock Films and *Beatlemania*

While the subject of rock on film is too vast to be discussed in much detail here, it must be noted that rock films operate very differently from staged rock musicals, and tend, on the whole, to be somewhat more successful (failed ventures like *Sgt. Pepper's Lonely Hearts Club Band* notwithstanding). Among other reasons, film appearances are likely to be more lucrative and less time consuming, and thus rock musicians are more likely to appear in them; cinemas are more capable of replicating the sound of original studio recordings than are most theaters; prerecorded music by original bands is regularly featured on film soundtracks, while the same is typically deemed unacceptable in the musical theater, which values live performance; tickets to the theater are often much pricier than those to movies, which are thus frequented far more often by young people; and unlike stage productions, films can be shown several times a day in movie theaters across the country, or on home systems, while theatrical productions are limited by time, space, and number of performances per week, and are rarely recorded for widespread distribution on video or DVD.

A more subtle difference between rock films and staged rock musicals lies with the fact that there seems to be less of a correlation between the success of rock films and the cohesion of their narratives. Whereas a lack of coherence in works like *Dude* and *Via Galactica* was enough to alienate audiences and force theater producers to close at huge losses, films like *Pink Floyd: The Wall,* the Led Zeppelin fantasia *The Song Remains the Same,* the Beatles' *A Hard Day's Night* and *Yellow Submarine,* and the concert documentaries *Woodstock* and *Gimme Shelter* remain in circulation on video and DVD, and are claimed as favorites by millions of rock fans. Arguably, the presence of the rock musicians themselves in these films becomes more important than a compelling story line, which fans who choose to can invent for themselves. Considering the widespread popularity of music video, of which the above-mentioned films are precursors, a lack of cohesive narrative is arguably preferable: on film, music is not necessarily made secondary to plot and characterization. Rather, more often than in musical theater, visual images, choreography, narrative, and direction can be made secondary to the music itself.

One notable theatrical exception was the touring show *Beatlemania,* different productions of which crisscrossed the United States in the middle and late 1970s. *Beatlemania* had a lengthy but rather unorthodox Broadway run, and its status as an "official" Broadway production remains somewhat marginal. The show arrived on Broadway in 1977 at a time when the commercial theater industry—and New York City in general—was faring so poorly financially that tourism had plummeted and producers were renting vacant theaters to rock concert promoters. Without ever officially opening, the Broadway company of *Beatlemania* bounced from the Winter Garden to the Lunt-Fontanne to the Palace Theatre between May 1977 and October 1979.

Unlike *Sgt. Pepper's Lonely Hearts Club Band on the Road, Beatlemania* attempted no plot, dialogue, or elaborate stage effects. Instead, four musicians, who were costumed to look and trained to sound as much like the original Beatles as possible, performed a concert of Beatles' songs while a montage of images evoking the 1960s was projected behind them. As a straightforward homage to the Beatles, then, *Beatlemania* certainly took fewer risks than *Sgt. Pepper's Lonely Hearts Club Band on the Road;* it also proved much more commercially viable.

The fragmented rock musical, whether derived from a familiar concept album or modeled after contemporary trends in rock music, proves problematic precisely because musical theater relies on linear narrative, visual stimulus, and character development, while concept albums tend to function most successfully without them. While a lack of linear narrative and an overemphasis on spectacle can be challenging in the theatrical realm, the foisting of additional narrative and characterization upon familiar concept albums proves just as problematic.

Black Musicals

If the 1960s saw rock 'n' roll mature into rock, the 1970s saw rock music's growing commercialization and fragmentation, as the music industry channeled the rapidly developing genre into increasingly specialized markets. Such partitioning influenced both the ways in which the producers of rock musicals marketed their properties and the ways these properties were described in the press. Whereas a seemingly endless number of productions featuring social commentary, youthful jargon, loose formats, electric instruments, and small, amplified ensembles were labeled "rock operas" or "rock musicals" in the late 1960s and very early 1970s, these terms became less popular in the 1970s, especially after so many self-described properties failed at the box office. The marketing of musicals featuring contemporary popular music styles was further complicated during the 1970s by the resurgence of black musicals on Broadway, many of which, like rock musicals, attempted to appeal to broader audiences by featuring contemporary popular music in their scores.

In *Black Musical Theatre: From "Coontown" to "Dreamgirls,"* historian Allen Woll acknowledges that although musicals by or about black people have been appearing on Broadway since the late nineteenth century, black musicals, whether by white or black authors, have always been designed to appeal primarily to white audiences.[131] This began to change in the late 1950s in much the way that the traditional musical began to change: as a result of innovations that were happening in tiny theaters Off and Off-Off-Broadway. Interested in creating musicals that would specifically address black concerns, African American playwrights, performers, critics, and producers argued that black writers had to free themselves from the demands of white audiences, who had for too long dictated the ways that musicals by and about black people were written and performed. In response to theater producers who argued that there was no black audience for the theater, black theater advocates insisted that the shows' creators were responsible for finding and cultivating a new generation of black theatergoers.[132]

The efforts to court a black audience for the theater gained enough momentum that by the late 1960s, innovations on the part of black theater companies Off Broadway had begun to exert influence on the Broadway realm. By 1970, black musicals began to proliferate on Broadway with a strength that had not been seen there since the golden age of the black musical in the 1920s.[133] Because black audiences were only just beginning to return to Broadway theaters, however, the most successful black musicals appealed to whites and blacks alike, with upbeat plots, lots of jokes, and catchy music carefully diluting any polemics. Shows like the plantation fable *Purlie* in 1970, and *Raisin,* the 1973 musical version of *A Raisin in the Sun,* both stuck to this formula, and enjoyed long, lucrative runs.[134] *The Wiz,* a black retelling of *The Wizard of Oz* set to a thumping soul and gospel score that opened at the Majestic Theatre in 1975 and ran for 1672 performances, seemingly ignored sociopolitical messages altogether (save that freedom is good and slavery is bad).[135] The most controversial musical of the 1971–72 season, *Ain't Supposed to Die a Natural Death,* was atypical in that it followed no such formula, did not appeal to white audiences—or to a majority of the city's white critics—and nevertheless managed a run of 325 performances.

Ain't Supposed to Die a Natural Death

Like many of the other fragmented musicals discussed above, Melvin Van Peebles's *Ain't Supposed to Die a Natural Death: Tunes from Blackness* was born in the recording studio and not on the stage, borrowed heavily from contemporary popular music styles, placed character and situation over narrative, and was written by a newcomer to Broadway. Born in 1932 in a suburb of Chicago and educated at Ohio Wesleyan University, Melvin Van Peebles is perhaps most often credited for inadvertently spurring the blaxploitation genre with his groundbreaking independent film *Sweet Sweetback's Baadasssss Song,* which he wrote, directed, starred in, produced, edited, and promoted in 1971. Van Peebles's designation as a cutting-edge filmmaker, however, tends to obscure his many other accomplishments: he has worked as an air force pilot, cable car driver, postman, options trader, journalist, novelist, playwright, painter, singer, actor, composer, and producer.

After his discharge from the air force in the mid-1950s, Van Peebles lived in Mexico, San Francisco, Paris, and Holland, where he painted, wrote, sang, and made short films. Shortly after returning to the United States as a French delegate to the San Francisco Film Festival in 1967, Van Peebles signed a recording contract with A&M records.[136] In 1968, A&M released his first concept album, *Brer Soul.* On this album, Van Peebles recited a series of original monologues—all of which focused on "the inner lives of the dispossessed"—over the brassy, improvisatory grooves that comprised the emerging subgenre of soul music known as funk.[137] In 1971, Van Peebles composed the score for *Sweet Sweetback,* which was performed by the then-unknown soul group Earth, Wind and Fire; he also released a second recording on A&M, *As Serious as a Heart Attack.*

Amidst this flurry of activity, Van Peebles's production associate Charles Blackwell suggested that his sound recordings could be turned into a Broadway musical. The result was *Ain't Supposed to Die a Natural Death,* which was launched for $150,000. The musical opened at the Ethel Barrymore Theatre on October 20, 1971.[138]

It was quite unlike anything else that had appeared on the Broadway stage. Although it resists classification as a rock musical—or, some might argue, as any kind of musical—its score was frequently described in the press as borrowing heavily from jazz, funk, and soul,[139] and at least one critic linked it unfavorably with other current rock musicals: shortly after *Ain't Supposed to Die a Natural Death* opened, the *New York Times'* Walter Kerr griped, in a particularly cranky opinion piece, "Have you noticed how many of our new musicals, rock or otherwise, are simply and unapologetically concerts? The beat begins, one song segues into another, after 16 or 18 or 20 numbers, we are released to go home."[140]

Conceived by Van Peebles to give voice to "the nightmare side of the American dream,"[141] *Ain't Supposed* is a collage of choreographed soliloquies drawn from his record albums. On stage, they were declaimed to live music—in much the same way that Van Peebles performed them on record—by characters who collectively represented the African-American experience at its bleakest. Set in the darkest corners of an anonymous ghetto, the musical is inhabited by pimps, prostitutes, alcoholics, junkies, hustlers, beggars, prisoners, and corrupt cops, as well as a number of underemployed and overworked men and women who have managed to steer clear of the most detrimental aspects of street life, but who nevertheless cannot wrest themselves from the poverty and discrimination that have confined them to the slums.

Although there are many moments of levity, *Ain't Supposed* is unapologetically harsh. It begins as the six-piece band—which, in the original production, was set in a galley above the stage—thumps out a dutiful but tinny rendition of "The Star-Spangled Banner." Once the show begins, the band does not stop, but instead provides constant accompaniment to the actors, who recite their monologues, occasionally repeating, shouting, or singing particular phrases for added emphasis. During the musical, overworked and underpaid men and women lament menial jobs; a prostitute hides five dollars from her pimp, who responds by beating her severely, taking her money, and demanding a kiss on the cheek; a death-row prisoner reminisces about the adventurous sex life he and his girlfriend enjoyed before he killed her; a young boy resorts to petty theft and is shot in the back while trying to escape; a young girl is lured into a life of prostitution, only to be raped by corrupt cops in the back of a patrol car; a pair of lovers sits on the stoop beneath a full moon and dreams about the future; a drunk begs for spare change; and a drag queen propositions a sailor on a dark street corner. At the end of the piece, a bag lady who has been wandering silently in and out of the action for the duration of the show walks downstage center and performs the monologue "Put a Curse on You," a polemic attacking "everyone who sits by and watches the degradation extant in our country without becoming outraged and moved to action."[142]

Ain't Supposed to Die a Natural Death received passionately mixed reviews. In *Women's Wear Daily,* Martin Gottfried raved that the production was "virtually flawless,"[143] while in *Newsday,* George Oppenheimer slammed it as "a compendium of ugliness, violence, tastelessness, and fury."[144] Unlike the fragmented musicals discussed above, however, the brunt of the criticism was not geared toward the show's emphasis on spectacle, its loud music, or its perceived lack of structure. Rather, the critics who disliked the show attacked its perceived messages.

Van Peebles's unflinching portrait of the black urban ghetto clearly put New York's overwhelmingly white theater critic corps off its guard. So many critics perceived *Ain't Supposed* as a "hate-filled," "anti-white" screed that the entertainment editor of *Amsterdam News,* a newspaper by, about, and for members of New York City's black population, wrote in a special review for the *New York Times,* "Some White critics seem to have the continuing and rather paranoid impression that any expression of love that does not mention Whites specifically is in fact an expression of hatred toward them. Which is, finally, a very sad comment on the state of their emotional health."[145]

Perhaps the most telling reviews of *Ain't Supposed* were the ones that admitted the most uncertainty. Several critics acknowledged, in assessing the show, that they were not sure that they had fully grasped its messages, and that Van Peebles's depictions of black life were a far cry from what they were comfortable with or used to seeing in the mainstream theater. "Black is coming to Broadway these days, and I mean real black, not just someone singing Ol' Man River—even though that's quite a magical song if you ever listen to it," Clive Barnes began fumblingly in his review for the *New York Times*. "I suspect that this is a fair picture of a 1971 New York street scene—not, dear friend, on the street where you live, but I suspect that people do, and rats and things like that," he continued, before concluding that *Ain't Supposed* would strike most white theatergoers the same way it struck him: "as a journey to a foreign country," and a most upsetting country at that.[146] Henry Hewes of the *Saturday Review* argued that the musical was a poor fit for Broadway in 1971: "Perhaps the best solution of all for a show that may be ahead of its time would be for the producers to store the scenery and costumes, and for Mr. Van Peebles to devise a way to make his exciting material as effective to a future Broadway audience as it was to a passionate minority of my colleagues," he concluded.[147] Richard Watts, for the *New York Post* wondered if "Mr. Van Peebles simply hates everybody," before calling the musical "confused, confusing, and ineffectual" and concluding that "white critics are not properly equipped to review certain black dramas."[148]

With *Ain't Supposed to Die a Natural Death,* Melvin Van Peebles not only effectively demonstrated that in 1971, the Broadway establishment was largely unprepared for a show that refused, in Gottfried's words, to present "the black man as something to ogle, celebrating a life style bred of servitude as if it were beautifully black."[149] Van Peebles also proved that regardless of what a group of white critics had to say, there was a large enough black audience to keep even the most controversial of shows running on the Great White Way. Van Peebles was not surprised when the reviews came out and attendance by white audiences plummeted. "I can't help it if they don't get it," he told journalist Tom Topor of the *New York Post*. "They want black theater to be either a tourist guide—you know, here's our beautiful black soul; or they want the hate trip. They don't want to look at things that aren't set up for them. I give a black image from a black point of view, so the whites and the blacks who want to be white don't like it."[150]

Rather than attempting to win over the traditional (white) Broadway audience, Van Peebles launched his own publicity campaign. He contacted every black church, school, civil rights organization, social club, and fraternal order he could find within two hundred miles of Manhattan, and encouraged them to buy blocks of tickets, which he made available on a sliding scale.[151] Although many televised talk shows that traditionally invited white Broadway personalities to perform numbers from their musicals did not extend the same sorts of invitations to Van Peebles, his repeated complaints to the press resulted in an invitation to appear on the *Today* show.[152] After sales for his musical began to pick up during the Christmas season, Van Peebles proclaimed January 1972 "*Ain't Supposed to Die a Natural Death* Month."[153] During the last seven months of the run, he made a practice of inviting black celebrities like Bill Cosby, Ossie Davis, Nipsey Russell, and Diana Sands to make guest appearances in the show. He organized discussions after matinees to improve business; Congresswoman Shirley Chisholm led one such discussion, and later announced her 1972 bid for president from the stage.[154] Due to the resultant turnout for the show, *Ain't Supposed to Die a Natural Death*, initially rumored to close within a week of opening, ran for almost a year before the dog days of summer forced it to close on July 29, 1972.[155]

The reception of *Ain't Supposed* was not only indicative of the vast racial divide that existed in the mainstream theater in the early 1970s, but of segregation in the popular music world, as well. It is tempting to romanticize early rock' n' roll as a style that helped unify Eisenhower's America because it was performed and consumed by both white and black youths. Yet although the American music industry supposedly moved beyond the rigidly segregated construction of its marketing techniques when it abandoned "race record" charts in the 1950s, and although there has been plenty of crossover between black and white audiences since then, American popular music remains highly segregated as a result of racial boundaries imposed by radio formats, retail practices, and the structuring of popular charts.[156]

Rock 'n' roll was marketed to white audiences practically at its inception, despite the fact that it was essentially popular music that had been made and consumed by black people for many years prior. Yet, as the scholar Russell A. Potter argues, while the rise of rock 'n' roll resulted in a huge new audience for black popular music, the music industry's "practice of knocking off cover versions of the songs of successful black artists, such as Pat Boone's relentless series of Little Richard covers, exacerbated tensions by siphoning off profits," especially since the white versions were given heavier rotation on the biggest commercial radio stations.[157] Thus, even as rhythm and blues—ironically renamed "rock 'n' roll," a euphemism for sex in black slang—reached a broader (whiter) audience, its black artists were being cheated out of the resultant financial windfall. By the time the 1960s rolled around, rock 'n' roll—newly shortened to "rock"—had become overwhelmingly identified with white audiences and, though there were notable exceptions, with white performers. Meanwhile, rhythm and blues developed in a new direction between the mid-1950s and the late 1960s, with the birth of soul music. In many respects, soul is to rhythm and blues as rock 'n' roll is to rock: more sophisticated, improvisational, introverted, moody, and experimental. Unlike rock through the 1960s and 1970s, however, soul and funk were strongly identified with African Americans.

With its amplified band churning out driving rhythms, solid basslines, improvisatory riffs, and rhythmic punctuation on brass, *Ain't Supposed to Die a Natural Death* could be as easily labeled a rock musical as any other to appear on Broadway at the time. Yet to call something a "rock" musical by 1971 would be to code it as a musical by and about white people, and *Ain't Supposed* was neither of these. It is thus unsurprising that the press failed to attach such a label to *Ain't Supposed*. It is similarly unsurprising that by the time *The Wiz* landed on Broadway in 1975, an overwhelming number of theater critics described it in the press as possessing a score influenced not by "rock" but by "soul."[158]

The "Death" of the Rock Musical

As the 1970s progressed, things didn't improve much on Broadway when it came to rock musicals. Following the highly anticipated, ultimately disappointing productions of *Soon, Earl of Ruston, Hard Job Being God, Dude,* and *Via Galactica* came even more poorly received, sparsely attended, long-since-forgotten shows that were in some way or another influenced by contemporary popular styles. These included the Andy Warhol–produced *Man on the Moon* (1975), with book, music, and lyrics by "Papa" John Phillips; *Lieutenant* (1975), a rock opera about the My Lai massacre that folded after nine performances; *The Rocky Horror Show* (1975), a hit in London and Los Angeles that closed within a month of opening at Broadway's Belasco Theater; *Rockabye Hamlet,* a musical version of the Shakespeare play that featured numbers with titles like "The Rosencrantz and Guildenstern Boogie" and "He Got It in the Ear" (1976); and *Got Tu Go Disco,* a disco version of *Cinderella* that opened and closed in late June 1979.[159]

This string of failures helped convince many members of New York's theater industry that with few exceptions, a successful rock musical was a contradiction in terms. As the number of rock musical fatalities climbed, producers grew wary of anything billed a "rock musical" or a "rock opera," and the appearance of such properties on Broadway diminished significantly. By 1979, the music scholar Eric Salzman would announce the death of the rock musical,[160] echoing theater writer Ethan Mordden, who in 1976 had sounded a similar death knell in his rambling *Better Foot Forward: The History of American Musical Theatre.*[161]

The notion that the rock musical was "dead" by the mid-1970s is, however, a misconception due, in the first place, to many musical theater historians' tendency to track Broadway trends while ignoring the many smaller musicals that appeared Off and Off-Off-Broadway. Such an oversight is especially problematic when it comes to rock musicals, which, with few exceptions, tend to fit more comfortably in smaller theaters that cater to selective audiences than they do in the largest and most commercial ones, and which are thus often brought to Broadway only after strong ticket sales justify producers' attempts to court wider audiences. In the second place, the fragmentation of the popular music market during the 1970s exerted strong influence on the ways that rock musicals were promoted as the decade wore on.

By the mid-1970s, producers and creators of rock-influenced musicals had begun to attempt to counter the dwindling success of rock musicals by avoiding descriptors that had appeared frequently earlier in the decade. Hence, by the end of the 1970s, gone were subtitles that had been appended to musicals like *Tarot: A Folk-Rock Musical* (1970) and *Grease: The New '50s Rock'n'roll Musical* (1972) early in the decade. Despite the dip in popularity of such subtitles, however, creators of musical theater continued to borrow freely from contemporary popular styles in creating new stage productions. Thus, many musicals that would likely have been described by creators or producers as "rock operas" or "rock musicals" at the turn of the decade were kept clear of such descriptors only a few seasons later. While rock musicals failed to take the American musical theater by storm, they certainly never disappeared.

The alleged "death" of the rock musical coincided with the dawn of a new era for New York theater. While the Off and Off-Off-Broadway realms exerted strong influence on what was seen as a creatively stagnant Broadway during the 1960s, this trend began to reverse itself at the turn of the decade. Although successful Off and Off-Off-Broadway productions

continued to transfer to Broadway, the rising costs of real estate and production forced many of New York's Off and Off-Off-Broadway companies to turn slowly away from innovation and toward financial stability,
which was achieved by appealing to broader audiences and raising ticket
prices.[162] As a result, although Off and Off-Off-Broadway remained less
commercial than Broadway, the distinctions between these realms began
to blur as the decade unfolded.[163]

The trend toward the commercial in all divisions of New York theater
was very gradual. Thus, compared with later decades, the 1970s were
much kinder to productions with limited appeal, especially those
mounted Off and Off-Off-Broadway. While reports of rising costs in all
realms were appearing even as the decade began, producers like the Off
Broadway impresario Joseph Papp could nevertheless afford to take risks
with an impressive number of new works.

Theater personnel in the Off and Off-Off-Broadway realms could also
afford to fail more gracefully during this decade. Whereas the collapse of
too many rock spectacles on Broadway led to a backlash that worked to
drive such talents as Galt MacDermot and Tom O'Horgan from the commercial realm, Off and Off-Off-Broadway flops from the period usually
escaped such ramifications. As discussed earlier, for example, in contrast
to high-profile flops like *Dude* and *Via Galactica,* which are still cited
among industry members and theater historians as two of the most laugh-
able disasters in Broadway history, poorly conceived Off and Off-Off-
Broadway flops like *Rainbow, The Ballad of Johnny Pot,* and *The House of
Leather* were merely given negative reviews and, once closed, quickly forgotten. These productions likely escaped similar ridicule in part because
they were much cheaper to produce and housed in theatrical realms
where riskier, more eclectic material was both expected and more readily
accepted.

The comparative freedom, during the 1970s, to produce risky theatrical
pieces was also due to the fact that theatrical production was radically different from what it would become only a few years later. Despite the fact
that real estate and production costs had begun to rise by the 1970s, this
nevertheless remained a decade during which it was relatively cheap to
produce theatrical productions and, as a result, somewhat less devastating
to producers when productions failed. In the 1980s, however, risks would
become much harder to take.

Interlude 3

Megamusicals

IN THEIR BOOK *The Broadway Musical: Collaboration in Commerce and Art*, Rosenberg and Harburg write that "the rising costs of a labor-intensive business (both blue and white collar), the tax burdens of city and state, the demands of individual and corporate investors in shows, and the rising expense of new technologies" all erupted at the beginning of the 1980s and "soared far beyond the general rate of inflation."[1] Between 1980 and 1982, production costs on Broadway increased by a whopping 62 percent, while the costs of operation rose by 45 percent.[2] The skyrocketing inflation had a particular impact on musicals, which are generally more expensive to produce than dramas.

Rising costs of production coincided with the development of a new division of labor and power among the creators of Broadway musicals. Traditionally, costs were managed solely by the producer. By the early 1980s, company managers, as well as visionary directors like Michael Bennett and Hal Prince, had become so important to productions that they began, with increasing regularity, to have a say in controlling costs. This new mode of cost control was, in many respects, refreshingly decentralized; unfortunately, it was also usually far less cost effective.[3]

In addition, the late 1970s and early 1980s saw the increased unionization of Broadway, as musicians, stagehands, carpenters, electricians, actors, directors, press agents, lighting designers, and choreographers all struggled for higher wages, better benefits, and healthier working conditions. Unionization has allowed for the protection of industry members who were traditionally underpaid and overworked; unfortunately, however, unions are often the victims of finger-pointing within the industry, since increased unionization has contributed to the rising costs of production.[4]

Rising costs did not influence the number of musical productions offered on Broadway in any given season; interestingly, the average number of musical offerings has not changed significantly since the early 1930s, although there has been a slight downward trend in recent years. Likewise, the ratio of flops to hits per season has hardly changed: over 70 percent of musicals to open on Broadway between the 1930s and the early 1990s have closed without recouping their initial investments.[5] What began to change on Broadway in the 1980s were the stakes, which would become much higher, as new musicals emphasizing the technologically spectacular would help uproot theatrical production from its local confines and transform it into international big business.

The approach to staged spectacle began to change with the rise of new technology and the influence of the cinema on the American theater. Whereas past productions emphasized elaborate costumes, scantily clad dancing girls, and immense casts, new technology led to shows that favored instead the latest in mechanically produced stage effects. Despite their tepid receptions, Tom O'Horgan's technologically progressive Broadway musicals proved enormously influential in this respect.

Cats and the Birth of the Megamusical

Megamusicals are not rock musicals per se; most tend to be too lushly orchestrated and too musically diverse for such a moniker. They may be viewed, however, as a highly significant offshoot of the rock musical, in that they are strongly influenced by the aural and visual aesthetics of rock and popular music, especially in their emphasis on spectacle and their composers' tendency to make frequent—if sometimes only fleeting—references to contemporary popular music styles. In "The Megamusical and Beyond: The Creation, Internationalisation, and Impact of a Genre," Paul Prece and William A. Everett identify the "typical" megamusical as thematically sentimental and romantic; most feature plots that "merge aspects of human suffering and redemption with matters of social consciousness" and are thus designed to evoke strong emotional reactions from audiences. Megamusicals tend to feature set designs, choreography, and special effects that are "at least as important as the music."[6]

Jonathan Burston identifies several "behind-the-scenes" characteristics of megamusicals, which are just as important as, if not more important than, their common aesthetics. He writes that megamusicals are "produced and controlled by a select and specific group of highly capitalised,

globally competent and now often transnational players" who have cultivated "specific commercial, technical, and aesthetic models of production." The result is a musical that is developed specifically for Broadway or
London's West End, but can then be franchised to theater companies
across the world, thus replicated "with unprecedented meticulousness
across a greater number of international venues than was common to the
field of theatrical production" in previous decades.[7] Cats is thus remarkable not so much because of its artistry, but rather because it was the prototype for the kind of slickly performed and produced big-budget musical
that would dominate Broadway through the 1980s and much of the 1990s.

Cats is essentially a cycle of poems from T. S. Eliot's Old Possum's Book
of Practical Cats, set to music by Andrew Lloyd Webber and held together
with a paper-thin plot. At the beginning, the godlike Old Deuteronomy
cat announces that by the close of the evening, one cat will be selected to
go to cat heaven (here called the heaviside layer) to be reborn. The musical concludes as the down-and-out Grizabella cat sings the musical's best-
known song, "Memory," before being awarded the dubious honor of
ascending into the heaviside layer on a giant, hydraulically mechanized
car tire that serves as the musical's most elaborate stage effect. What falls
between the introduction and the conclusion is a revue of songs and
dances in styles ranging from swing ("The Invitation to the Jellicle Ball")
to English dance hall ("Mungojerrie and Rumpleteazer") to operetta
("Growltiger's Last Stand") to rock 'n' roll ("The Rumtum Tugger"), all
of which are performed by actors dressed and made up to look like cats.

Flush from the international success of Evita, Lloyd Webber teamed
with theater producer Cameron Mackintosh, and recruited an impressive
team to help him bring his new musical to the stage. The creative staff
enlisted to work on Cats included the esteemed Royal Shakespeare Company director Trevor Nunn, the choreographer Gillian Lynne, and the set
and costume designer John Napier. Cats opened at the New London Theatre in the West End on May 11, 1981, and then at Broadway's Winter Garden Theater on October 7, 1982.[8]

While many musicals fail to win audiences due to a weak plot or an
overdependence on spectacle, Cats' revue-like form and stunning visuals
proved assets to the production. The show's costumes, makeup design,
and innovative set—which extended well into the auditorium, allowing
the audience to enjoy a cat's-eye view of a (decidedly sanitary) garbage
dump filled with oversized candy wrappers, soda cans, and worn-out

shoes—arguably won more critical praise and sold more tickets than the music itself. As the *New York Times* critic Frank Rich wrote, "*Cats* proved as no production had before that there was an infinite tourist audience for a theatrical attraction (as opposed to, say, a circus, Las Vegas revue, or Radio City Music Hall pageant) in which spectacle trumped . . . content and no English was required for comprehension, whether by young children or foreign visitors."[9]

Cats enjoyed unprecedented success, opening in twenty-six countries and over three hundred cities worldwide, and spawning numerous national and international touring companies. By the time it closed in the West End (in May 2002 after a twenty-one-year run), and on Broadway (in September 2000 after an eighteen-year run), it had become the most internationally profitable theatrical venture in history.[10] In North America alone, *Cats* is estimated to have been seen by over 35 million people.[11]

The success of *Cats* made Cameron Mackintosh and Andrew Lloyd Webber remarkably powerful on both sides of the Atlantic. Either working individually or in tandem, the two would be responsible for a number of megamusicals that would open through the 1980s and early 1990s in New York, London, and, via franchise, around the world. Megamusicals to attain worldwide success after *Cats* include Schönberg and Boublil's *Les Misérables* (1987) and *Miss Saigon* (1991), and Lloyd Webber's *The Phantom of the Opera* (1988) and *Sunset Boulevard* (1994), all of which were produced either by Cameron Mackintosh or by Andrew Lloyd Webber's production company, The Really Useful Group Ltd.

The Stylistic Impact of the Megamusical

As the scholar Philip Auslander points out, a franchised live performance "takes on the defining characteristics of a mass medium: it makes the same text available simultaneously to a large number of participants distributed widely in space."[12] In this respect, the megamusical has brought musical theater in general a step closer to the mass media, not only in the ways that it is produced, but in terms of its aesthetic makeup. Megamusicals are often criticized for "dumbing down" the theater, by luring audiences with scores built of maddeningly simplistic, redundant melodies; anachronistic orchestrations that strive to make every production—whether set in revolutionary France, Saigon during the Vietnam War, or

Hollywood at the beginning of the 1950s—appealing to listeners of adult-oriented radio stations through the use of electric instruments and propulsive rhythms; thin, often treacly plots; and emphasis on visual spectacle over content. The term *spectacle* here denotes scenic technology that has, in recent decades, become sophisticated enough to allow the simulation of special effects previously only possible on film. Examples include the giant, ascending car tire at the end of *Cats;* the chandelier that hurdles through the theater and crashes onto the stage at the end of act 1 of *The Phantom of the Opera;* and the helicopter that lands onstage and takes off again during the evacuation scene in *Miss Saigon.*[13] Yet what is perhaps most significant here is the way in which both the mass media and the rock musical have influenced the aural aesthetics of the musical theater in general, and the megamusical in particular.

Once it emerged in the middle of the twentieth century, rock 'n' roll was not only frequently blamed for the decline in popularity of the American musical; it was also often singled out as being directly responsible for what has since become a widespread reliance on microphones and amplification in the theater. Such blame is warranted, in some respects, since the development of postwar popular music is virtually inseparable from the electronic technology that has developed alongside it. Thus, among the many elements of contemporary popular music to work their way into the postwar musical theater, one of the most overarching has been the increased presence of amplification.

In 1968, the musical *Promises, Promises*—the score of which did not feature rock, but rather the smooth, tightly constructed, slickly orchestrated Brill Building songs that its composer, Burt Bacharach, built his career on—became the first Broadway musical to feature a miked orchestra pit: every member of the band, along with four backup singers who sat in the pit through the show, had a microphone.[14] Other postwar musicals that sought inspiration from contemporary popular music, like *Hair* and *Jesus Christ Superstar,* relied almost exclusively on electric instruments, thus creating the need for new ways to transport singing voices from the stage to the audience without the risk of permanent damage to the performer.

While the postwar practice of amplifying musicals was the direct result of an interest, among theater personnel, in emulating contemporary popular music styles, the practice of enhancing the sound of live theater did not lose any momentum in theater circles during the mid-1970s, despite the fact that terms like *rock musical* and *rock opera* had fallen out of fashion. Instead, the burgeoning megamusical, which appeared on the theater scene at roughly the same time as the radio microphone, took up where rock musicals had left off.

Rock musicals staged in the 1960s and 1970s were ahead of their time, at least when it came to sound design; companies who staged them were forced to rely on unwieldy, aurally inconsistent handheld microphones, which kept a clear, well-balanced sound exasperatingly out of reach. A number of problems were solved, however, with the advent of radio microphones, which were invented in the mid-1960s and steadily improved upon through the 1970s and especially the 1980s. Radio mikes are small and not hindered by electrical chords; they can thus be neatly concealed in the wig or costume of a performer.

This innovation in sound has had a number of important ramifications. Perhaps the most obvious is the relative liberation of actors, who were once required to hover around microphone stands, or to sing into handheld mikes while being ever-mindful of their potentially hazardous extension cords. Yet the advent of the radio microphone has had other implications. As Jonathan Burston writes, the amplification of individual performers "allows for a general increase in sound levels from the pit, as individual voices no longer rely on their own volume-generating capacities in order to compete successfully with orchestras' higher volume levels." Since volume levels are now mixed by a sound designer stationed at a centralized soundboard that is often placed at the rear of the theater, musical input from actors and musicians can be significantly increased. The result is theatrical productions that are, in Burston's words, "cinema-sized," in that they can emulate the same levels one expects in movie theaters equipped with "surround sound."[15] Radio microphones have had a somewhat less obvious but equally important impact on the soundscape of the American musical theater: they have helped alter that which is expected of the Broadway singer.

The embrace of microphones for use in recording popular vocal music between the 1930s and 1950s resulted in the development of a new style of singing known as "crooning." No longer required to project from the diaphragm, as old fashioned "belters" did in the days before amplification, crooners like Bing Crosby, Frank Sinatra, and Elvis Presley were able to create a sense of intimacy with their listeners that was, ironically, cultivated by singing "first and foremost *to* the microphone," and only secondarily to the real or imagined audience.[16] The increased reliance, on Broadway, first on standing microphones in the 1960s and 1970s, and then on radio microphones since the 1980s, allowed for musical theater performers to cultivate the same "crooning" sound.

Steve Sweetland, a New York–based voice teacher who counts several Broadway performers among his students, notes that while radio microphones are purportedly used to protect singers from strain, reliance on such technology has nevertheless resulted in new problems for singers:

> Absent the microphone and certainly the body mike, most of the people performing today would not be. Frankly, it's potentially very damaging, the way most singers sing today, thinking they are going to be boosted and aided by microphones. They assume they can whisper. They do a TV soundstage performance and crank up the microphones and assume that's going to carry them. But the kind of energy required to do some of these shows eight times a week—they have to put forth whether they are singing and speaking properly or not. That's where the discrepancy comes in. If they could stay in their little shells it wouldn't hurt them. But they can't.[17]

Radio microphones have thus contributed to the decline of the traditional "belter" and the proliferation of singers best equipped not for the stage but for the recording studio.

In the years since the dawn of the megamusical, the recording studio is regularly emulated on the Broadway stage in other respects, as well. Burston notes that advances in sound technology now allow sound designers to reproduce "a sonic environment identical to that of adult-oriented rock as experienced on FM radio. Here, timbres are carefully 'scrubbed' of all surface noise, producing what is often called a 'pure' sound, or . . . a 'studio sound.'" Further, now that sound designers can mix the sound levels of each performer from the sound board, sound design for the musical theater has shifted away from "techniques which enhanced the structural acoustics of a given theatrical venue," and toward an interest in making actors who appear live onstage sound as if they had been prerecorded.[18]

Due to their timing, megamusicals have been able to enjoy a sophistication in sound design—and thus to borrow liberally from contemporary popular styles—in a way that the earliest rock musicals could not. Burston argues that the sonic aesthetic of the megamusical—a "global" pop writing and singing style that he labels the "FM sound"—borrows liberally not only from the inoffensive popular stylings of recording artists like Kenny G., Michael Bolton, and Céline Dion, but also from early rock musicals like *Jesus Christ Superstar* and *Godspell*, which, like megamusicals, "also took their stylistic cues from popular music radio." The difference, however, lies in the fact that while early rock musicals offered a "sanitised but still occasionally vigorous 'rock'n'roll' sound," the scores of megamusicals are often "more compatible with the aesthetic norms of a more specifically soft rock sound,"[19] due in large part to their lush orchestrations, frequent choral numbers, and reliance on simple, repetitive, folksy melodies that are often devised from pentatonic scales.[20]

The rock musical's failure to have the impact that the megamusical would a decade later is due in part to the fact that rock music had not yet become fully integrated with the traditional Broadway sound, and was thus not yet properly "softened" for theater audiences, as well as to the fact that it preceded the very technology it required. It is thus the successors of rock musicals, and not rock musicals themselves, that have exerted the most direct influence on the developing sound of the musical theater in general. While microphones have been used on the Broadway stage since the 1960s, and have been the subject of hot debate for almost as long,[21] the sound of musical theater became aesthetically standardized only after it became a global business concern. As a result, while amplified productions were once a rarity, Broadway musicals that are *not* wired for sound are now uncommon.

The fact that the rock- and pop-influenced scores typical of 1980s megamusicals have become emblematic of Broadway at present is, perhaps, inevitable. By the time Lloyd Webber reached the height of his influence, rock 'n' roll and its offshoots had predominated for nearly twenty-five years. Thus, while the style might have been easy to ignore in its early years, it had become so widespread and diversified by the 1980s that even the most traditional of theater composers were subject to exposure. As Clifford Lee Johnson III, director of the musical theater program at Manhattan Theatre Club, remarks,

> Pop music shed its Tin Pan Alley veneer almost completely in the fifties and sixties, and a lot of the people working in theater were angry and jealous, so they resisted it. So starting in the late fifties and early sixties,

there's a whole lost generation of music-theater writers. There were people who tried to write popular songs, but most composers turned against it and tried to maintain that 1920s and '30s jazz beat. They just said, "Theater music is *different,* so you are just going to have to suck on this stupid rhythm forever." There were only miraculous, sporadic crossovers during that time period. But a generation later, you have a group of writers who grew up knowing and understanding rock 'n' roll and pop, and who also know and love the craft of theater music. So they are able to mix the two. Now you hear a lot of musicals that don't sound like rock music, for the most part, but you hear chord changes and phrases that sound like at least they are from 1970 or 1980, as opposed to 1920.[22]

The megamusical, then, not only offers more sophisticated sound than its predecessors, but also a more thorough blend of popular music and traditional theater fare. Whereas rock musicals often feature raw, amplified voices backed by electric instrumentation throughout, rock's direct influence on megamusicals tends to be comparatively tame: an occasional guitar riff, the use of twelve-bar blues form in a single number; an electric guitar, keyboard, or bass guitar intermingled with an otherwise standard pit orchestra; the occasional use of vocal techniques that might be heard on FM radio amid songs otherwise performed by conservatory-trained vocalists.

The Economic Impact of the Megamusical

The franchising of megamusicals allowed theater producers to transcend specific locations, and thus to make musical theater into a global business with the potential for unprecedented profit-making. Rising production costs in New York City in the early 1980s and the rise of the megamusical can be seen as mutually influential. Because the cost of production rose ever-higher on Broadway, as many musicals grew larger and more reliant on technology, investments became harder to recoup. Producers thus grew increasingly dependent on income generated from international and touring companies, which helped justify soaring production costs back in New York.

The act of franchising theater thus works in two ways. In the first place, franchises purportedly guarantee that patrons across the world will be able to see an "authentic" Broadway or West End production without having to travel terribly far from home. The result is a new interest in carefully replicating every aspect of a production that premieres in New York or London before bringing it to any number of theaters across the country or across the world. This explains the use in the theater industry of terms like *cloning* and *McTheater* to describe megamusicals.[23]

The franchising of theater also works to safeguard producers who invest in such spectacles in the first place, since national and foreign productions can help shows that flop on Broadway return investments and ultimately make profits.[24] Such protection becomes increasingly necessary as production costs climb, since shows that are more expensive to mount take longer to recoup. A number of informants for this project have mentioned that it is not uncommon for producers to open musicals on Broadway even though they expect them to flop, specifically so that they can launch official Broadway tours, since any show branded with the words "official" and "Broadway" will sell more tickets outside of New York City.

While the megamusical was in some respects the logical outcome of higher production costs, the subsequently raised ticket prices reduced the regularity with which local theatergoers could attend productions.[25] In fact, during the 1980s, the rising costs of production and the reactions to such costs by theatergoers became something of a double-edged sword: as the cost of production skyrocketed, producers of musical theater became more reliant on the idea of spending more money to make more money, which resulted in higher ticket prices for ever-larger, technology-driven spectacles. Yet while such spectacles proved hugely popular with the city's seemingly inexhaustible tourist supply, many local theatergoers became either less willing or less able to buy increasingly expensive tickets for smaller, more inexpensively produced shows. As critic Frank Rich asks, "Why pay the same high ticket price for a show . . . that didn't have a levitating spaceship or a falling chandelier but only good songs, compelling characters, or provocative drama?"[26] In the shadow of the megamusical, then, the "modest hit" became less of a staple on Broadway during the 1980s.[27]

4 🎸 Spectacles of the 1980s

In the early 1980s, as production costs soared and the megamusical took root on Broadway, Off and Off-Off-Broadway reasserted their positions as foci for the adventurous, cutting-edge theater that Broadway was seen to lack. At the end of the 1981–82 season, Otis L. Guernsey Jr., editor of the *Best Plays* series, argued that Broadway was no longer a center for original new productions:

> An alternative seems to lie in evolving Off Broadway into the principal bearer of creative theater, raising the price of the top ticket to more than $20 and pushing the production cost well up into six figures, hoping it will become economically feasible to maintain such a theater in the dozens of auditoriums scattered throughout the city. If this sounds like past Broadway mistakes—raise prices and costs and hope for the best—it should serve as a warning to Off Broadway against playing follow-the-leader over the same cliff. Right now, good plays and willing audiences exist in abundance Off Broadway, even at $14 to $20 a seat. Whether this will enable Off Broadway to establish an economically stable outlet for its creative energies is still very much an ongoing question.[1]

Unfortunately, even as Guernsey was recording his concerns about the future of New York's less commercial theater realms, Off and Off-Off-Broadway were beginning to react to the pressure of rising production costs. Ticket prices Off Broadway, like those on Broadway, rose progressively through the decade, and many productions began to reflect the sheen of increased commercialism traditionally expected of Broadway productions, especially when it came to visual spectacle. The distinctions between "commercial" and "nonprofit" theater, which had begun to blur in the 1970s, continued to do so through the 1980s, as megamusicals attracted the attention of increasingly large entertainment companies, members of which began to take new interest in producing live theater. As the 1980s progressed, and shows on Broadway grew more spectacular, the direction of influence—from Off and Off-Off-Broadway uptown to Broadway—began slowly but surely to reverse itself.

Little Shop of Horrors

A fitting example of an Off Broadway show that reflected this turning of tides is *Little Shop of Horrors,* with book and lyrics by Howard Ashman and music by Alan Menken. Based on the 1960 cult film by B movie king Roger Corman, this rock 'n' roll horror musical was workshopped at the tiny, ninety-eight-seat WPA Theater Off-Off-Broadway in the spring of 1982. While there, it caught the attention of Bernie Jacobs, then the president of the Shubert Organization, and his producing partner, David Geffen, then the president of Geffen Records.[2] *Little Shop* was quickly moved to Off Broadway's Orpheum Theater, where it reopened on July 27, 1982; the film version, also produced by Geffen, would be released four years later.

Set in Mr. Mushnik's flower shop in an unnamed urban ghetto during the Eisenhower era, *Little Shop* recounts the strange and oddly tender tale of the schlemiel Seymour Krelborn, who works for Mr. Mushnik as a salesman. Seymour pines away for his fellow employee, the beautiful but enormously insecure Audrey, who is dating a sadistic, abusive dentist. As the musical begins, Mr. Mushnik is considering closing his shop, since business is horrible and only getting worse (it seems that very few people are in the habit of venturing to skid row to buy flowers). Seymour, however, unveils his new discovery: an exotic little plant that, when placed in the shop window, becomes a tourist attraction that soon gives Mushnik's a much-needed boost in business.

Conflict sets in when Seymour learns that his plant—which he names Audrey II in honor of his secret love—is a carnivore. On occasion, Audrey II will settle for a snack of rare roast beef, but it is much more partial to human blood. At first, Seymour pricks his fingers to keep Audrey II happy, but as the plant grows larger and larger, it begins to demand much more than just a few measly drops. Oddly, it also begins to sing its demands to Seymour in a style strongly reminiscent of the soul singer Otis Redding.

Partway through the musical, Seymour musters up his courage and confronts Audrey's abusive boyfriend, the dentist. As luck would have it, the dentist dies of a laughing gas overdose shortly after Seymour arrives at his office. Seymour decides to feed pieces of the dentist to Audrey II, thereby hiding the evidence and keeping the plant quiet for a few days. What with the dentist out of the way, Audrey realizes her love for Seymour. The new couple enjoys a few brief moments of happiness before Audrey II gets hungry again. In the final act, Audrey II devours Mr. Mushnik, Audrey, and Seymour, before—according to the finale—mutating into hundreds of tiny little plants that move on to consume the rest of the world.

Functioning as a kind of informal Greek chorus in *Little Shop* are three young, black women, all of whom happen to be named after prominent 1960s girl groups: Chiffon, Crystal, and Ronnette. These women, inhabitants of the same rundown neighborhood that is host to Mushnik's flower shop, comment flippantly on the antics of the main characters—all of whom are white—in bouncy, three-part harmony; break into choreographed dances reminiscent of the pony, the twist, and the mashed potato; and provide regular vocal backup for the other characters in the form of countless "bob-sha-bops," "sha-la-las," and "chang-da-dos." Once the entire cast has been devoured by the plant, this trio of young women provide the moral of the story: no matter how tempted you may be, don't feed the plants!

Little Shop of Horrors enjoyed strong reviews, and, once it arrived at the Orpheum, a healthy run of 2,209 performances. While this strange little musical's talented cast, cheerful girl-group sound, and macabre plot most certainly had a hand in charming critics and theatergoers alike, there is no question that one of its biggest attractions was essentially a huge, movable prop: Audrey II, the man-eating plant. Designed and operated by the sculptor, actor, and puppeteer Martin P. Robinson (perhaps most famous for playing Mr. Snuffleupagus on "Sesame Street"), the original Audrey II appeared on the *Little Shop* stage in the form of four different puppets—two that were worked by hand, and two that were large enough to be manipulated from within.[3] Initially tiny, the plant grew significantly during the course of the performance, mutating by the end of act II into an enormous, tentacled pod with ferocious jaws that gobbled up the entire cast and snapped at the audience before the final curtain.

The reliance here on "special effects" was not lost on some critics, who voiced concern over the theater's need to imitate, in Walter Kerr's words, "its much younger and less sophisticated brother."[4] Kerr argues that despite a talented cast and some cute, catchy songs, *Little Shop* absent the plant is not a very interesting musical at all. "In the theater," he writes, "special effects can be dandy on an incidental basis. Beware, however, the evening that depends on them for its life's blood."[5] Kerr might, arguably, have been a bit hasty in targeting *Little Shop of Horrors* for criticism; after all, an Off Broadway musical that relied so heavily on spectacle was, at the time, relatively atypical. Yet as the decade continued, Broadway—as well as the mass media that was influencing its musicals—would continue to contribute to changes Off Broadway.

Dreamgirls

While the 1982 production of *Little Shop of Horrors* remained Off Broadway during its entire run (it was finally brought to Broadway in October 2003, where it ran at the Virginia Theater for 372 performances), another spectacle-laden musical produced by the Shuberts and David Geffen and featuring a fictional 1960s-style girl group was drawing crowds to Broadway. *Dreamgirls,* the latest offering from famed *Chorus Line* director-choreographer Michael Bennett, had opened at the Imperial Theater on December 20, 1981. Despite the fact that *Dreamgirls* featured a score representative of American popular musical styles from the 1960s and early 1970s, it was never dubbed a "rock musical" in the press. In part, this is because a vast majority of its mixed reviews focused instead on the show's gimmicky lighting, high-tech stagecraft, lavish costumes, and sentimental plotlines, all of which edged it toward megamusical status.[6] Further, however, like *Ain't Supposed to Die a Natural Death* and *The Wiz,* the musical's cast was comprised almost entirely of black actors; those critics who did apply descriptors other than "megamusical" thus tended to refer to *Dreamgirls* as a "soul," "rhythm and blues," or "Motown" musical, and not a rock musical.

Despite its mixed reception, *Dreamgirls* received a fair enough share of raves to alert potential spectators who had not already booked advanced tickets based solely on Bennett's reputation. "When Broadway history is being made, you can feel it," Frank Rich gushed at the beginning of his review for the *New York Times.*[7] *Dreamgirls* became a huge commercial success and ran for 1,521 performances before closing in August 1985.

Dreamgirls follows the career trajectory of a fictional black female singing trio from their inception in a Chicago ghetto in 1962 to their farewell performance a decade later. At the start of the show, the Dreamettes compete in a talent contest at Harlem's Apollo Theater. Although they lose the contest, they are approached by a manager, the Machiavellian Curtis Taylor, Jr., who pushes the group to the top of the charts. Determined to cross the music industry's notorious color barrier, Taylor makes major changes to the group, including shortening its name to the Dreams; altering its sound from hard-edged (black) rhythm and blues to mainstream (white) pop; and coldly replacing Effie, its hefty, gravel-voiced founder and lead singer—and also his lover—with the slimmer, softer-sounding Deena, who he feels will be more appealing to white audiences. While the Dreams' ascent is thus rocked by heartbreak—broken families, ruined relationships, crushed hopes—one of the larger issues that *Dreamgirls* tackles is cultural assimilation. As the Dreams "blunt the raw anger of their music to meet the homogenizing demands of the marketplace," Frank Rich writes, "we see the high toll of guilt and self-hatred that is inflicted on those who sell their artistic souls to the highest bidder."[8]

Of course, the fact that the plot of *Dreamgirls* was padded with shimmering costumes, mile-high wigs, state-of-the-art lighting, and a slick set consisting largely of sliding panels, towers, platforms, stairways, and bridges did not hurt ticket sales. As with *Little Shop of Horrors,* this reliance on visual spectacle was not lost on the critics. In his review for the *New Republic,* Robert Brustein wrote that the directorial emphasis of *Dreamgirls* was on "sights and sounds, on fluorescent signs, white handheld mikes, and magnificently gussied-up gowns. You find yourself following the story less than the quick changes, and leave the theater humming the wigs and costumes rather than the songs."[9]

Megamusical though it might have been, *Dreamgirls* was also something of a giant step backward to the pre-1970s black musical, in that its all-black cast contrasted sharply with an all-white creative team. Such a division, which had been rare on Broadway since the late 1960s, raised the hackles of culture critics and members of the press, especially in light of the fact that the plot of *Dreamgirls* revolves entirely around black entertainers who cannot succeed unless they tailor their sound and image to appeal to a white mainstream. "The white structure that demands so much soul drain is never really seen; it exists as an abstract ghost off-stage," Stanley Crouch wrote in the *Village Voice.* "A harsher examination would have symbolically questioned the way in which the show itself reached Broadway—white generals mapping out the strategy for singing, dreaming, and suffering black troops to take the bright hill of the musical smash."[10] Likewise, Robert Brustein concluded in his *New Republic* review that more than anything, *Dreamgirls* taught him that "despite the occasional nod toward social matters, Broadway is still primarily interested in black people if they can display a nice sense of rhythm, along with a little singing and dancing."[11]

These critics make an important point. *Dreamgirls*—and *Little Shop of Horrors,* for that matter—are shows that were ultimately patronized by the white, middle-aged people who have always made up the vast majority of theater audiences in New York City. With this audience in mind, it is perhaps not surprising that there is such frequent reference, in contemporary musicals, of girl groups in general and the Supremes-era Motown sound in particular.

Evoking Girl Groups

Beginning in the late 1950s, a number of independent music producers, including the profoundly influential Phil Specter and Berry Gordy Jr., began to cultivate trios of young, female, predominantly black vocalists, who became known as "girl groups." Singing trios like the Shirelles, the Chiffons, the Crystals, the Ronnettes, and the Shangri-Las became enormously popular by the early 1960s. Girl groups were initially used to record the songs of Brill Building songwriting teams like Carole King and Gerry Goffin, Barry Mann and Cynthia Weill, Jeff Barry and Ellie Greenwich, and Neil Sedaka and Howard Greenfield, who were so named because they worked in and around the Brill Building, at 1619 Broadway, during the 1950s and early 1960s. The girl group sound and image also influenced Gordy, founder of the Motown empire, who reached something of a commercial and stylistic pinnacle with his girl group, the Supremes, by the middle of the decade.

Girl groups not only made an impact as a result of their sound—which emphasized bright harmonies, frequent call-and-response between a lead vocalist and a two-voice "chorus," and heavy syncopation that was often punctuated by hand claps or a jangling tambourine—but also, especially in the case of the Supremes, as a result of their image. Berry Gordy saw to it that his performers were provided not only with dance training, but also with lessons on etiquette; the result was a group of recording artists who not only sounded good, but who were also always beautifully dressed, immaculately groomed, and exceedingly graceful as they moved through tightly choreographed numbers on the concert stage or in front of television cameras. As darlings of the Motown empire, the Supremes—in shimmering dresses, coiffed hairdos, tasteful makeup, and elbow-length gloves covering arms that were, in a signature dance move, frequently outstretched with palms perpendicular to the floor—represented the epitome of style in their heyday.

Gillian Gaar, author of *She's a Rebel: The History of Women in Rock & Roll,* writes that the importance of the girl group image and its impact on audiences has traditionally been overlooked by critics and scholars, "who tend to regard girl groups as interchangeable, easily manipulated puppets, while the ones with the 'real' talent were the managers, songwriters, publishers, and producers who worked behind the groups."[12] This is particularly the case since so many girl groups had remarkably short careers, and because young female singers were used so interchangeably that many girl groups were groups in name only.

While the importance of girl groups has thus been downplayed in the male-oriented popular music world, their emphasis on smooth vocals, infectiously danceable rhythms, hummable melodies, tightly choreographed dance routines, and physical beauty all translated with ease to the song-and-dance medium of musical theater. Indeed, within years of their inception in the popular music world, girl groups showed up on the Broadway stage. During the number "Black Boys/White Boys" in *Hair,* a trio of black women in blond wigs and glittering evening gowns danced like the Supremes atop a platform as they sang the praises of white men, while beneath them, a trio of white women bedecked in minidresses and thigh-high boots pretended to be the Shangri-Las as they danced and sang of their attraction to black men.

While Berry Gordy's Motown empire certainly helped break down color barriers in the popular music world, its founder's philosophy—that topical issues, especially controversial ones, had no place in popular music—resulted in frequent criticism that charged Gordy and his company with being too disengaged from the civil rights struggle of the time, and with being more interested in catering to white audiences than in appealing to black ones.[13] Of course, Gordy was not alone in believing that popular music should steer clear of controversial topics: the Brill Building songwriters, too, were known for witty lyrics, catchy melodies, and slickly produced recordings, but hardly for their stinging social commentary. While Brill Building and Motown groups certainly appealed to a fair share of black audiences—and employed a significant number of black musicians—their economic success ultimately depended on serving the demands of white audiences. It is these very same audiences who, having come of age by the early 1980s, were supporting the American musical in the largest numbers, and were again being entertained by trios of young, black women who charmed them, but did not necessarily make them think too deeply about contemporary societal issues.

While both *Dreamgirls* and *Little Shop* thus relied in large part on spectacle to attract audiences, then, at least some of their appeal was also clearly based in nostalgia for popular music styles of the not-so-recent past. As Simon Frith argues, the connection between nostalgia and popular music should not be overlooked: "It is a sociological truism that people's heaviest personal investment in popular music is when they are teenagers and young adults—music then ties into a particular kind of emotional turbulence, when issues of individual identity and social place, the control of public and private feelings, are at a premium," he writes. As people grow older their relationship with popular music tends to become less intense. This, Frith argues, suggests not only that "young people need music, but that 'youth' itself is defined by music . . . [Y]outh music is socially important not because it reflects youth experience (authentically or not), but because it defines for us what 'youthfulness' is."[14] In short, popular music is associated with youth not only because young people listen to it, but because music contributes to the very construction of what has been culturally deemed as young.

In *Our Musicals Ourselves,* John Bush Jones writes that importance of nostalgia—"the psychic equivalent to comfort food"—to the musical theater, especially since the 1970s, also cannot be underestimated.[15] Ever since *Grease* relived the simple and innocent—if also conformist and dull—1950s onstage nightly for audiences living through the 1970s, many musicals—including *Dreamgirls, Little Shop of Horrors,* and, for that matter, more recent shows like *The Who's Tommy, Smokey Joe's Café, Mamma*

Mia! and *The Donkey Show*—use popular styles of the recent past to evoke nostalgia among audiences who were, for the most part, children and young adults when those styles were born. The role that nostalgia played in *Little Shop of Horrors,* for example, was duly noted by Frank Rich in his review. Bloodthirsty plants aside, he wrote, *Little Shop* was ultimately about "that increasingly quaint-seeming decade of the 1950s."[16] Similarly, Sylviane Gold of the *Soho Weekly News* wrote that by resurrecting the 1960s, *Dreamgirls*

> allows us to look back and to understand, at last, the fundamental ways in which the doo-wops and oooh-aaahs shifted our culture, our consciousness. And when I say "our," I don't mean it in a general way. I mean *us,* the kids who turned on those radios. *Dreamgirls* is the first Broadway musical that is really about—and really for—the rock generation. . . . Eyen and Bennett would have us believe that their show is how the big bad music business changed the black sound, but they end up showing us how *we* were changed. And when, at the end, Effie in shimmering black, and Deena and the Dreams in shimmering white, are reunited to tell us that they are dream girls, the dreams of our youth come back in a poignant, heart rending rush. Couldn't we have tried a little harder?

Like popular music itself, the contemporary rock- and popular music–influenced musicals *Little Shop of Horrors* and *Dreamgirls* drew from past styles not only to allow audiences to relive bittersweet memories of what was, but sometimes, also, to ponder what might have been.

When Megamusicals Fail: The Case of *Carrie*

As the 1980s progressed, smaller, less visually spectacular musicals were becoming harder to launch; their dwindling numbers were indicative of a period during which, critics charged, the theater industry was passing on innovative productions in favor of the newest trends in stage technology. Despite soaring production costs and a new fascination with cinema-like "special effects," however, musicals still needed to connect with audiences to sell tickets. Indeed, while megamusicals proved highly influential, both economically and stylistically, not all have been successful. Through the

1980s, amid the unprecedented international success of musicals like *The Phantom of the Opera* and *Les Misérables*, Broadway was littered with ventures that spared no expense and nevertheless failed to become international phenomena. While megamusicals were alluring to investors because of their potential for unprecedented returns, the opposite applies, as well: with megamusicals, the prospect for success increases, but so does the threat of disaster.

The musical *Carrie* is perhaps the most fitting example, here, of ways in which increasingly large productions had the potential to yield increasingly catastrophic results. Stephen King's 1974 novel about a lonely, telekinetic teen who takes revenge for the cruelties inflicted upon her by her classmates and her religious fanatic of a mother was adapted for the stage by Lawrence D. Cohen, who had also supplied the screenplay for Brian DePalma's 1976 film version. Michael Gore composed the music and Dean Pitchford, who would later author the screenplay for the film *Footloose,* wrote the lyrics. *Carrie* ran for three weeks in Stratford, England, before landing in April 1988 at Broadway's Virginia Theater, the interior of which was painted black for the occasion.[17]

According to Ken Mandelbaum—whose book *Not Since "Carrie": 40 Years of Broadway Musical Flops* not only describes the musical in detail but uses it as the touchstone for all Broadway flops before and since—there was very little about *Carrie* that was not completely inept. Actors cast as high-school students appeared to be in their thirties or older and were clad inexplicably in either togas, studded leather jackets, or neon body stockings; the set for Carrie White's home consisted of nothing but a trapdoor and a chair, and that for the high school a series of rotating, mirrored side panels; fire shot from Carrie's hands, lightbulbs exploded over her head, and various grooming items floated around her as she readied for her prom, and yet her telekinesis was never explained or even verbally alluded to; lasers, strobes, smoke, pyrotechnics, and flashing hydraulic lifts abounded, and yet the famous prom scene was reduced to a mirror-ball secured to the floor, a small bucket of what was supposed to be pig's blood but by most accounts looked like strawberry jam, and a cast who pretended to be in the throes of electrocution by doing cartwheels in slow motion across the stage. To add to the confusion resulting from poor casting, staging, and costuming, *Carrie* was sung-through, and the lack of dialogue proved additionally befuddling for spectators unfamiliar with the story.[18]

Even before *Carrie* entered its preview period in New York, the musical was grist for the local rumor mill, especially once news broke that Barbara Cook, who played Carrie's mother, had quit the production during its badly received Stratford run after she was nearly decapitated by a piece of flying scenery.[19] Gossip that the first Broadway performance of the musical would be its last was stoked when the curtain at the first preview was delayed for a half hour. This rumor was quashed as *Carrie* limped toward opening night, but the show was nevertheless subject to further indignities during its preview period. Mandelbaum writes of an audience divided during early performances, the curtain calls of which were greeted with a raucous mix of cheers and boos.[20]

Carrie opened on May 12, 1988, to the cruelest of critical pans—Frank Rich compared it with the Hindenberg[21]—and closed after five performances.[22] The musical thus earned the dubious distinction of surpassing *Dude* to become the most memorable and costly flop in Broadway history. The investments that were lost as a result of these failed productions are indicative of how much more expensive it had become to launch the most spectacular of Broadway productions: whereas the producers of *Dude* were vilified as wasteful and incompetent when that musical lost its $800,000 investment in 1972, *Carrie* lost $8 million less than two decades later.[23]

While *Carrie* is perhaps the most extreme example, the vogue for megamusicals in general began to wane by the end of the 1980s, when even the once-charmed Andrew Lloyd Webber and Tim Rice experienced major disappointments. In 1987, a production of Lloyd Webber's soul-influenced, $8 million musical *Starlight Express,* which was a hit in London and in Germany,[24] opened in New York. It lasted 761 performances, which was not embarrassing by Broadway standards, but was nevertheless not long enough: *Starlight Express* became the first Lloyd Webber venture on Broadway to fail to recoup its investment.[25] In 1988, the $6.6 million *Chess,* Tim Rice's collaboration with former ABBA members Benny Andersson and Björn Ulvaeus, also closed at a loss, despite the publicity generated by Murray Head's recording of the song "One Night in Bangkok," which reached number 3 on the *Billboard* Top 40 in 1985.[26]

As Scott Warfield points out in "From *Hair* to *Rent:* Is 'Rock' a Four-Letter Word on Broadway?" *Chess* is not only a good example of a failed megamusical, but also a good example of a show that appropriated rock music as its primary idiom for no apparent reason. A musical about a

Cold War–era chess championship between a Russian and an American, *Chess* featured a score that went heavy on the power ballads and up-tempo pop anthems that ABBA was known for; as Frank Rich wrote, the result was that "'for three hours, the characters on stage yell at one another to rock music."[27]

While the megamusical saw Broadway's absorption of contemporary popular music during the 1980s, it did not result in the extinction of the more aggressively amplified and orchestrated rock musical. Rather, the occasional rock musical continued to emerge through the 1980s and well into the 1990s. As was now typical of the subgenre, those that opened on Broadway usually proved disappointing; self-described rock musicals like *Marlowe* (1981), *The News* (1985), and *Leader of the Pack* (1985) all closed within months of opening;[28] even the much-heralded *The Who's Tommy* (1993) closed after barely recouping its investments. As they had through the 1970s, rock musicals continued to appear more regularly Off and Off-Off-Broadway, where small, offbeat shows like *Starmites* (1980), *Lenny and the Heartbreakers* (1983), *Surrender/A Flirtation* (1985), *The River* (1988), Todd Rundgren's *Up Against It* (1989), *Return to the Forbidden Planet* (1991), and *Rent* (1995), among many others, ran with differing degrees of critical and commercial success.

With megamusicals on the wane, the late 1980s saw Broadway poised for yet another change. By this point, even the most successful megamusicals had begun to outlast their creators, who were having trouble repeating their early successes. As the 1990s progressed, Broadway would become increasingly corporate, and the creation of megamusicals would be taken to new levels.

Interlude 4

Economics and Marketing

BEGINNING IN THE LATE 1980s and especially through the 1990s, a number of dramatic changes took place both in New York City's Times Square area and in the commercial theater industry. These changes were spurred by the announcement, in the mid-1990s, that the Walt Disney Company would become active in Times Square as an investor, real estate owner, and theater producer. Since Disney's arrival, Times Square has seen a significant increase in business activity by a variety of entertainment conglomerates.

A great deal of writing has been devoted to the implications of the Times Square renovation.[1] There has also been a fair amount of scholarly investigation into the "Disneyfication" of some of the neighborhood's entertainment venues.[2] Yet little attention has been paid to the overall influence that corporations have exerted on the commercial theater industry itself.

The Renovation of Times Square

While heavy construction did not begin until the mid-1990s, plans to rebuild Times Square—which had become prey to strip clubs, porn houses, and massage parlors during the 1960s and 1970s—had been in the works since the 1980s, under the administrations of Mayors Ed Koch and David Dinkins. During the mid-1980s, the city planned to use the neighborhood as an extension of midtown Manhattan's business district, but this project stalled late in the decade when the commercial real-estate market softened.[3] Times Square's many commercial theaters had not been part of this revitalization plan, but they became central to the revised one, which envisioned Times Square as a cleaner, more tourist-friendly enter-

tainment district or, as Steve Nelson calls it, a "formerly indigenous theatrical district transformed into a romantically idealized tourist version of
its former self."[4]

This revised plan was contingent upon the lucrative relationship
between entertainment and retail.[5] Potential investors were lured with the
promise of profit to be found in connecting Times Square's theater heritage to its potential value as a site for advertising and selling.[6] The City
and the State of New York, hoping to profit from the increase in tourism
that the presence of media conglomerates would bring to the rejuvenated
area, courted the Walt Disney Company.

Hoping to elevate Disney's sagging image from a company solely interested in making money into a company respected for fueling the performing arts, Disney CEO Michael Eisner struck a deal with the City of
New York in 1994. Disney would spend roughly $6 million to renovate the
New Amsterdam, a dilapidated old theater on Forty-second Street built in
1903 that had served as a home for the Ziegfeld Follies and then a movie
house before falling into disrepair. Disney would enjoy exclusive use of
the New Amsterdam, which it now occupies under a forty-nine-year lease
and uses to house the stage version of *The Lion King*.[7] The city and state
agreed to lend Disney an additional $28 million in low-interest loans in
return for 2 percent of all ticket receipts from the theater.

In exchange for renovating a theater that promised to be costly to
maintain, Disney was encouraged to expand its presence in Times Square
through the development of other properties, including the ESPN Zone, a
dining and sports-related entertainment venue;[8] a street-level studio for
Disney-owned ABC television; and new musicals, to be developed by Disney's own theater division and staged in other Broadway theaters.[9] Com-
peting entertainment conglomerates quickly followed Disney's lead into
the area. By the end of the century, corporations including Cablevision,
News Corp., Hallmark, and SFX-Entertainment (which was acquired by
Clear Channel Communications in 2000) arrived in Times Square as
investors in theatrical properties, as real estate owners, or as purchasers of
advertising space on the well-lit facades of neighborhood buildings, all of
which are obliged by zoning laws to advertise as intensely as possible.[10]

The result has been a remarkable transformation: in less than a decade,
a decaying and notoriously sleazy neighborhood has become re-imagined
as a slick vacation destination for international travelers. While critics
argue that redevelopment has traded local flavor for new status as a

"global crossroads, populated by transnational corporations catering to tourists,"[11] advocates of redevelopment cite a more attractive, visitor-friendly neighborhood, the curtailing of the sex entertainment industry, and the hundreds of jobs created by the appearance of new theme restaurants, shopping centers, megastores, cinemas, and television studios, all of which now serve alongside the area's commercial theaters as tourist attractions in their own right.

Inviting corporations into Times Square is not quite as outlandish as it seemed when the deal with Disney was first announced, and gripes about Times Square as Disney's newest theme park began to circulate. In the first place, as noted in previous chapters, such denizens of the film and music industries as Robert Stigwood and David Geffen had already begun to enter the theater business in decades prior. In the second, beginning in the 1980s, real estate values in New York City had skyrocketed to such an extent that theater maintenance and production had become prohibitively expensive. For amounts of money that had risen far too high for independent producers by the late 1990s, corporations could not only afford to renovate theaters, but could also fill them with their own properties. The musical versions of *Beauty and the Beast* and *The Lion King,* for example, each reportedly cost Disney about $15 million. While such a sum is reasonable for a corporation accustomed to gambling four or five times as much on a television or film property, the shows were the two most expensive musicals in Broadway history upon opening in 1994 and 1997, respectively.[12]

The media companies that have helped make Times Square into a revitalized tourist attraction have taken an active role in working the Broadway musical back into the web of American popular culture from which it was severed in the 1950s. Building on the pioneering efforts of producers like Cameron Mackintosh, entertainment conglomerates that followed Disney into theatrical production have not only begun to purchase or develop their own theatrical properties; they can also market and franchise these properties internationally with relative ease, since most own film studios from which to borrow material, recording studios in which to record original cast albums, and a variety of periodicals, television studios, and radio stations from which to advertise productions. Such access to the mass media has extended far beyond the reach of Broadway's less-moneyed old guard in the years since the decline of Tin Pan Alley. Rather than relying heavily on the annually televised Tony Awards ceremonies for national exposure, as theatrical producers have done in past decades, shows with corporate backing can now be hyped internationally in myriad ways long before a theatrical property begins its run.

While corporations have built on models introduced by past producers, their reach proves infinitely more powerful, due to the application of a business tactic commonly known as "synergy." Synergy allows a company to generate stockholder value and revenue, both by selling a particular product and by simultaneously integrating it into a web of related products. Thus, a company like Disney can use one of its properties—for example the film *The Lion King*—to sell any number of others: videos, *Lion King*–related rides at Disney theme parks, merchandise at Disney stores, and the musical adaptation, whether on Broadway, on tour, or in cities around the world. Synergy allows a company to sell itself along with any product it hawks. The Broadway version of *Beauty and the Beast*, for example, can be mentioned in Disney films and television shows, or advertised on Disney-owned radio stations. Disney musicals can also serve as advertisements for one another: for example, the Broadway production of *The Lion King* makes at least two overt references to *Beauty and the Beast*, which is conveniently playing a few blocks north.

The application of business synergy to the musical theater helps explain why so many Broadway shows to open since the mid-1990s are staged versions of popular films, many of which combine the technological innovations typical of megamusicals with familiar titles, characters, plot lines, and, in some cases, songs from soundtracks, which are reorchestrated and incorporated directly into the plot. Movies that have been adapted for the Broadway stage include *The Sweet Smell of Success, Thoroughly Modern Millie, Footloose, Saturday Night Fever, The Full Monty, The Producers, Dirty Rotten Scoundrels,* and *Monty Python's Spamalot.* In most cases, the adaptations are overseen by the people who own the rights to the original films.

The lure of familiarity cannot be underestimated. A majority of audience members interviewed at performances of both *Footloose* and *Saturday Night Fever* said that they had purchased tickets to these shows specifically because they knew and liked the music from the film soundtrack, or because they had seen the movie. While neither of these productions fared particularly well, an increasing number of theater producers are nevertheless finding it safer to invest in familiar titles than to take chances on unknown material. As producer Marty Bell puts it, recognizable titles are attractive "because they're pre-sold. Everybody's trying to find a way to be safe in a business you can't be safe in."[13]

There is some indication that familiarity is in fact becoming expected of musical productions. While walking through Times Square one evening in September 2000, I overheard a group of British tourists discussing the Broadway version of *The Full Monty*. One remarked that although it had been "Americanized" and featured none of the disco hits featured on the film soundtrack, "it was *still* really good." Familiarity becomes additionally important since a rising number of visitors to New York speak little English and are thus interested in recognizable titles when shopping for Broadway shows. Of course, film adaptations rely on synergy, too: the film sells the musical and vice versa, both sell related merchandise, and the producers profit from all sales.

Because they can expand their reach beyond local audiences, corporate producers take advantage of a fact that the commercial theater industry has known for a long time, but with few exceptions has been unable to afford to exploit: theater audiences are no longer as local as they were even thirty years ago. Producer Tom Viertel explains:

> We cater to a tourist audience now that is ever-renewing, which is why something like six or seven of the seventy . . . shows that have ever run a thousand performances in Broadway history are all running right now. . . . In the "golden age" of Broadway, if you will, the audience was essentially local, except for very rare occasions when something would transcend that. When you ran out of local audience, you closed. That's not so true anymore, particularly of musicals. . . . In musicals there has become, rather quickly, a tradition of people coming to town, seeing shows, and leaving, and then new people coming to town and seeing shows and leaving. So you have this ever-renewing domestic and foreign audience. So there is the possibility of longevity that there never used to be.[14]

The integration of musical properties into preexisting webs of international commerce appears to be working well for Broadway's corporate producers. Due in large part to the heavy marketing of an already-familiar property, for example, the staged version of *The Lion King* generated a $20 million advance in ticket sales in 1997.[15]

Just as the advent of the megamusical helped make musical theater more accessible to a larger population, the international reach enjoyed by media companies new to Times Square has benefited the commercial theater in some respects. According to the League of American Theatres and Producers, Broadway contributed an estimated $2.8 billion dollars to the city's economy during both the 1996–97 and 1998–99 theater seasons. These numbers represent a 40 percent inflation-adjusted increase from the 1991–92 season, which was, despite the economic recession, itself surprisingly strong.

Despite a dramatic drop in tourism after the World Trade Center attacks on September 11, 2001, which led to a sharp decline in profits during the 2000–2001 season, Broadway's numbers have only continued to climb: during the 2002–03 season, Broadway as an industry contributed $4.3 billion to the city's economy. This represents an inflation-adjusted increase of 45.7 percent from the 1998–99 season.[16] The presence of entertainment conglomerates has also allowed for the reclamation of a desirable demographic that the musical theater lost when rock 'n' roll usurped Tin Pan Alley. Due to the increase of youth-oriented marketing and subject matter, as well as the many reduced-rate tickets that corporations can afford to offer, attendance at commercial theaters by people under the age of twenty has been rising slowly but steadily after decades of decline.[17]

The presence of corporations as theater producers has had a less obvious but equally important influence. Because conglomerates can spend more money to appeal to an ever-widening pool of tourists, they can keep shows open for longer stretches, despite even the most scathing criticism. In this respect, corporations are contributing to the decline in power of the local theater critic, who mere decades ago could single-handedly close a show the day after it opened. "There has never been a bigger divergence between critical and public opinion," theater critic and historian Ken Mandelbaum insists. "In my lifetime—probably never in the history of musicals—have shows gotten such bad reviews and been so wildly popular."[18]

While the declining importance of the local critic and the triumph of the corporate musical might not be cause for celebration among aesthetes, it has allowed for a significant boost in employment. The staged version of the 1984 film *Footloose* provides an excellent example here. During its tryout in Washington, D.C., and again when it arrived on Broadway in October 1998, *Footloose* was labeled a "musical chore," a "flavorless marshmallow of a musical," and "sickening," among other unkind appellations that would have been fatal in the past.[19] Nevertheless, the musical ran for 709 performances, due largely to aggressive marketing by its producers, Cablevision and Dodger Endemol Theatricals.[20] Catherine Campbell, a member of the original cast, remembers that company members were hugely relieved to learn that the bad reviews would not close the show:

> Broadway is now like a tourist spot—like Disney World, it really is. And there's room for all kinds of people now. It's not just intellectual, elite people that go to the theater anymore. . . . There's a part of me that misses what it used to be, because I am a person who loves brilliant theater. I love to go to something and be shaken to my core. But I'm not everybody. There's a whole lot of people out there who deserve what *they* want, not just what *we* want. Critics in New York say, "This is what you should like," but . . . they're obviously wrong, because people are still buying tickets to shows that the critics bombed. I see the joy that people stand up with at the end of the play, and I think, "What a wonderful thing to give to people." I've never felt warmth from an audience like I do in this show. So even though we were killed by critics, it makes it worth it. Which is nice, because, I tell you, ten to fifteen years ago, if you got bad reviews, you closed the next day. That's what commercialism has done for Broadway: a lot more actors have jobs.[21]

While not as fully developed or as widely used at present, a few strategies aimed at "critic-proofing" shows have recently been attempted in the commercial theater. In a few cases, corporations have revamped struggling musicals in mid-run. For example, *The Scarlet Pimpernel,* which ran between 1997 and 2000, was closed by its producers—Hallmark among them—in mid-run; the show was recast, revised, and reopened in "new and improved" form, resulting in a longer run than the original version would have allowed.[22] In other cases, companies have attempted to criticproof musicals by test-marketing them before they open. Tom Viertel notes that when the production company Livent (later a subsidiary of SFX-Entertainment) was developing the 1998 musical *Ragtime,* producers held focus groups during which a select group of spectators were asked "what they liked about the show, what they didn't, [and] what they would change."[23] But for these rare exceptions, however, most of the approaches that media companies are taking in producing Broadway shows have been used in the theater industry for decades, albeit on much smaller scales.

Corporate Approaches in Relation
to Past Industry Techniques

Long before Disney, Cablevision, and Clear Channel showed up on Broadway, the so-called Big Three"of New York theater—the Shubert, Jujamcyn, and Nederlander organizations—functioned as theater owners and producers, and thus have long made a practice of developing or handpicking shows to put into their own theaters. In hopes of appealing to the largest potential audience, these producers have traditionally relied in some part on familiarity to sell tickets. One can find hundreds of past musicals based on popular novels or stories, for example; while the trend is certainly on the rise, films have inspired stage musicals at least since the 1939 film *Ninotchka* inspired Cole Porter's 1955 hit *Silk Stockings,* which itself was made into a film in 1957.[24]

Further, producers have attempted to thwart the power of critics for decades. Long before Cameron Mackintosh, and later Disney, began developing international marketing campaigns and selling franchised productions to foreign producers to offset the influence that poor reviews might have on audiences in New York, producers like Melvin Van Peebles and David Merrick were devising creative ways to extend the runs of shows.[25] Nor is synergy new to the commercial theater. As early as the 1970s, producers like Robert Stigwood were staging properties on Broadway—like *Jesus Christ Superstar*—that had already earned international names for themselves in other forms. The 1980s megamusical simply proved even more than *Superstar* had that musicals could be made into international commodities through strategic marketing campaigns aimed at widening audiences. Marketing strategies that once set megamusicals apart from other musicals are now being even more liberally applied. Since corporations moved to Broadway, the term *megamusical* has thus become somewhat obsolete: any musical can now be sold internationally, as long as it has a corporate-sized budget.

In increasing numbers since the 1990s, theater producers have been developing marketing strategies unique to each musical. Tom Viertel notes, for example, that his Lieber and Stoller revue, *Smokey Joe's Café,* had a commercially successful run despite poor reviews due in part to a promotional relationship with the local "oldies" radio station, which frequently gave away free tickets to the show and sponsored on-air guest appearances by cast members.[26] While corporations have more money and a broader reach, most of their strategies are not much different from those applied by the theater industry in the first place. The scale might be new, but most of the techniques are not.

One might conclude, then, that rather than transforming it, corporations have merely given the commercial theater a much-needed financial boost. Broadway productions have always been commercial ventures, after all; media companies have simply made them even more commercial than the Shuberts, Merricks, Stigwoods, and Mackintoshes could manage on their own. With such logic in mind, it is perhaps surprising that the response to the presence of media companies in the realm of commercial theater has been highly ambivalent among journalists, scholars, and many members of the theater industry itself.

A Critique of "Theatrical Corporatization"

Critics of increased corporate presence have not collectively duped themselves into thinking that Broadway was ever anything but a place to make money. Broadway musicals have always been big business, so the fact that the business is getting bigger is not the focus of concern. While opponents are often quick to acknowledge, and even to appreciate, the economic boost that conglomerates have given the industry, most add that this very boost is wreaking havoc on the already delicate balance struck in theater between art and commerce, which seems to be tilting further and further from art. The conundrum is perhaps best summarized by Steve Swenson, a theater technician who has worked in New York since the early 1990s. "Everyone's really happy that there's so much work right now," he says. "The problem is, there's so much crap being staged that it's sort of hard to care much about the work you get, once you get it."[27]

The perceived decline in quality is often linked to the increase in production budgets. While shows like *The Lion King* and *Beauty and the Beast* help increase the amount of money that Broadway makes in a year, these costly productions have raised the stakes even higher than megamusicals did a decade prior. As the price of musicals escalates, many independent producers find that they simply cannot compete. A need to vie with larger companies has begun to change the way old-time theater producers do business. The rising costs and emphasis on synergy have led to a shift from the desire to perfect a property and toward the desire to sell that property in as many ways as possible. Many producers are thus less concerned about the quality of a show than they are in secondary income generated from that show's related merchandise.[28] Jack Viertel, Tom Viertel's brother and the creative director of Jujamcyn Theaters, argues,

> *The Lion King* was the first shot out of the barrel. Once that worked, you knew it was a matter of time before MSG and Radio City and Universal and Hallmark and all these people said, "Wait a minute, this is a good thing, I want to be part of it." And once those companies that are used to spending $40 and $50 million to create a product come to Broadway and see Broadway as a sort of beginning of a profit center for a huge product, rather than the play being the play, then that's it, it's changed. It's going to change the whole landscape.[29]

With this in mind, rumors like the one about Disney's *Aida* being inspired by the company's need for an excuse to market a black doll are as plausible as they are risible.[30]

In many respects, the arrival of entertainment conglomerates in Times Square has done less to help theater than it has to help the conglomerates themselves. Tom Viertel notes, for example, that corporations have benefited most from the marketing strategies being applied on Broadway:

> Disney is a very marketing-heavy company, but their capacities to market are so specific to them that while they have borrowed from us, it has been virtually impossible for us to borrow from them. I mean, we don't own a theme park in which to give away tickets to our shows, or offer opportunities for people to see the shows at discounted prices. The synergy involved when you own a television network, several cable networks, [and] a half-dozen theme parks . . . is unimaginable from our perspective. So . . . basically it has been a one-way street, where they have taken a number of the techniques that . . . independent producers have pioneered, and adapted them, because they are perfectly good techniques, and why shouldn't they use them? But we can't really do much of what they do.[31]

Many members of the theater industry have responded to the changing landscape by developing projects viewed as relatively "risk-free"—for example, by following the lead of corporate producers and adapting movies for the stage. Other projects currently deemed "safe bets" are revivals, which have been particularly abundant on Broadway since the 1990s.

Yet while "crowd-pleasers" might be good for business, they are not necessarily indicative of a healthy state for the theater. On the contrary, fetishizing the familiar can work to the disadvantage of new creations, which become increasingly marginalized. In this respect, what is currently happening to the commercial theater can be compared with what has been happening to classical music in this country.[32] As in the music industry, the theater industry is increasingly forced to take economics into consideration, and less able to bring new work to Broadway since developing new projects is expensive, risky, and enormously time-consuming.[33] While innovative work is becoming scarce on Broadway, original shows that do open there often prove unable to compete with the familiar or the spectacular. Further, just as it is difficult to lure audiences away from spectacle, it is hard to argue with the market for nostalgia. Statistics on Broadway seasons from 1984 to 2004 indicate that seasons offering the fewest new productions often make the most money.[34]

Although the revitalized Times Square area has seen the renovation of a number of theaters, as well as the construction of new rehearsal space, access to performance venues remains competitive. The growing glut of shows that producers refuse to close has begun to cause something of a shortage of theaters, the largest of which are dominated by either long-running holdovers or by corporations like Disney. According to Tom Viertel,

> Independent producers can't really compete with the Disneys and Cablevisions for the types of attractions that will now go into the 2,000-seat theaters. Those are likely to cost $15 to $20 million because *The Lion King* set the bar that high. The only people who can do that are large companies who have other fish to fry besides simply making a profit out of the endeavor itself. That leaves the rest of us looking at a number of theaters that aren't big enough to accommodate that kind of attraction. To take an example, a theater like the Beck [now the Al Hirschfeld Theater], which is 1,433 seats—in the old days, this would have been plenty big enough to house what was thought to be a large musical. You could have put *Les Miz* in the Beck and it would have been a perfectly fine thing to do. They almost did put *Phantom of the Opera* there. But those shows are small by comparison with a show like *The*

Lion King. And now what is considered a top-of-the-line musical attraction has inflated in size by almost double . . . So a theater like the Beck has ceased to be appropriate for the largest attractions. These now have to go into houses that are 1,500 seats and up. There are only a handful of houses like that . . . on Broadway, many housing long-running attractions that aren't showing any sign of slowing down. This is forcing a number of difficult situations to occur. Some theaters, which were typically never musical theaters, are being turned into musical theaters for musicals willing to accept the additional risk of having small capacities. The alternative is not having a theater at all. . . . [But] when you're sitting in a theater with a 1,000-seat capacity and you have a running cost that suggests you should be in a theater with a 1,400-seat capacity, your approach to promotions has to be . . . different because so much promotion involves trading tickets for exposure . . . [But] the notion of giving away a significant number of tickets when you only have a thousand tickets to sell a night is fairly terrifying.[35]

In an atmosphere in which the best-selling productions are also often the biggest productions, a question arises as to what type of audience is being created for the theater. While it is perhaps good news that record numbers are flocking to theaters in New York, or to see international tours of Broadway musicals, it must be remembered that showing people their favorite films live on stage, no matter how innovative the adaptation, is not necessarily going to create lifelong theatergoers. The approach could just as easily lower the standards of what is expected from theatrical production.[36] The question as to what future audiences will expect of theater becomes more pressing since corporations are the ones that can most easily afford to offer reduced ticket prices and court young people with special advertising campaigns.

Despite these issues, many argue that Broadway's move toward commerce and away from art is not only inevitable, it is also unproblematic. "Whether art needs to survive on Broadway is a good question," Jack Viertel muses:

I'm not sure it does need to for anybody but people like me who want it to survive. As a business, it may not need to. The problem is, of course, in the movie business, you can make a $200 million movie, but it's still possible to make a $6 million movie. In the Broadway theater

. . . you can *only* make the $200 million movie. You can't really make the $6 million movie. . . . You can maybe do it Off Broadway, or in a resident theater, but you can't on Broadway, because the economic constraints are such that it's impossible. . . . The question that everyone has to answer . . . is, does that matter? Does it matter if there is no real quality art on Broadway? It matters to me because I work on Broadway and that's what I'm interested in. But it may not matter in the long run.[37]

The Relationship between Commercial and Nonprofit Theater

These issues would matter less if the commercial and nonprofit theater realms were distinct. If this were the case, Broadway could continue evolving into a museum for revivals and recycled films, while the non-profit realm could concentrate on developing new musicals and plays. The corporatization of Broadway, however, has affected the not-for-profit realm, which is being used increasingly for commercial purposes. In another trend that has been spurred by the presence of entertainment conglomerates as theater producers, the divide between commercial and nonprofit theater is blurring.

Although they have always influenced one another, the nonprofit and commercial realms of American theater have historically remained at a wary distance. Commercial theater has traditionally prioritized entertainment suitable for mass audiences, while the nonprofit sector has prided itself on placing artistic innovation before economic gain. The nonprofit theater remains the primary cultivator of new American drama and a site for the development of innovative musical theater, but those who work in the nonprofit realm are underpaid when compared with their commercial counterparts.[38] Nonprofits, like their commercial counterparts, need money to survive; this has begun to translate into drawing audiences with surefire hits that have a chance of crossing into the commercial realm.

The commercial and nonprofit theater worlds have thus begun to inch away from the adversarial relationship they have had in the past, and toward a partnership: the commercial realm looks to the nonprofit one for new works and smaller houses to test Broadway-bound material, while the nonprofit realm seeks a greater share of the financial rewards found in the commercial realm. As a result, more nonprofit groups have begun to host what are essentially workshop versions of shows intended for the commercial realm. In return for housing early versions of Broadway-bound productions, nonprofits accept what is known as "enhancement money" from producers interested in test-marketing productions before attempting a Broadway opening. Nonprofit companies share production credits, while corporations foot most of the bill.

Partnership has its benefits. Nonprofit houses now produce musicals and bigger plays than they could otherwise afford, and a move to Broadway can put a struggling nonprofit theater on the map. On the other hand, such relationships threaten to stifle creativity. In response to arguments that the growing partnership between the nonprofit and commercial realms is ultimately harmless, Ira Weitzman, former director of musical theater at Lincoln Center, scoffs, "Does the fact that this money is coming from commercial sources influence the end product? Of course it does."[39]

In such an atmosphere, it is perhaps not surprising that the most successful rock musicals to be staged recently in New York City have cropped up in spaces that are increasingly far from Broadway, and even, to some degree, from the traditionally nurturing realm of Off Broadway. As the distinctions between Off Broadway, Broadway, and the regional theater blur, Off-Off-Broadway has become home to offbeat productions like *Hedwig and the Angry Inch* (1998), about an East German victim of a bungled sex-change operation, and *The Donkey Show* (1999), an adaptation of Shakespeare's *A Midsummer Night's Dream* set in a discotheque in the 1970s. Both of these productions found success in performance spaces located on the literal and figurative fringes of Manhattan: *Hedwig* ran at the dilapidated Jane Street Theater in the farthest reaches of the West Village, while *The Donkey Show* made its home in an abandoned discotheque near the West Side Highway in Chelsea. Shows like these usually boast ticket prices that are dramatically lower than their Broadway counterparts, thus attracting a much-coveted young audience with relative ease.

Over the past thirty years, rock has merged with Broadway fare in the commercial theater, while less diluted forms of rock and popular music continue to emerge in innovative new productions that attract more specialized audiences. While the large number of casualties on Broadway in the 1970s still keeps producers wary of rock musicals, plenty of productions continue to experiment with rock music in theaters far from Broadway. This formula extends to practically all theater productions in New York: the more experimental or risky a piece is, the more likely it is to find its way to an Off or Off-Off-Broadway house. Since these houses, like regional ones, are increasingly influenced by economic factors on Broadway, however, experimental productions are potentially being placed in peril.

Like the Times Square area in which it is based, the commercial theater industry has seen a number of monumental changes in a very short period of time. These are indicative of a general process of corporatization, whereby fewer and fewer organizations control an ever-widening amount of any given product. In a trend that began in the late 1970s and has only accelerated in the past half-decade due to the presence of media companies in Times Square, an increasing number of "risk-free" Broadway productions are developed, produced, and marketed to appeal to ever-widening audiences. While the megamusical in the 1980s and the corporatization of theater through the 1990s have allowed the Broadway musical to move back into an entertainment mainstream that has become dominated in the past half-century by the film, television, and recording industries (all of which were similarly corporatized decades ago), the American theater takes its share of the spotlight at a cost.

Although Broadway has been enjoying an unprecedented financial windfall, theatrical productions in New York and across the country are evolving from creative forms of artistic expression into products developed by committee and suitable for synergistic appropriation by the entertainment conglomerates that produce and market them. In short, stylistically and economically, theater is becoming more like mass-mediated entertainment than ever before. While this process of corporatization is perhaps less problematic on Broadway, which has always been a center for commercialism, the issue becomes more complicated due to the fact that the most commercial realm of American theater is influencing the country's many nonprofit houses. Corporations might be helping theater, then, but arguably not as much as theater is helping corporations.

While corporatization has certainly limited artistic expression in the American theater, it has yet to cause its death. New musicals and plays are still being staged across the country; many theatrical productions still regularly succeed or flop as the result of audience response, critics' reviews, or both, despite the best efforts of marketing experts new to the theater; and, perhaps most importantly, independent programs that nurture young artists continue to be developed.[40] Optimists thus might argue that creative expression will always find its way. Just as music continues to be made and disseminated on the grassroots level, innovative theater continues to dot the landscape. For every staged screenplay or big-budget revival, there is a *Donkey Show* or a *Hedwig and the Angry Inch,* both of which succeeded despite their lack of marketing tie-ins.

Nevertheless, as corporations continue to fill the vacuum left by the dwindling and censorious National Endowment for the Arts, there is less opportunity for young composers and playwrights to be nurtured in environments that value creativity and innovation over moneymaking and broad appeal. As long as costs continue to spin out of control, corporations continue to offer recycled films in place of innovative musicals, and regional theaters continue to be used as breeding grounds for Broadway-bound ventures, the American musical will only continue to be compromised.

5 🎸 Rock Musicians in the Musical Theater: The 1990s

IN DISCUSSING SOME OF THE MANY DIFFERENCES between the rock and musical theater worlds, the actor Michael Cerveris, who originated the title role in *The Who's Tommy*, relays the following anecdote:

> The night before the big press opening, the big debut where we were going to show the media a rehearsal, we had this party where we put a band together with Pete [Townshend] and me and some guys from the *Tommy* band, and some other guys from the cast, and we played this party and did a little rock show. The next morning was sort of important. We were going to have all the national network news crews, and it was the first time the public was going to see anything. It was two or three o'clock and I said, "I should probably get home, I guess" and [Townshend] said, "Well, actually, probably what you should do is, I should take you out and we should stay out drinking all night and you should come in looking like hell, and sing about five minutes into the first song and then stop and just say, 'No, no, no, fuck it, I hate this, I hate *you*, I hate it all' and then just walk out. *That* would be very rock-'n'roll. But I guess we can't really do that." But there was at least part of him that thought that this really might be the thing to do.[1]

Yet as Clifford Lee Johnson III, director of the musical theater program at the Manhattan Theatre Club, notes, one of the most overarching obstacles to creating and performing successful rock musicals is the fact that rebelliousness does not translate well to the theater stage, just as a lack thereof does not work well in the rock realm.[2] As this chapter demonstrates, decades after *Hair* opened in 1968, rock and the musical theater remain distinct enough performing arts genres that most of the rock-influenced musicals to open in New York City during the 1990s confronted a broad number of obstacles in the process, despite wildly divergent critical and commercial receptions.

The Who's Tommy

On April 22, 1993, Broadway saw the return of the fragmented rock musical when *The Who's Tommy* opened at the St. James Theater. Although the musical received more critical acclaim than Ken Russell's disjointed film version of *Tommy* from 1975, it nevertheless faltered in its ability to allow rock music to take center stage. Further, despite director Des McAnuff's close association with Pete Townshend and his struggle to remain true to the original piece, the musical was ultimately perceived by many rock fans to be too saccharine for their tastes, and at the same time deterred many theatergoers who preferred more traditional Broadway fare.

Tommy, like *Jesus Christ Superstar,* began life as a concept album that spawned a number of incarnations before eventually landing on Broadway. Also like *Jesus Christ Superstar, Tommy* proved difficult to translate into visual terms, due to an ambiguous, nonlinear plot that alternately explores the inner life of its central character and offers loose descriptions of significant people and events he experiences. *Tommy* differs from *Jesus Christ Superstar,* however, in that its creators had no initial interest in developing a staged production of the concept album. Rather, *Tommy* was, from inception, intended to be a project that would challenge rock musician Pete Townshend and his band, the Who, and broaden its audience; its designation by the band as a "rock opera" was, Townshend has acknowledged, "a bit facetious."[3]

Prior to *Tommy,* the Who was largely a purveyor of single records. Formed in 1964, the band enjoyed a string of hits on the singles charts, first in their native England and later in the United States. Within a few years, however, the band's interest in singles had begun to flag. "We'd had a fun pop-group career, a string of hits all of which were wonderful—we never made a bad record—and suddenly we ran out of songs," Townshend recalls.[4] Hoping to keep the band members interested in making music together, Townshend began to compose larger-scale works. The first of these, "A Quick One While He's Away," was a ten-minute-long "mini-opera" that appeared at the end of the Who's second album, released under the title *A Quick One* in England in 1966 and *Happy Jack* in the United States in 1967. Bolstered by the challenges that "A Quick One" posed, Townshend began revising old songs and writing new ones with the aim of recording a concept album of songs that functioned independently, but that told a story when played in sequence.[5]

The result was *Tommy,* a double-record album that tells the disjunct and allegorical tale of Tommy Walker, born in England at the end of World War I to a woman whose husband is missing in action and presumed dead. When Tommy's father suddenly returns home a few years later, he finds that his wife has taken up with another man. A scuffle ensues; the Walkers kill the suitor, and then realize that their son has witnessed the murder. In a panic, they tell Tommy that he imagined the entire incident, and that he must never utter a word to anyone about what he thinks he saw.

To his parents' horror, the traumatized little boy responds by losing his ability to see, hear, and speak. Although completely sealed off from the world, he experiences a complex inner life. He retains a curious ability to perceive himself in the mirror, which he stares into for hours on end. He is also an extraordinary pinball player; despite his inability to see or hear, he becomes the national champion as an adolescent.

Tommy's extended family takes advantage of him. He is sexually molested by his drunken Uncle Ernie and physically abused by his sadistic cousin Kevin. Tommy's parents take him to countless healers who attempt to treat him in ways ranging from the conventional to the bizarre. One specialist determines that Tommy's problems are entirely psychological, but no one is able to come up with a cure. Eventually, Mrs. Walker's frustrations get the best of her. Tired of watching her son stare into the mirror day after day, she smashes it, inadvertently freeing Tommy from his trance.

The newly transformed Tommy is heralded as a messiah. He begins to make public appearances, and opens a pinball camp, where his followers are greeted by the opportunistic Uncle Ernie. Once inside, visitors are told that they will find enlightenment if they cover their eyes, plug their ears, cork their mouths, and play pinball. Tommy's followers quickly grow tired of this path, however, and violently turn on him, thus leaving him again as isolated as he was when he was blind, deaf, and dumb.

Despite a few accusations of pretentiousness in the press and among fans, *Tommy* was a big hit in both the UK and the United States upon its release in 1969. The album went double-platinum and spent forty-seven weeks on the Billboard album charts. It also yielded a number of hit singles, including "Pinball Wizard," "I'm Free," and "See Me, Feel Me," all of which remain in heavy rotation on classic rock radio stations.

Like *Jesus Christ Superstar*, *Tommy* spawned several stage versions in the years following its release. Tours by the Who were often devoted to live renditions of the album in its entirety,[6] and a ballet interpretation was staged by Les Grands Ballets Canadiens in 1971.[7] The album sold so well that a second version—recorded by the Who with the London Symphony Orchestra and Chamber Choir, and featuring guest vocals by Ringo Starr, Richard Harris, and Rod Stewart, among others—was released in 1972. Ken Russell's film version, featuring members of the Who, Ann-Margret, Oliver Reed, Jack Nicholson, and a slew of rock musicians in featured roles, was released in 1975.

Despite many requests for rights to adapt *Tommy* for the musical stage—and endless reports of unauthorized stagings in England and America—Townshend never had much interest in pursuing such projects.[8] In 1991, however, he broke his wrist in a biking accident, and was forced to curtail his guitar playing. During the long period of recuperation, he took note of one request for rights from the PACE Theatrical Group. Deciding that such a project might help him keep his mind off his inability to perform, Townshend granted the theater producers rights to *Tommy*, provided that he had a say in the choice of director.

The PACE group introduced Townshend to Des McAnuff, then artistic director of the La Jolla Playhouse and a director known for drawing on rock music to inspire much of his work. Townshend and McAnuff hit it off, and Townshend agreed to collaborate on a staging of the rock opera.[9] Their initial collaboration proved fruitful: *The Who's Tommy*, so renamed in a nod to the other surviving members of the Who, was both a critical triumph and the biggest commercial success in the La Jolla Playhouse's ten-year history when it opened there in the summer of 1992.[10]

Although musical adaptations of sound recordings have proven disappointing in New York in the past, executives at Jujamcyn Theaters were nevertheless convinced that moving *The Who's Tommy* across the country to one of their Broadway houses could only result in further success. Whereas shows like *Jesus Christ Superstar* had opened in New York without the benefit of an out-of-town run, *The Who's Tommy* was already playing to sold-out houses in Southern California. Further, while *Superstar* was staged only a year after the album was released—and was thus very likely a victim of overpromotion—*Tommy* was almost twenty-five years old, and had thus long since proven its durability. Finally, *Tommy* was already familiar to many baby boomers, who grew up listening to the album or watching Ken Russell's 1975 film version, and who now comprised a significant segment of New York's theatergoing public.

Jack Viertel, artistic director at Jujamcyn Theaters, remembers that the La Jolla production appealed to him not only as a businessman, but also as a member of the baby-boom generation. "Jujamcyn did *Tommy* because we loved *Tommy* and thought it was a terrific production," he notes. "It was absolutely great—the audience just *screamed*, you know. I am of the era of *Tommy*. I saw the Who perform *Tommy* at the Psychedelic Supermarket in Boston in 1969. So I just really wanted to do it, and so we did it."[11]

Moving the acclaimed production from one coast to the other initially seemed to pay off. When it opened on Broadway, *The Who's Tommy* diverged from previous fragmented rock musicals staged in New York City by receiving glowing reviews from most theater critics, including the exceptionally influential Frank Rich of the *New York Times.* Audiences responded enthusiastically, as well. Right after the reviews came out, eager theatergoers rushed the box office at the St. James Theater and formed a line that snaked around the block. Within twenty-four hours of opening, *The Who's Tommy* set a Broadway record by selling $494,897 worth of tickets in a single day.[12] It therefore came as a surprise to many members of the theater community when, on June 17 1995, it closed after a run of 899 performances.[13]

While a two-year run on Broadway in the early 1990s was certainly not an embarrassment, it was also not a great success, especially for a show that won such adoration in the press and broke box office records when it opened. Jack Viertel admits that *The Who's Tommy* was the source of much bewilderment among industry executives. "It was a terrific production and it turned out to be barely a hit," he muses. "We thought it would run for 150 years, and it didn't run for 150 years—it ran for two."[14] In the end, *The Who's Tommy* made just enough money to recoup its initial investment and earn its investors a 10 percent profit.[15]

A number of theories have been offered regarding the fate of *The Who's*

Tommy. One is that for all its baby-boomer appeal, the musical was not reaching a broad enough audience.[16] Scott Zieger, one of the musical's executive producers, surmised that a two-pronged marketing approach, aimed at both young people and at Broadway's traditional audience, would have saved the show, but that the producers could not afford two campaigns.[17] Still other insiders argued that the producers had "committed theatrical suicide" by periodically slashing ticket prices in an attempt to lure audiences. From January to April 1995, for example, the producers offered half-price discounts on advance tickets, which caused a sharp increase in attendance at the show. But every time tickets were returned to their normal price, sales would drop again. Rather than pay full price, many potential audience members—especially the younger, more financially strapped ones—would simply wait for another round of deep discounting. "Why would anyone pay full-price when they could have gotten it for half-price?" asks veteran producer Arthur Cantor. "You have to have a mix of full and discounted prices in order to survive . . . shows cannot survive on half-price tickets—especially musicals."[18]

Jack Viertel, who remains unsure as to why *The Who's Tommy* did not enjoy a longer tenure on Broadway, hypothesizes that the disappointing run was in part a result of the fact that Broadway musicals are rarely afforded the "next-big-thing" status that fuels popular culture, and that when they are, public interest tends to flag too quickly to ensure the long run of any production:

> I think the show didn't cross over to a traditional theatergoing audience. I also think there is something about the other audience, that goes to rock'n'roll events, which has a very short attention span. I mean, they go to what's hot that minute, and then six weeks later they expect something else to be hot. So the idea of having thought that *Tommy* was hot the day it opened, and then thinking about going to see it a year later is just not something—they had moved on. They either saw it, or they missed it. If they missed it they were into—you know, they were on their way to a Nine Inch Nails concert.[19]

Of course, Viertel's theory about the "other" audience applies to consumers of popular culture in general, and extends to theater spectators in particular. The very term *popular culture* implies a series of ever-changing fads and fascinations; just as one popular music group or clothing style or film may be "hot" one week and not the next, Broadway shows often lose their status as "hot" tickets after they have been running for a while and the initial rush at the box office subsides.

While all the existing theories about the early demise of *The Who's Tommy* are certainly viable, ample evidence indicates that despite its hearty reception among theater critics and its initial box office records, the musical disappointed many people who were unable to accept a Broadway version of a classic rock album, no matter how carefully adapted, visually spectacular, or Pete Townshend–approved it was. Despite noble attempts by Des McAnuff to remain true to the original concept album, *The Who's Tommy* became a theatrical production that utilized rock music, whereas the concept album was a rock production that utilized the theater.[20] While this distinction is perhaps obvious, it is also crucial to understanding why the musical did not become the long-running attraction its producers hoped it would: no longer "real" rock and never a "traditional" musical, *The Who's Tommy* alienated members of both camps.

Although Townshend and McAnuff worked hard to retain the spirit of the concept album when adapting the musical, *The Who's Tommy* changed in some subtle but important ways. McAnuff and Townshend were faced with the challenge of negotiating *Tommy*'s lack of narrative without alienating critics and ticket-buyers who were fond of the original album. McAnuff touches upon this paradox by noting that although he detected "substantial gaps in the story line that needed to be addressed in order to realize a full theatrical presentation of the piece," he also felt that the ambiguities "inspired a willing audience to fill in its own personal detail." Aware that he and Townshend would be walking a very fine line in doing so, McAnuff strove to preserve the strengths of the original recording by purposely leaving in some of the ambiguities, while at the same time trying to "flesh out and expand" the diffuse story line.[21]

Hence, rather than foisting additional narrative upon the album in hopes of making it clearer for theatergoers, McAnuff chose instead to take a more visual approach to the stage adaptation, adding dialogue and changing the music or lyrics only when absolutely necessary. To this end, McAnuff writes, the design team for the production

was called upon to play a role that theatre designers rarely undertake: that of storyteller. In other words, the show's creators weren't simply requiring the design artists to create ambiance, a sense of period, locale, class, character, and all of the conventional duties usually given to designers—we were asking them to literally help us develop the fundamental narrative throughline. . . . We made a decision to employ stagecraft and . . . a number of different theatrical storytelling techniques to allow the libretto to do what it had done on the initial recording: Advance the piece thematically without expecting it to develop in the manner a conventional musical might. It was our belief that this was crucial if we were going to retain the purity of the original libretto, which had its own unique poetry. Despite the considerably detailed story we expected to tell, we didn't want to clutter *Tommy* up with added recitative.[22]

Stunning lights and colorful slide and video displays were thus used to help propel the story line of *The Who's Tommy*. This approach allowed the adaptation to remain true to the original in several respects. With very few exceptions, songs remained both intact and in the order that they appeared on the album; further, the flow of the music was rarely interrupted by added dialogue. Tiny Sennheiser microphones worn on the bodies of the actors contributed to a sound design that allowed for the loud volumes and intricate guitar work expected of classic rock, as well as the clarity of voice required of musical theater.[23] Lyrics were only occasionally changed, and the setting was updated from World War I to World War II. Characters were developed, and their actions clarified. The actions of Uncle Ernie, Cousin Kevin, and the LSD-addled Acid Queen—who, Townshend's lyrics imply, is responsible for Tommy's sexual initiation—were significantly toned down, as were all overt references to drug and sexual abuse. A single song—"I Believe My Own Eyes," written by Townshend for the characters of Mr. and Mrs. Walker—was added in hopes that it would shed light on the emotional lives of Tommy's parents.[24] A decidedly upbeat ending was added, in which Tommy grows uncomfortable with his role as a popular idol, turns his back on wealth, power, and status, and returns to his estranged family in hopes of reconciliation.

Finally, when the musical moved from La Jolla to Broadway, the title character was altered, due in part to complaints by the Who's bassist, John Entwistle, and lead singer, Roger Daltrey, both of whom perceived the initial stage version of Tommy as too passive. Michael Cerveris elaborates:

In La Jolla Tommy was totally just a victim of the whole machinery, this pure, innocent spirit that went through the whole experience just kind of being otherworldly and very light. And they realized, partly because of comments from Roger and John and Bill Curbishley, the Who's manager, that Tommy needed to be responsible for some of what happens. He needed to participate in the whole demagogue machinery, he needed to get off on it more and become a bit of a rock monster. The first act changed almost not at all, [but] the second act had a twenty-minute section that was reworked, and culminated in the whole big exploding pinball thing. Part of it was that they had more money to do it—but the really important thing was giving Tommy a dark side.[25]

Several members of the theater press who saw *The Who's Tommy* in both La Jolla and New York reacted positively to these changes. Frank Rich, for example, wrote that they improved the flow of the musical.[26] The rock press, however, was not nearly as pleased; many critics wrote that they were particularly dismayed by the new ending.

The original concept album has a highly ambiguous conclusion: Tommy is rejected by his followers and left to face an unknown future. While Ken Russell's film clears up some of the ambiguity by having Tommy's followers murder his parents during a violent revolt, the future of Tommy himself remains unclear. The musical adaptation, however, concludes after Tommy reconciles with his extended family, and forgives them for any past mistreatments inflicted upon him. Such an ending, combined with the overall tendency on the part of the production to tone down references to sex and drug abuse, prompted many rock critics to attack Townshend and McAnuff for bowing to conservative values and pandering to Broadway producers. In an angry editorial in the *New York Times*, rock critic John Pareles wrote that the new ending and muted references to sex and drugs worked to transform "a blast of spiritual yearning, confusion, and rebellion into a pat on the head for nesters and couch potatoes." The result, in his eyes, was a Broadway musical tame enough to be "almost Reaganesque in its tranquility."[27] A few months later, McAnuff responded angrily to accusations that *The Who's Tommy* was too sanitized. "That's a real little boy up there," he snapped when *New York Times* reporter Janet Maslin asked him about a scene during which Uncle Ernie sings the song "Fiddle About" before, it is implied, he molests ten-year-old Tommy. "Does anyone actually need me to abuse that child to get the point across?"[28]

Few explanations, however, were offered about the new ending. Michael Cerveris remembers that the decision to emphasize the power of family was made by Townshend himself, and was never intended to espouse conservatism. Rather, the change was reflective of Townshend's own personal growth, and was meant to add emotional depth to the characters of Tommy and his family:

> I don't know if Pete changed things as much as he gave them one out of the multitude of answers that they might have had before. And he did change some things—because at the time he wrote the record, so much was about the spiritual journey, and finding your way towards meaning through gurus and drugs and everything else—and at this point in his life he had come to think a little differently, and to recognize the family story. Now he is a father, and he has been for most of the time between now and then—and he has come to the conclusion that you can spend your whole life rejecting everything you grew up with and waste a lot of energy, or you can just try to come to terms and move on. A lot of people felt that the end of the Broadway show was a cop-out; just a touchy-feely ending. That wasn't ever what we were trying to say. I understand how it looks like that because it ends so quickly, and so much is thrown in at the last minute. But I think the idea is that Tommy starts to understand that people can do harmful things without being harmful people, and realizes he has to try and make amends, and doesn't know quite what to do except that going home is the way to do it. So he invites everyone to come home, and asks them what it is they want, and they say, "We want to be like you," and he tells them that that is not the point, and of course, people don't want to hear that—they would rather it be some tablet they could take, or media they could watch. And so they walk out, and he has to come to terms, and the show doesn't really end there. It ends after he has confronted everybody and says, essentially, "I don't hate you anymore," but not necessarily, "All is forgiven and everything's fine." And the end of the show is him sitting with his past selves onstage, staring into this empty mirror, and there's no guarantee that it's all going be happy for Tommy in the future. People have told me they thought it was such a touchy-feely ending, but I think they didn't get it. I don't really blame them, because, like I said, it happened awfully fast.[29]

While additions and changes to the rock musical might have upset many people who were fond of the original concept album, they were nevertheless not clear enough to satisfy theatergoers who were unfamiliar with it. Ken Mandelbaum, for example, notes that for all its strengths, *The Who's Tommy* left him cold:

> He did a great job of staging it, Des McAnuff, but I don't get the piece. I think a lot of people felt what I did—they sat there bewildered by this incomprehensible story. While the production was visually wonderful to look at, I'm interested in being emotionally grabbed in some way—being transported, delighted. I have always felt that emotion is a gigantic factor in the appeal of musicals. People like musicals because they make them cry, or they make them totally delighted in a way that other works don't really do. *Tommy* didn't have that.[30]

In keeping with Mandelbaum's criticism, critic Jeffrey Stock wrote in *Pulse,*

> The show's sets and lighting out-spectacle all the recent Broadway spectacles, but somehow it doesn't feel like a musical. There isn't a single character that escapes from all those great old tunes to connect emotionally with the audience. . . . When [Roger] Daltrey saw an early version of the show in La Jolla, his first response was "Tommy's got no balls." Apparently the finished product is much improved on that account, but a cipher with balls is still a cipher.[31]

A final problem that plagued *The Who's Tommy* is similar to the one that has plagued other adaptations of sound recordings: the cast and pit band could not compete with the original recording. As in *Jesus Christ Superstar,* the lyrics and melodies of *The Who's Tommy* survived more or less intact, but singers and musicians nevertheless often had to diverge from the concept album. In order to preserve their voices, actors in the musical could rarely exhibit the raw vocal power that makes singers like Roger Daltrey so distinctive. Cerveris acknowledges that although Townshend went out of his way to make the company feel that they had "a legitimate right to stand on the stage and sing these songs," one of the most challenging aspects of his role was "singing songs in a big public forum that had been made incredibly famous by other people."[32]

While the sound recording's instrumentation and orchestrations were emulated in the stage version, the score was nevertheless subject to a handful of necessary alterations. Mark Stewart, who served as lead guitarist in the Broadway orchestra pit, explains:

> There were some things that were rearranged. Certain motives—like in the structure of the guitar solo, the elements were all there, but the structure was moved around. . . . There were some other things, too. For example, to function in the musical, certain things were moved around or extended. We had to treat it like theater: what do we need so that we can go from point A to point B on the stage? We want to do this on the stage—will the music accommodate it? If not, how can we change it, add to it, subtract from it? So there were modifications, but for the most part [the score] was pretty straight ahead. There was a little more lead playing in the show than there was on the album because Townshend was much more of a rhythm guitarist. . . . [But] we certainly were true to the record.[33]

Nevertheless, the resultant sound was often unfavorably compared to the original recording in the music press. For example, in his review of the musical for *Rolling Stone,* Anthony DeCurtis argued that no matter how aggressive the music, a pit band hired to provide accompaniment for a Broadway musical cannot compare with a rock band:

> The lesson *The Who's Tommy* teaches is that in coming to terms with the requirements of the theatrical stage, rock . . . must not allow its visceral power, its instinct for anarchy, to be blunted. Take the case of Luther Rix, the orchestra drummer who performed the thankless task of having to reproduce Keith Moon's parts for *The Who's Tommy.* He's a first-rate musician, certainly well-trained, probably, in strict terms, a "better" drummer than Moon. He did everything right, but what he couldn't manage—and was smart enough not even to attempt—was Moon's innate wildness, the vertiginous sense that he might take a song in any direction at any moment, just for the kicks. They can't teach that at the conservatory, just like they can't teach the splendid singers who sang *Tommy's* songs so technically well the yearning, cord-ravaging strain of Roger Daltrey's and Pete Townshend's voices.[34]

While, on the one hand, members of the music press did not warm to *The Who's Tommy,* the show seemed unable, on the other, to appeal to many traditional theatergoers, who avoided the production for fear of loud volumes, lewd subject matter, or both. Lead guitarist Mark Stewart fielded complaints from both theater and rock camps during his term with the production. "The standard, stereotypical complaint about *Tommy,*" he recalls, was that for "theater people, it wasn't enough theater; musical people, it was not enough musical; and rock people, it was not enough rock. It ended up being somewhere in the middle."[35] While the middle ground clearly failed *The Who's Tommy,* it worked wonders for the next rock-influenced musical to show up on Broadway: *Rent.*

Rent

One of the most successful rock-influenced musicals in recent years—and, in fact, in the history of the rock musical subgenre—is *Rent,* with book, music, and lyrics by Jonathan Larson. Because of its phenomenal success, as well as several stylistic and structural similarities, *Rent* is regularly compared with *Hair.* Yet these two musicals are ultimately very different, particularly in terms of their marketing and impact.

Rent was originally developed at the New York Theatre Workshop on East Fourth Street in Manhattan. A retelling of Puccini's *La Bohème* set in the early 1990s, Larson's musical follows a group of young, East Village idealists over the course of a single year. Like *Hair,* the musical attempts to provide a snapshot of a particular place and time, and tackles themes that would seem unapproachable by traditional musical theater standards, including AIDS, heroin addiction, and homelessness. Also like *Hair,* the original staging of *Rent* featured regular breaks to the fourth wall, and did away with elaborate sets in favor of a sparse, curtainless stage exposed to the wings and set with a minimum of props. In place of the totem-pole featured in *Hair,* the stage of *Rent* boasted an immense sculpture of junk, wire, and Christmas-tree lights, which was used, depending on the scene, to symbolize the facade of an apartment building, a Christmas tree, and a church. *Rent* was perhaps most similar to *Hair* in its use of amplification and its musical presentation. It made use of standing microphones set downstage left and right, as well as radio microphones worn conspicuously over each actor's face. The actors were accompanied by a five-piece band that sat onstage in a confined structure resembling a huge wooden crate with most of its slats kicked away.

Also like *Hair,* despite themes that might initially strike some as extreme or alienating, *Rent* was able to transcend its subject matter and appeal to mainstream theater audiences in several ways. First, for all its taboo subjects, *Rent* relies heavily on a number of classic musical theater structures and images. The romantic leads, Roger and Mimi, are flanked by two other couples. One, the ever-quibbling Joanne and Maureen, functions primarily as comic relief; the other, the optimistic, HIV-positive drag queen Angel and his devoted boyfriend Tom Collins, is tragic. In keeping with tradition, act 1 closes with a lively, full-sized production number, "La Vie Bohème," during which the budding romance between Roger and Mimi is established. In its noisy celebration of youth and nonconformity, the number is reminiscent of the anthem "Hair" from the musical of the same name; simultaneously, however, its lyrics—built almost entirely of long lists—pays obvious homage to the works of Stephen Sondheim.

Don Summa, the press agent for *Rent,* adds further that Mimi's entrance in act 1—during which she dances down a staircase as she sings the song "Out Tonight"—clearly invokes the classic musicals *Hello, Dolly!* and *Mame,* in which the title characters both make their entrances in much the same way. Whether purposely or inadvertently, Larson structured his musical in a way that references a Rodgers and Hammerstein classic: Whereas the 1954 musical *The King and I* features a first act that spans a year and a second act that spans a day, *Rent*'s first act takes a day and its second spans a year. Finally, Summa argues, the significance of the title should not be overlooked: "he called it *Rent.* I mean, you know, *clearly* he was thinking about *Hair.*"[36]

It is also significant that the musical diverges from its source at the conclusion. Whereas *La Bohème* ends when the consumptive Mimì dies in the garret bed of her bereft lover Rodolfo, who bellows her name to no avail, *Rent* features an ending more befitting its traditionally upbeat genre. The HIV-positive Mimi, now homeless and sleeping in the park, is found by Joanne and Maureen, who bring her to Roger and Mark's East Village squat. Although she seems, initially, to be nearing death, she is miraculously revived when Roger sings the love song he has composed for her on his electric guitar. The lovers resolve to savor every moment they have together as the musical ends.

Nods to more traditional musical theater aside, *Rent*'s broad appeal is due in part to the fact that despite the amplification, emphasis on vamped accompaniment, and reliance on electric guitar, electric bass, and drum set, *Rent*'s score—like that of *Hair*—borrows from a variety of different styles, including slow ballads, salsa, tango, and gospel. Despite the stylistic and thematic similarities that may be drawn between *Hair* and *Rent*, less risk was involved in moving the latter from Off Broadway to Broadway. In some respects, the comparative lack of gamble was the result of highly atypical momentum generated during *Rent*'s initial run at the New York Theatre Workshop. *Rent* outlasted the initial hype, however, as a result of savvy marketing techniques that snowballed during the period between the musical's premiere on Broadway and the end of the millennium.

Despite *Hair*'s hit status when it opened Off Broadway in 1967, Michael Butler was rejected by most members of the Broadway establishment in his attempts to bring *Hair* uptown. He did so at the risk of failing to find an audience. By contrast, Broadway's major producers fought feverishly over *Rent* weeks after it had opened Off Broadway.[37] Even before it entered previews at the New York Theatre Workshop in early 1996, *Rent* generated a tremendous amount of hype as the result of a tragic backstage story. After watching the final dress rehearsal of his musical on January 24, 1996, Jonathan Larson died of an aortic aneurysm in his apartment at the age of thirty-five.[38] The media took great interest in this tragedy. The fact that *Rent*'s many HIV-positive characters juxtaposed youthful vigor with the specter of untimely death made the sudden demise of its composer particularly poignant, and *Rent* thus became central to countless human-interest stories. The barrage of media attention—combined with strong word-of-mouth and the glowing critics' reviews that appeared after the musical opened Off Broadway on February 13, 1996—resulted in such a furious demand for tickets that within three weeks of its opening, producers announced that *Rent* would be moving to Broadway.[39]

Rent was restaged at the Nederlander Theater on West Forty-first Street, where it reopened on April 29, 1996.[40] The musical won an impressive array of awards, including the Tony, New York Drama Critics Circle, Drama Desk, Outer Critics Circle, and Drama League awards for best musical, as well as the Pulitzer Prize for drama. International and touring companies for *Rent* sprang up across the globe; these reflect the increased interest in theatrical franchising. Whereas different productions of *Hair* were custom-designed to fit the flavor of each host city, *Rent*'s producers stipulated that all productions of *Rent* were designed to be as nearly identical to the Broadway version as possible.[41]

Early in its run, there was little question that despite its tragic foundations, the media blitz surrounding *Rent* was good for business.[42] While the intense hype might well have steered its initial reception, *Rent* was nevertheless buoyed significantly as a result of the application of innovative advertising and marketing techniques. In the days of *Hair*, a musical's commercial success depended much more on strong reviews and word-of-mouth than on the few local advertisements run for any given production. *Rent*'s move to Broadway in the spring of 1996, however, was accompanied by a flurry of both local and international advertising, which had by this point become much more important to the theater industry.

In March 1996 an advertisement consisting of nothing but a stenciled logo surrounded by blank space appeared in the Arts and Leisure section of the Sunday *New York Times*, as well as on buses, taxi cabs, and billboards throughout the metropolitan area. This minimalist campaign helped sell $750,000 worth of tickets to *Rent* in three days.[43] At roughly the same time, a line of clothing inspired by the musical was placed on sale in a special boutique on the second floor of Bloomingdale's in Manhattan,[44] and fashion spreads featuring the cast appeared in *Newsweek, Time Out New York,* and *Rolling Stone* magazines.[45] The advertising blitz boosted sales for the already hot show; in the short time that it took to move *Rent* from the New York Theatre Workshop to the Nederlander, the musical generated a $6 million advance.[46]

While *Hair* became a phenomenon because it was the first musical to successfully merge rock and Broadway fare, *Rent* succeeded *despite* its affiliation with a musical subgenre that had fared notably poorly in its three decades of existence. Tom Viertel argues that in modern marketing campaigns, avoidance of the terms *rock musical* and *rock opera* remains crucial to a musical's success. "I don't think you would market anything as a rock musical anymore in part because rock is so fragmented," he notes. "You could describe something as a rock musical back in the days of *Hair*, when rock 'n' roll was basically one strain of music. But within three years of *Hair*, it was not one strain of music anymore, and now everything in rock is a niche." *Rent*, Viertel argues, is an example of "a theatrical composer utilizing rock forms. Not that *Rent* doesn't qualify as a rock musical. But what we're hearing is theatrical composers borrowing forms to make a point. Larson didn't have any currency as a rock writer. He was a theatrical writer."[47]

Viertel's opinions are mirrored by those of Don Summa, the press agent for *Rent,* who went to great lengths to avoid labeling the musical during its development. Although the theater press insists on using labels like *rock musical* and *rock opera,* history taught him to adamantly oppose applying such terms to *Rent:*

> I never like to call *Rent* a rock musical . . . because for the people who really care about the music and know about the difference between rock music and—they're not going to see this as rock music. It certainly has rock motifs, and uses rock rhythms, but, I mean, you have pop, you have gospel, you have a tango—this isn't a rock musical. My problem with "rock musical" is that it doesn't get the people who like rock to come, and it doesn't get the people who like musicals to come. So who's gonna come? People who are interested in rock music aren't gonna go to Broadway, and people who are interested in musicals don't care about rock music. That's why I think *Rent* is successful—because it's not really a rock musical. The press loves to call it a rock musical or a rock opera. But . . . I just didn't think that was going to sell it to anybody.[48]

Whereas the creators of *Hair* flaunted its rock influence by incorporating the description into its title—thus inadvertently coining the phrase—those responsible for selling *Rent* made an effort to avoid pigeonholing the musical for fear of limiting the audience.

Rosenberg and Harburg note that in most cases, "the real distance between not-Broadway and Broadway is several hundreds of thousands of dollars and a carload of glitz."[49] *Rent,* however, is a notable exception. Once on Broadway, *Rent*'s sparse set and low budget worked to its advantage by contributing to its long run in the years after the hype surrounding its opening and the impact of the initial advertising campaign waned. Summa notes that because *Rent* is cheap enough to break even at only 60 percent capacity, the show can withstand dips in attendance that would be fatal to most Broadway shows.[50]

Befitting its low-budget bohemianism, *Rent* moved into the long-unused Nederlander Theater, which was badly in need of renovation. Because of its fraying carpets, fading curtain, peeling paint, worn seat covers, and unfortunate location—the corner of Forty-first Street and Seventh Avenue, just down the block from the magnificently ugly Port Authority Bus Terminal—the dilapidated Nederlander was hardly the most sought-after performance space in New York. Nevertheless, it made the perfect home for *Rent*. Expensive renovations were unnecessary. In fact, the auditorium was made even more dilapidated to fit the musical's grungy, downtown aesthetic.

In the years before Times Square's renovation, *Rent* fit perfectly at the Nederlander, in part because even its exterior and immediate surroundings seemed appropriate for the musical. Summa, in fact, believes that the "aura" surrounding *Rent*'s new home made the show even stronger than it had been Off Broadway. "The show seemed stronger in a Broadway house, and I never thought it would have," he says. The Nederlander sits on a block "that was not unlike an East Village block—it was kind of run down, it was—still is—inhabited by homeless people." Not only was the Nederlander the right theater, concludes Summa, but "the block was the right block."[51]

Ironically, while the Nederlander remains appropriately dilapidated, the renovation of the Times Square area in the years since *Rent* moved uptown has not damaged the musical's appeal. In his article "New York's Facelift," Mark Sussman notes that during the mid-1990s, *Rent* simply became yet another attraction in a neighborhood transformed into a theme-park version of its former self:

> In Jonathan Larson's *Rent*, life below 14th Street is thoroughly reified into a high-speed montage of sex, drugs, AIDS, and art relentlessly humanized into an MTV version of Bohemia. . . . Homeless folks fight cops in riot gear. "La Vie Bohème" plays a hip "Downtown" to Times Square's new and improved Uptown. The characters, mostly with wealthy, caring parents, live in upbeat poverty according to the legends of the 1980s and 1990s East Village. . . . AIDS and aesthetics are both neatly contained issues: the AZT goes down easily. The demonstration chant "ACT UP! FIGHT BACK! FIGHT AIDS!" is appropriated as a song lyric, a chorus that doesn't bear repeating. The Underworld has been placed many limo-lengths away. Safe consumption replaces excessive and illicit consumption. The danger of carnival—which keeps many life-long New Yorkers far away from Times Square on a New Year's Eve—is being effaced and contained by this new cultural and commercial zoning.[52]

In this respect, *Rent* is very like its predecessor. Just as *Hair* appealed to the vicariousness of its mainstream audience, *Rent* fit into its new surroundings due to its upbeat, ultimately unthreatening depiction of squatting, drug addiction, and AIDS. Even further, the musical became a tribute to an East Village that ceased to exist when that neighborhood underwent its own gentrification in the late 1990s.

As they did with *Hair,* many critics received *Rent* with myriad ecstatic superlatives and the declaration that it would revitalize the American musical theater. Indicative of a growing fear of taking risks, however, is the fact that despite its huge success, *Rent,* unlike *Hair,* spawned few imitations on or Off Broadway. Michael Cerveris believes that *Rent* follows in too long a line of disasters to convince producers that rock musicals will ever be safe investments. "After *Tommy,* every other thing I was called in for or sent a tape of was some pop or rock opera thing," he laughs. "There's a lot of that stuff being written—it's just not getting produced. And one of the reasons is that they look at *Tommy,* which was one of the most successful of those things. It made its money back, but then it closed. *Rent* may make people feel a little safer, but it may not."[53] Indeed, if *Rent* managed to renew an interest in rock-influenced Broadway musicals, Paul Simon's *The Capeman* succeeded just as quickly in quashing it again.

The Capeman

In the late 1980s, the singer-songwriter Paul Simon grew interested in developing a Broadway musical, in large part because he found all extant musical theater unsatisfying.[54] He thus commenced work on *The Capeman,* about the Puerto Rican gang member Salvador Agrón, who became tabloid fodder when he murdered two white teenagers on August 30, 1959, in the Hell's Kitchen section of New York City. Less interested in telling a story than in bringing his music to Broadway audiences, Simon immersed himself in numerous Latin popular genres. These, combined with a heavy dose of the rock 'n' roll he grew up listening to during the 1950s in Queens, influenced the musical's score. Eager to create accurate characters, as well as to escape again being labeled a "cultural carpetbagger," as he was after the releases of his albums *Graceland* (1986) and *Rhythm of the Saints* (1990), Simon developed a friendship with the Nobel Prize–winning, Saint Lucia–born poet Derek Walcott shortly after conceiving of the project. The two men collaborated on the book and lyrics over a seven-year period.[55]

The initial buzz about *The Capeman* was strong among members of the theater industry, but rumors about Simon's inability to relinquish control of his work soon began to scare off potential investors, and to cause concern among the producers, many of whom either pulled out of the production or downgraded their financial commitments as the budget for *The Capeman* crept toward $13 million.[56] Unlike Pete Townshend, who collaborated closely with but ultimately ceded control to director Des McAnuff during work on *The Who's Tommy,* Simon had trouble switching hats from singer-songwriter to musical theater collaborator, and his rigid control of the production proved destructive.

Simon's attention to detail was skewed. A notorious perfectionist who allegedly spent eight hundred hours over two years making the Simon and Garfunkel album *Bridge Over Troubled Water,* he approached *The Capeman* as if it were a record, not a musical.[57] In hopes of generating interest in his project among investors, Simon spent close to $1 million making studio recordings, tapes of which he played for interested parties. In lieu of coming up with a script and a score, Simon planned to record a finished version of the musical, which a cast and pit band would then replicate for the stage. As journalist Stephen Dubner wrote, "this was the first signal that, although Simon was writing a musical that he wanted to play on Broadway, he felt no compunction to play by Broadway rules."[58]

Similarly unorthodox was Simon's obsessive attention to musical detail at the expense of all other aspects of his production. During the process of developing *The Capeman* for the stage, emphasis was placed on the "authenticity" of the music and its performers. In hopes of making his musical as "authentic" as possible, Simon regularly sat in with prominent Latin musicians, and eventually hired a number of them to work with him on the musical. The Broadway company of *The Capeman* thus boasted, among others, Oscar Hernández as keyboard player and conductor; Oriente López as assistant conductor and keyboard, flute, and accordion player; Marc Anthony and Ruben Blades as the young and middle-aged Salvador Agrón, respectively; and Ednita Nazario as Agrón's mother. Attaining ideal sound, even during the rehearsal process, was clearly a priority for Simon, yet such perfectionism proved a hindrance. A company member anonymously told the press that Simon once kept the cast and band waiting for a half hour while he moved a tambourine around the room to determine where it sounded best.[59] While such activities may be viewed in the rock realm as examples of artists taking control of their own creations, they were dismissed as erratic and annoying in a theater rehearsal.

Adamant about maintaining full artistic and financial control over *The Capeman,* Simon either alienated or refused to hire several esteemed directors. Both atypically and tellingly, the director was the last member of *The Capeman*'s creative team to be hired. Simon's difficulties in relinquishing even enough power to decide upon a director caused word to spread through the industry that Simon was looking not for a director but for a glorified stage manager.[60] He initially settled on the Argentine-born Susana Tubert, but she would serve as only the first of *The Capeman*'s directors. Tubert was replaced by Eric Simonson, who was then replaced by the show's choreographer, Mark Morris.[61]

Due to the constant hiring and firing, as well as the creative team's communication breakdowns, rehearsals for *The Capeman* plodded on for an unusually long time. Natascia Díaz, who originated the role of Yolanda, remembers that while rehearsals went on for six months, little in the way of direction was ever provided:

> Mark Morris had no concept of how to talk to actors. If you've never directed before, you don't just come in and say, "Oh, yes, well, I'm a big star." That's how he came in. For the first month it was cute, and it was like, "Well, he's a genius, he's allowed to be like this." Second month, it was, "We're getting tired of being insulted here." The level was not to be believed. Not to mention that he would leave for weeks on end to work with his dance company. And this Broadway show is left hanging, and we're getting directed by his little dance assistant. It was unbelievably frustrating. And [Ruben Blades, Ednita Nazario, and Marc Anthony] were in another world. . . . I mean, of course they cared, but it was like—the theater people were in the ensemble, and they were just coming to Broadway as singers. So God bless them for finding their way as they did. And people seemed to just stand by and let it happen, so it died a long death. Six months. You don't need to rehearse six months for a Broadway show that you have been in workshops for. There was a miscommunication.[62]

Once it was realized that Morris had failed to hone the musical, seasoned director Jerry Zaks was brought in during the final month of rehearsals in a last-gasp attempt to address some of the production's many problems.

The Who's Tommy director Des McAnuff found Zaks's involvement in Paul Simon's show to be sadly ironic:

> Theatre is a collaborative art form, as we know, but rock artists are used to controlling everything for an album, and that's a good thing—you want to keep the record company away. But in the theatre, it just does-n't work that way. You want a designer who is smarter than you about design, and you want a director who has vision. Simon, a man who has made a career of exploring different cultures, seemed to have not much interest and little respect for Broadway, a culture he grew up near to, in New York. The greatest irony is that he ended up with Jerry Zaks trying to fix his show, which seems to be the exact opposite of the kind of artist he wanted to work with.[63]

Zaks's attempts to fix The Capeman failed in the end. The Capeman opened at the Marquis Theater on January 29, 1998, after a preview period that was extended several times over three weeks—never a good sign on Broadway.[64] When it finally did open, The Capeman was trounced by crit-ics, many of whom cited the music as the production's greatest strength, and the convoluted narrative and obvious lack of direction as its most insurmountable problems. Vincent Canby, for example, wrote in the New York Times that "as a show, The Capeman is a great album."[65] As a the-atrical piece, however, The Capeman suffered as a result of poorly devel-oped characters, plot lines that led nowhere, scenes that made no sense, and actors—particularly Blades and Anthony—who were clearly unsure as to what they should be doing most of the time.

Nor did The Capeman sell particularly well. Months before it opened, the musical's advance was moderate, at best.[66] The poor reviews and the show's inability to stir much interest among theatergoers proved fatal; The Capeman closed on March 28, 1998, after fifty-nine previews and sixty-eight regular performances.[67] While Simon's solo album of songs from The Capeman sold well among his fans and earned critical accolades, Simon proved incapable of crossing over to the theater world. Although his work in the Broadway realm does not seem to have influenced his relationship with his fans, his inability to collaborate and his obsession with musical "authenticity" did little more than earn him a reputation within the theater industry as a rebellious troublemaker.

Hedwig and the Angry Inch

At about the same time that *The Capeman* was nearing the end of its ill-fated run on Broadway, the musical *Hedwig and the Angry Inch* was gearing up for a much happier two-year stint Off Broadway at the Jane Street Theater. This quirky little musical, which featured a book by John Cameron Mitchell, and music and lyrics by Stephen Trask, opened to critical acclaim and strong commercial interest on February 14, 1998. It has since been mounted by regional, college, and community theaters across the country and abroad. A film version, adapted and directed by Mitchell, won awards at the 2001 Sundance Film Festival before opening nationwide in theaters in the late summer of that year. More a monologue with songs than a fully-fledged musical, *Hedwig* borrows liberally from Plato's *Symposium* in recounting the tale of its title character.

Abandoned at a young age by his sexually abusive father and raised alone by his mother in East Germany during the 1970s and 1980s, Hedwig—born Hansel Schmidt—lives in an apartment so small that he plays and listens to his adored American pop records in the oven. As a young man, he wins the affections of an American GI who agrees to marry him and take him to the United States if he agrees to a sex change operation. The doctor botches the operation, and Hansel awakens to find a thickly scarred mound of flesh where his penis had been, hence the "Angry Inch" of the show's title.

Hansel, renamed Hedwig and self-identified as a female after the surgery, marries the GI and accompanies him to the United States, only to be abandoned in a Kansas trailer park where she dejectedly watches the fall of the Berlin Wall on television. Making a living by prostituting herself and performing songs in restaurants around the park, Hedwig meets Tommy Speck, a gawky adolescent Army brat, Jesus freak, and aspiring rock star. Hedwig grooms Tommy for stardom and gives him the stage name Tommy Gnosis, after the Greek word for knowledge. The two become romantically involved, but because of his own confused sexuality, Tommy refuses to kiss Hedwig on the mouth, and will only make sexual overtures by approaching her from behind. When Tommy finally reaches between Hedwig's legs, he is so horrified by what he finds that he abruptly leaves her.

Tommy takes all the songs that he and Hedwig wrote, and uses them to become a superstar. The heartbroken Hedwig, meanwhile, struggles in obscurity. Desperate to maintain some control over her life, she marries a talented Serbian-Jewish drag queen named Yitzak, forms a rock group made up of Slavic immigrants, and names her band the Angry Inch. She keeps the band and Yitzak in line by threatening to have them deported whenever they defy her. Hedwig further inflicts her despair on Yitzak by refusing to allow him to perform in drag, despite the fact that he regularly tries to steal her wigs when she is not watching.

Hedwig remains obsessed with Tommy. She and the Angry Inch follow him across the country, playing music in dive bars near his much larger, more respectable performance venues. When not barking at her band, squabbling with Yitzak, or imparting her life story to the audience, Hedwig repeatedly kicks open a stage door so that she can listen bitterly to what she tells her audience is a sold-out concert that Tommy is giving across the waters at the Meadowlands. Yet her attempts to hear any acknowledgment of her influence on his life are rewarded only with earfuls of Tommy praising himself. Eventually, Yitzak defies Hedwig by spitting in her face, which catalyzes an emotional breakdown. The ambiguous ending of the show suggests at once that Hedwig and Tommy were two parts of the same person, and that Hedwig has found the strength to forgive Tommy, release Yitzak from virtual slavery, and stand alone as a self-respecting, emotionally sound individual.

Hedwig and the Angry Inch offers one of the most successful blends of rock and musical theater elements to date, in large part because the creators chose not to fully integrate the two divergent genres. Rather, rock and musical theater elements are presented side by side. Throughout the show, Hedwig, surrounded by Yitzak and the Angry Inch, tells her tale in monologue form, with only occasional lines spoken by the other characters. Most of the show's eleven musical numbers are far more aggressively amplified and rendered than most songs on the theatrical stage. They are performed, as good live rock songs often are, with no regard to the clarity or precision typically required of the musical theater. While some of the songs function to further the plot of the show, others are freed from narrative trappings and are used instead to punctuate Hedwig's many changing moods.

"The fundamentally weird thing about musicals is that people sing in the middle of everyday life and you have to kind of step out of reality," Michael Cerveris muses.[68] By structuring their piece as a "rock cabaret" instead of a fully fledged musical, however, Mitchell and Trask circumvented this problem. *Hedwig and the Angry Inch* unfolds as if it were a gig in a dive bar; Hedwig's monologue comes off as the drunken ramblings of a lead singer taking frequent breaks between songs.

Hedwig and the Angry Inch's balance of rock and musical theater is a result of the unique nature of collaboration between its creators. John Cameron Mitchell, an actor who made his name on Broadway in musicals like *Big River* and *The Secret Garden,* and Stephen Trask, a rock musician who led the house band at the gay downtown club Squeezebox, struck up a friendship on a flight between Los Angeles and New York. After discovering that they had mutual likes (rock and theater) and dislikes (all extant rock musicals), the two decided to collaborate on "a play that translated the visceral charge of live rock into theater that wasn't watered down or sanitized."[69] Mitchell developed the Hedwig character while Trask wrote music and lyrics. Rather than workshop their production in a traditional manner, they honed their project at Squeezebox, where Mitchell would appear as Hedwig before a tough audience of drag queen regulars who were notoriously icy to newcomers.[70] As the bit developed into a full-length piece, Trask's band, Cheater, became Hedwig's backing band, the Angry Inch.

Trask and Mitchell tinkered with *Hedwig* for four years. An early version of the show, directed by Peter Askin, ran for a month at the Westbeth Theatre in Greenwich Village in 1997, after which its creators began to shop for a more permanent venue.[71] After searching high and low for a site that offered a proper balance of theater and rock club aesthetics, the two stumbled upon the Jane Street Theater at the Hotel Riverview. A long-abandoned ballroom that had been made into a cabaret-style theater, the room was deemed dilapidated enough to serve *Hedwig* perfectly. An added draw was the remoteness of the space: originally a seaman's hotel, the Riverview is so close to the Western rim of Manhattan Island that it was used in 1912 as an emergency shelter for surviving members of the *Titanic.*[72]

Hedwig and the Angry Inch was initially a hard sell for its press agents, but their noble efforts eventually paid off. *Hedwig* opened to positive reviews, and these, along with a few appearances on television talk shows, attracted theatergoers. Rock denizens like Pete Townshend, David Bowie, Lou Reed, Laurie Anderson, Bob Mould, and Joey Ramone went to see the show, as well; their attendance helped add to the show's legitimacy in the rock press and among rock fans.[73] Finally, although taking out advertisements in the print media is expensive, press agents Tom D'Ambrosio and James Morrison placed the few that they could afford strategically: lists of the many celebrities who attended performances of *Hedwig* appeared alternately in the theater and music sections of periodicals like the *Village Voice,* the *New York Times,* and *Time Out.*[74]

The visual aesthetic of *Hedwig and the Angry Inch* is heavily influenced by the glam rock movement, which proved advantageous to the show's reception. Glam, which arose in the early 1970s was, in part, a response to the highly machismo posturing found among performers of hard rock. Adherents such as the New York Dolls, T. Rex, Mott the Hoople, Roxy Music, and David Bowie recorded brief, hook-based songs that were executed live in a highly theatrical manner by performers in either androgynous or overtly feminine costumes. In tribute to the glam movement, the cast of *Hedwig* was clad, for the most part, in eye-catching, gender-bending costumes. As the show began, John Cameron Mitchell as Hedwig marched down the aisle in gaudy, glittering makeup, a feathered white-blonde wig, fringed cowboy boots, and a huge multicolored cape on which were scrawled the words "Yankee, Go Home" down one side and "With Me" down the other. Beneath the cape, which Mitchell tossed from his shoulders after the first number, Hedwig wore a tight-fitting minidress covered in fringe. Beneath that was a black leather bustier.

As the Angry Inch, the members of Cheater wore costumes that were somewhat less eye-catching, so as not to draw attention away from the title character. Nevertheless, various band members were clad in studded, sleeveless denim or see-through mesh; fringed leather jackets; shiny, skin-tight plastic or vinyl pants; gravity-defying two-toned wigs; and black lipstick and eyeliner. In a nod to punk aesthetics, the one character who appeared in the most baggy, formless clothing—shapeless black pants, a ripped T-shirt (ironically sporting the *Rent* logo), a vinyl jacket, and a bandanna covering limp, stringy hair—was the only female cast member, Miriam Shor, who originated the role of Yitzak.

The aspect of glam that most benefited *Hedwig and the Angry Inch* was its overt disregard of authenticity, and its self-conscious embrace, instead, of camp and artifice—in short, its theatricality. As Ethan Smith wrote in a cover story about *Hedwig and the Angry Inch* in *New York Magazine,* glam lent itself perfectly to the musical because "*Hedwig*—like the entire pop subgenre from which it borrows its ambitious sound—is about androgyny, life in a borderline state of being, and the inevitably disappointing pursuit of glamour."[75] Ironically, while glam has traditionally celebrated its inauthenticity, its influence on *Hedwig and the Angry Inch* made the show appealing to many rock musicians and fans who usually dismiss such pieces as inauthentic. The musical caught the attention of the glam rock icon David Bowie, for example, who enjoyed the show so much that he became a producer of the Los Angeles production.[76]

While glam aesthetics were a huge influence on John Cameron Mitchell in developing the character of Hedwig, however, they did not influence Trask's music in the least. Among his chief musical influences, Trask lists John Lennon and Paul McCartney, Willie Nelson, Chuck Berry, Duke Ellington, Cecil Taylor, Henry Threadgill, Lou Reed, and Captain Beefheart.[77] While Reed dabbled briefly in glam aesthetics during the 1970s, none of these musicians could be classified easily as representative of the glam movement. Thus, while glam had a strong impact on visual elements of *Hedwig,* Trask borrowed from a much broader sampling of popular styles in composing its score.

The songs from *Hedwig* reveal their composer's keen understanding of the hooks, bridges, verses, and choruses that are the building blocks of most Western popular music. A majority of the songs that make up *Hedwig*'s score are built on bluesy, recurring guitar riffs, I-IV-V ostinatos, driving 4/4 meters, and a verse-chorus structure in which the lead singer delivers the verses, and the rest of the band provides backup during the choruses. The score reveals a wide variety of influences. Songs like "Tear Me Down," "The Origin of Love," "Wig In a Box," and "Wicked Little Town" borrow from the arena rock power ballads of the late 1970s and 1980s by beginning gently and slowly on acoustic instruments, only to build in tempo and intensity through the gradual introduction of power chords on the electric guitar. The lyrics to "The Origin of Love," which describe Hedwig's mother's philosophies, reveal an interest in the fantastic and mythological and are thus evocative of music by the heavy metal forerunners Led Zeppelin; at the same time, the fuzzy reverb of the guitar parts is reminiscent of the Velvet Underground's sonic soundscapes. The bluesy, bouncy "Sugar Daddy," with its trebly, highly syncopated guitar arpeggios, is a playful rockabilly song. And driving rhythms, furiously shouted lyrics, squealing, distorted guitar parts, and repetitive two- or three-chord accompaniment make "Angry Inch" and "Exquisite Corpse" paeans to punk and its offshoot, grunge.

While its visuals pay tribute to a subgenre that gleefully disregards rock's imagined authenticity, then, *Hedwig* borrows musically from subgenres that tend to embrace it. In particular, the raw, angry energy and "Do It Yourself" (DIY) aesthetic of punk and grunge has caused those subgenres to be placed in particularly high esteem by many rock critics and historians. It is likely that Trask and Mitchell kept this in mind when developing the musical's powerful finale.

Late in the musical, Yitzak, tired of being taunted by his emotionally abusive wife, spits in Hedwig's face. The incident is devastating for the lonely, powerless Hedwig, who spirals into an emotional breakdown that begins during the number "Hedwig's Lament." This song serves as an introduction to the much angrier, more aggressively rendered number "Exquisite Corpse." During "Exquisite Corpse," Hedwig yanks off her wig and most of her clothes, removes the tomato "breasts" from her bustier and smashes them against her naked torso before flinging them to the ground, kicks over her microphone stand, and flings herself to the floor as a strobe light pulses insistently through the theater. When the character stands up again in the dead silence that follows the number, he reveals himself to be the emotionally exhausted, disoriented, and deeply ashamed Tommy Gnosis. He and Hedwig have been parts of the Platonic whole all along.

This sequence not only serves as the musical's dramatic climax, it reflects a profound respect for and understanding of rock's ideological relationship to authenticity. A living homage to glam for most of the show, Hedwig literally and figuratively removes her makeup at the end, thereby exposing herself both physically and emotionally to her audience. Although a fictional character, Hedwig is thus transformed from a campy, second-rate glam act to an "authentic" rock artist who has shared herself so completely that (s)he becomes one with the audience. The very last number, "Midnight Radio," drives this home: during the song, Hedwig-as-Tommy frees the delighted Yitzak, who walks off stage with Hedwig's discarded wig and quickly returns dressed as a woman in a black cocktail dress. Just as Hedwig is transformed from glam queen to rock king, Yitzak is transformed from a gender-bending cross-dresser to a classic rock mainstay: a female backup singer. During the last, repeated refrains of

"Midnight Radio," Tommy-as-Hedwig, echoed by Yitzak-as-backup singer, prompts the audience to raise up their hands and wave together in rhythmic solidarity with the band as the performance concludes.

Its commercial and critical success notwithstanding, *Hedwig* was not without its internal complications. In the first place, although it was acclaimed for capturing the spirit of live rock music more competently than most staged rock musicals, the performances were nevertheless compromised. Trask and his band were onstage for the entire show, but remained largely silent and motionless during the lengthy segments of monologue between songs. With little to do during these interludes, the band often seemed stiff, uncomfortable, and bored. When they were playing, band members had to take precautions so as not to distract attention from the title character. Because they could not disrupt the mix, which was amped at much lower levels than those at rock shows tend to be, the band had to learn to play in a way that Trask remembers was "unnatural" and "terribly constraining."[78]

In the second place, although he was heralded by journalists as an "authentic" rock musician who had composed an impressive score for the production, Trask was often given short shrift in the media covering the reception of the show. Early in the run of *Hedwig and the Angry Inch*, Tom D'Ambrosio noted with some surprise that "for a rock musical, all anybody cares about is John Cameron Mitchell from a press point of view.[79] Understandably, the flamboyance and quick-witted humor of Mitchell-as-Hedwig proved somewhat more appealing than Trask, who played a more marginal, decidedly less ostentatious role onstage as Skszp, the Angry Inch bandleader. Yet even the rock press, which duly cited Trask's involvement in New York's rock scene as evidence of the show's purported authenticity, tended to show less interest in Trask than in Mitchell. This is made clear in David Fricke's *Rolling Stone* feature on *Hedwig*, which boasted a full-page color photograph of Mitchell as Hedwig on the first page, and a black-and white photograph of Trask that took up a mere eighth of the second page.[80] Such emphasis is typical of the musical theater; actors tend to receive more media attention and credit for a successful production than those in behind-the-scenes roles. Yet the opposite is usually the case in the rock world, where performers are typically lauded both for their musicianship and the originality of their songwriting.

Two different informants affiliated with the production, both of whom requested anonymity, noted that the comparative lack of media attention was initially painful for Trask, who acknowledged as much in the press. In an interview for the *Village Voice,* Trask joked that it was "weird after years of trying to be a rock star myself to be in the Dave Stewart half of this very Eurythmics relationship."[81] Trask described his acceptance of this role a bit more soberly in an interview for the online network Gay.com. "The most compelling theme of Hedwig's life was her lifelong desire, struggle, and ultimate failure to become a rock star," Trask responded when asked about the inspiration for the show's final number. "Since that was also my story, I was able to write 'Midnight Radio' from a very personal view point. And I cried every time we played it for the first month of the show.[82]

Trask's secondary role in the reception of his show was matched by the secondary role he played onstage nightly at the Jane Street Theater. As a bandleader, Trask was used to being in charge, but as a member of the cast of *Hedwig,* he was often placed in the role of accompanist. Trask's difficulty accepting a less central role was in evidence on a number of occasions, in particular during a shoot for MTV News at the Jane Street Theater on the afternoon of February 10, 1999, and at an album release party sponsored by Atlantic Records at the Bowery Ballroom on the evening of February 17, 1999.

At the Bowery Ballroom, the *Hedwig* company played a concert to celebrate the release of the original cast recording. During the show, Trask called a great deal of undue attention to himself. He fidgeted; he was easily distracted; he fumbled with the mike; he kept making all sorts of unnecessary technical commentary. "You can cut the guitar mike, now!" he snapped at one point, after emphatically motioning to the booth several times that it needed to be turned up a notch. This behavior was consistent with that during the MTV shoot, when Trask repeatedly complained that his mike was too soft, the engineers kept informing him that the soft mix was necessary to keep the sound from distorting on video, and Trask would listen to them only to complain minutes later that his mike was too soft. At both events, Trask appeared restless, and more interested in calling attention to himself than in getting through a song.

After struggling for years to find success as a rock musician, Trask was likely somewhat dismayed to find himself forced into the background by the flamboyant figment of someone else's imagination. Like countless other theater composers before him, Trask had written an entire score of songs that had become famous without him. At the Bowery Ballroom release party, it was Mitchell as Hedwig that audience members flocked to, cheered, and asked to sign their free promotional CDs, while Trask remained out of the spotlight. The lack of attention had to sting.

Making matters worse for Trask was the fact that despite the blessings bestowed upon his songs in the rock press, the cast recording of the show failed to cross over into the popular music market. Shortly after *Hedwig and the Angry Inch* opened, Trask and Mitchell began negotiations with record companies interested in recording the cast album. Aware that most cast albums are "recorded live in one day," which struck him as "a ridiculous way of recording," Trask began to devise ways to distinguish the album from other cast recordings. Hoping to fashion the songs into a concept album that would stand apart from the show, he enlisted indie rock producer Brad Wood to work on the project.[83] Trask finally chose to make the recording with Atlantic Records, which in 1975 had approached the original cast album of *The Wiz* by following the pattern of popular music recording: laying down rhythm tracks first, instrumentals second, and vocals last, over a period of weeks.[84]

Personnel at Atlantic attempted to market the *Hedwig* cast album to a broad audience, in hopes that it would move beyond its theater moorings. "We're totally downplaying the theater aspect for radio," Senior Vice President of Marketing Vicky Germaise told Smith Galtney of *Time Out New York*. "That would just give them another excuse not to play it."[85] To further distinguish the album from the show, Trask said, he and Mitchell chose not to include any "goofy dialogue bits you find on cast albums—[they make] the record seem less like a work of art unto itself and more like a souvenir for a different work of art."[86] Trask also decided to add a new song, "Random Number Generation," which he wrote for the original Yitzak, Miriam Shor. Finally, in a nod to *Hedwig*'s punk roots, Trask invited Danny Fields, a record executive who had managed both the Ramones and Iggy Pop, to write the liner notes.

The efforts that went into marketing the album initially seemed to pay off. Like the show itself, the cast recording of *Hedwig* earned rare accolades in the rock press. In keeping with the defensive habit rock writers have of justifying what little attention they give to staged rock musicals, Barry Walters of *Rolling Stone* gave the album three-and-a-half out of five stars and noted that while "rock rarely makes it to the theatrical stage with balls intact," the *Hedwig* album "makes for the brainiest, catchiest concept album since Liz Phair's *Exile in Guyville.*[87] The New York–based late-night disk jockey Vin Scelsa embraced both the show and the album; more than once, he invited the company to perform on his show, mentioned the production frequently during his broadcasts, and played cuts from the album when it was released.[88]

Nevertheless, the album failed to catch on with a broader audience. Michael Cerveris argues that the fault lies with a music industry that is overly obsessed with target audiences and niche marketing:

> I've been asked why the music business hasn't embraced *Hedwig* more. The record has sold like most cast albums, but it hasn't been a big crossover hit; you don't hear it on the radio. I think that comes down to the music business' resistance of anything performance oriented, or its distrust of it. So if anything comes from the theatre, it's automatically fake, artificial. But there's a long history of that—David Bowie, the most obvious one—of performance, or style in rock music. But the other way around—there's this snobbism. But, you know, the Sex Pistols were totally a performance art project; the Rolling Stones met in art school. So musicians and creative people have always known that it's a show—even if the show is to stand stock still with bright lights behind the amps lining the audience. I was talking to Pete Townshend about this and saying, "Do I need to focus more on music to be taken seriously?" He said, "In some ways, it's true: as long as you're connected with the musical theater world, the music business is going to be resistant to you. If you can find a way to use the exposure without being identified with it, that could be useful—and good luck to you."[89]

Indeed, the simple fact that the music was originally the score for a piece of theater seemed to have kept it from crossing over to a larger audience. All attempts that were made to divorce the songs from the show seemed especially futile once the album was made commercially available: the cast recording of *Hedwig and the Angry Inch* never made it to the "popular music" section of most major record stores. Rather, it was grouped with all the other musicals in the "soundtrack" section.

Despite the critical and commercial success of *Hedwig and the Angry Inch,* Stephen Trask found his dreams oddly compromised when his songs became most closely associated with a fictional character. Although embraced by the theater world, and, perhaps more impressively, by a majority of hard-won rock critics, Trask's songs were ultimately unable to transcend their status as parts of the score to an Off Broadway show. There is no aesthetic reason that the show's music, with its catchy hooks, moody lyrics, and aggressive delivery, should not have won the interest of rock audiences. Yet by very nature of its association with the musical theater, the *Hedwig* album became a specialty item that was tolerated and even respected, but never fully embraced in the rock world.

Bright Lights Big City

A musician and songwriter who encountered some of the greatest difficulties in bridging the gap between rock and the musical theater was Paul Scott Goodman, composer of the musical *Bright Lights Big City*.[90] Throughout his life, Goodman's interests were split evenly between rock and the musical theater. Despite his mutual respect for the forms, however, he was bluntly rejected by both rock and musical theater camps when he appeared onstage at the New York Theatre Workshop in early 1999 as a performer in his own musical.

A Scotland native, Goodman was born to parents who were actively involved in the Scottish-Jewish amateur theater group in Glasgow. Goodman participated in many of their productions as a child; during his adolescence he began playing guitar and performing in rock bands. Interested in merging his passions for rock and the musical theater once he reached adulthood in the 1980s, he moved to New York and enrolled in the BMI Lehman Engel Musical Theater Workshop. After writing a few small-scale musicals, Goodman was encouraged by his mentor, the musical book writer Peter Stone, to adapt Jay McInerney's 1984 novel *Bright Lights, Big City* for the stage. Goodman began work on this project in August 1996.[91]

Three months later, Goodman, along with New York–based musician Annmarie Milazzo, sang through an early version of the musical for James Nicola, the artistic director of the New York Theatre Workshop.[92] Impressed, Nicola agreed to see Goodman's project through a number of staged readings and a workshop. *Rent* director Michael Greif staged the workshop and was later tapped for the full production.[93]

In developing *Bright Lights Big City* for the stage, the creative team was faced with a unique challenge: Goodman cannot read or write music. This touches on an important distinction between rock and the musical theater: the former is, at least ideologically, rooted in oral tradition, while the latter is not. "Rock critics have consistently derided orchestral or symphonic fusions as pretentious and bourgeois, while exalting the nihilism of punk and alternative bands as the best way to purify and revitalize rock-and-roll," Paul Simon pointed out in a 1998 opinion piece in the *New York Times.* "Perhaps the deeply ingrained oral tradition in rock has left an indelible mark on the psyche of its musicians: beware the written form, the manuscript paper with notes, clefs, and musical direction in Italian. It's a credo of rock that raw is true."[94] Yet while composers from the popular music world who are not musically literate, for example Frank Wildhorn, are slowly becoming more present in the musical theater world, they nevertheless remain exceptions to the rule. Goodman's approach to the score of *Bright Lights Big City*—which he committed entirely to memory as he wrote it, only putting it on tape once he felt that it was finished—was thus highly distinctive.[95] To compensate for his inability to put notes to paper, Goodman retained the help of Annmarie Milazzo, who was cast in the production and also served as the musical's vocal arranger. He also enlisted Richard Barone, a New York–based popular musician and producer, who joined the project as the orchestrator and musical director.

Barone's role in the *Bright Lights Big City* creative team quickly proved even more idiosyncratic than Goodman's. Accustomed to recording music, Barone was not much more adept at notating it than was Goodman. As he explains,

> The way I worked on *Bright Lights* was the way I would work on my own album. I had Paul come over with his guitar. I set him up to record the whole show with just him singing all the parts. I set up my living room as a recording studio, which I often do for new material . . . in the role of producer. So he came over, I set him up, he let loose and did the entire show. . . . I [then] used the tape to build on. I added all the parts onto that tape—the string parts, guitar parts, bass, percussion and keyboards—I added it all to the original tape of Paul. . . . His performance was something that was important to me. It really worked for me because it had the spirit of the show throughout—the spirit of his compositions. In other words, he didn't really have to write it down. The tape wrote it down for him and I just built on that. The way any orchestrator would build on it on paper—I did it on tape.[96]

While such practices are the norm in the popular music realm, the lack of written music proved problematic when the time came to teach the score to the cast and band. Thus, Joe McGinty, musical director of the popular concert series Loser's Lounge, was hired as the conductor. During the first weeks of rehearsals in January 1999, McGinty and Barone worked furiously to transcribe the entire score from tape to paper.

The number of people working on the *Bright Lights Big City* score was no more challenging than the unorthodox approach that Barone took as musical director. Interested in attaining the best sound, Barone had a habit of tinkering with the tempi and instrumentation of songs, even after Greif had "set" a particular piece for a particular scene. Martha Donaldson, the stage manager, remembers,

> We would do a piece of music and we would set it. We would say, "It's going to be four counts." And then the very next day we would do it again and it would be different. Richard would say, "I just thought maybe you might like it better if . . ." And it was like, "No, we decided *yesterday* what it is." It was funny because I know that he thought that if he did this that we would like it better, and maybe we wouldn't quite notice. And it was like, "Yeah we notice, you can't *not* notice, it was four counts yesterday, it's eight counts today! We notice!" . . . Things were not written down, and not only were they not written down, but we had Joe McGinty, who plays piano and reads music, we had Richard Barone, who plays a number of different instruments but who does not read or write music, we had Annmarie teaching vocal arrangements and who knows more than any of those guys but also does not read or write music. It was very, very frustrating, and then there's Richard Barone not really understanding that when we set something, it's *set.* When you say, "That's that," then that's what it is. You don't change it the next day, you don't do it differently the next time. The tempo is not different every single time we do it, it's the *same.*[97]

Just as Paul Simon annoyed the cast and crew of *The Capeman* by spending too much rehearsal time trying to figure out the proper placement of a tambourine, Barone's interest in attaining the best possible sound for the songs might be expected in the studio, but only proved confusing in rehearsals for a musical theater production.

A further problem lay in working with Paul Scott Goodman, who was not only busily putting the finishing touches on his musical during the rehearsals, but was also appearing as a character in the show. His presence onstage in his own piece was the result of decisions made on the part of the creative team in hopes of tackling one of the largest problems encountered while adapting *Bright Lights, Big City* for the stage: the novel's distinctive voice. Set in New York City in the early 1980s, McInerney's book is narrated by a privileged, unnamed young writer, whose mother has recently died and whose wife, a model, has even more recently left him for another man. Depressed and alone, the Gatsbian narrator enters a self-destructive spiral of drinking, cocaine snorting, casual promiscuity, and all-night club-hopping, which eventually costs him his job as a fact-checker at *Gotham* magazine (a thinly veiled *New Yorker*). The narrative, which follows the writer from the depths of despair back to emotional health and the chance for happiness, is not particularly unique. Yet the novel is one of the few written in second-person singular: the protagonist addresses himself throughout as "you."

During the early stages of the project, it was decided that Goodman's initial sing-through of his musical was moving enough that he should serve as a sort of alter ego to the stage incarnation of the novel's central character, therefore addressing the problem of translating the novel's distinctive voice for the stage. Goodman was cast as the Writer, a narrator character who delivers many of the novel's descriptive passages and provides added insights to the protagonist. Goodman's role as an actor, however, led to even greater difficulties than the novel's distinctive voice had.

In the first place, Goodman speaks with a thick Scottish accent. In early workshops, his presence onstage as the alter ego for an American man confused spectators.[98] After the workshops, the creative team set about trying to explain Goodman's presence onstage by adding a short speech that he delivered at the start of the show. During its run at the New York Theatre Workshop in 1999, the musical began when Goodman walked onto the stage with his guitar, introduced himself to the audience as the writer of the musical, and explained that McInerney's character reminded him a lot of himself as a young man when he first moved to New York. He made a similar speech at the end of the show, thanking everyone in the audience for attending before sending them on their way. While these speeches might have helped explain Goodman's presence onstage, they did nothing to address a much larger problem: Goodman's inability to shed the qualities that befit rock musicians, but that are not considered appropriate in the theater.

Onstage for most of the musical, serving both as the lead character's alter ego and an acoustic guitar-strumming narrator who bridged the gap between the cast and the band (which was set on a platform high above center stage), Goodman regularly exhibited an inability to follow stage directions. He had a penchant for both verbal and musical improvisation, and would often get carried away while accompanying songs during rehearsal. Although he clearly enjoyed exploring his songs from various angles, Goodman's improvisational style became problematic during tech rehearsals, when the company moved from rehearsal rooms to the stage in the weeks before previews began. Especially once the cast was joined by the band, Goodman's instrumental flights of fancy frequently worked to throw off the rest of the company. Goodman's fondness for musical improvisation was distracting enough that the band devised a number of "safeties," or specific cues, to protect themselves from being confused by his digressions at the beginnings of musical numbers.[99]

Goodman's love of improvisation was matched by a distaste for adhering to stage directions. Acting, he admitted, was hard for him: "Hit your mark every night, do the same thing every night. As a performer that's tough for me. I like to go with the moment onstage. If I feel a certain way and want to say something, I want to be able to say it," he notes. "Acting is a discipline, but it's not for me. Imagine what it was like being Yul Brynner and doing *King and I* five million times? I don't even need to be doing it for three months and I get bored with it already."[100] Yet doing the same things in the same ways each night is enormously important in the theater world, where company members rely on one another for cues.

Stage manager Martha Donaldson remembers that part of the production's problems lay in the fact that Goodman was always treated as an outsider, and thus never truly meshed with the rest of the company:

I feel as though the issue of who he is in the play was never developed. I don't feel as though anybody ever said, "Okay, this is the deal with this character. The things that he is saying are because of this. The reason he is here is because of that. . . . This is why he has to be present at all times." None of those things were ever established, near as I can tell, unless Michael [Greif] had secret meetings with Paul to tell him what he was all about. He was just there, and it was a given that he had to be there, and his basic direction was, "You're there. Now you're gonna be over here. You are gonna go over here, and you are gonna sit next to him and you're gonna watch him." That was basically the direction that he received. . . . He wasn't treated like an actor. He was treated like he was the writer and he was also in it. . . . He wasn't taught anything that he needed to know that would have helped his performance. It wasn't established that he was one of a twelve-person company.[101]

Goodman habitually forgot his lines, cues, and blocking, all of which proved frustrating for the rest of the company. Assistant director Leigh Silverman remembers,

It was always a struggle for Paul to be consistent. It was a struggle for everyone. The lighting designer would design lights around where Paul was and the next night Paul would not even come out onstage. The idea behind Paul being onstage was to preserve the second-person narrative, which is so intrinsic to the book. . . . I think [Paul] is a lovely man, and I loved having him there. But he's out of control. He's a loose cannon. There is a discipline that goes along with the theater that has to do with consistency and a focused energy on keeping your performance fresh every night, but keeping it exactly the same. Being able to walk that line between doing little things that keep it fresh for you, versus doing it the same so that you are getting the same quality and the same movements every night. Patrick Wilson [who originated the lead in the musical] is the god of this. Patrick keeps his performance so fresh—he hits the same mark, his foot always goes up in the same place, always, every night, the exact same thing. But his quality of performance is so high because he keeps it so fresh for himself. Paul does not understand that. It's like a different language. He's a rock 'n' roller. So he does something different every night. For everything.[102]

One cast member who requested anonymity argues that Paul Scott Goodman's inability to meld with the rest of the cast was not his fault, but that of the creative staff who attempted to force him into the mold of a professional actor:

When you put Paul in a situation where there's a lot of rules, I don't think that works for him. So he was neither here nor there. Either use him like he is, or don't use him at all. Because he's not an actor, he's a performance artist. And that energy you could really harness, or you should just leave it out. It ended up very much in the middle. You can't hide him. They tried to take away that he was very eccentric, but a little bit crept out, so then people had the reaction of, "What's that? Who's that? Some guy with a Scottish accent standing on the stage."[103]

While a songwriter who performs his or her own songs onstage is allowed the luxury of a distinctive performing style, Goodman's flamboyant presence did not translate to the stage of *Bright Lights Big City*. With his shaggy mop of hair, his thick accent, his reedy and occasionally unintelligible singing style, and his penchant for black or blue fingernail polish, Goodman often seemed to be occupying a different stage from the rest of the obviously trained and carefully groomed cast.

When *Bright Lights Big City* opened on February 24, 1999, it was typically ignored by rock critics and was greeted with mixed-to-poor reviews by theater critics. Most compared the musical unfavorably with the New York Theatre Workshop's previous rock musical, *Rent,* and almost all cited Goodman's presence as a major shortcoming. Peter Marks, in his review for the *New York Times,* wrote that Goodman, as the "scruffy, guitar-strumming troubadour," was so miscast as to be "pointless."[104] In a particularly cruel pan, Sam Whitehead of *Time Out New York* wrote,

> Thank God that every yahoo who feels a connection to other people's words doesn't also feel the need to parlay the bond into a show. If Goodman has one thing going for him throughout his theatrical debacle, it's that he definitely looks as if he's done all the boozing and blow necessary to somehow figure as a hard-living player in the decade of excess that *Bright Lights* came to symbolize. With a craggy, washed-up smile, he awkwardly strolls the stage acting like a detached emcee and guiding the audience through the infamous week of drug-fueled despair that brought McInerney's autobiographical hero . . . to his knees. And given eye-rolling lyrics that rely on strained, sophomoric rhyme schemes . . . it's not long before you too are brought to your knees. If only it were in an intoxicated haze.[105]

While critical and commercial reception do not always reflect one another, the audiences who attended performances of *Bright Lights Big City* had similar reactions.

The role of the singer-songwriter in the rock realm is vastly different from that of the songwriter in the musical theater. Whereas in the rock realm it is perfectly appropriate for a songwriter to perform his or her own music, the singer-songwriter is comparatively nonexistent in the musical theater, where to perform one's own music onstage—especially poorly—can be perceived by spectators as the epitome of egotism. A commentary about *Bright Lights Big City* that was posted online by an anonymous contributor to the fan-site Sondheim.com neatly summed up such opinions:

> *Bright Lights Big City* was written by a fellow named Paul Scott Goodman. . . . He is also in the show, playing someone named Paul Scott Goodman. This is a curious device, to say the least. I don't think this "author serving as narrator" is a good idea for the musical theater. Why, can you imagine if Stephen Sondheim came out at the beginning of *Passion* and said, "Hi, I'm Steve Sondheim and I wrote this show" and then proceeded to walk up to the naked Clara and Giorgio and start singing about what we're going to see?[106]

Many audience members approached at random during preview performances of the musical admitted that they were thoroughly confused by the goings-on onstage.

A few audience members, questioned at different performances, commented that because they had never read the book, the musical made little sense to them, and that Goodman's presence was especially confusing. During the performance on the evening of February 4, 1999, I sat behind a handful of audience members who regularly stifled giggles at the sight of Goodman on the stage. Walkouts during the performance and at intermission were not infrequent. After the performance on the evening of February 15, as I walked across town, I listened to the reactions of a couple who had seen the same performance, and who were walking a few paces ahead of me. They had greatly disliked the production and were especially critical of Goodman, whose presence onstage struck them as unforgivably arrogant. "Get *over* yourself!" one of them shouted. "They *have* to take him out of there!" agreed the other.

Without question, negative critical and commercial reception bruises the morale of a performing company, and this was certainly the case with *Bright Lights Big City*. The poor reviews and ticket sales took a particular toll on Goodman. His bitter disappointment at the negative reception manifested itself in even more erratic onstage behavior than he had exhibited before the opening. Stage manager Martha Donaldson elaborated:

After the reviews came out, [Paul] became morose and despondent, and refused to wear his costume, and refused to follow his blocking, and refused to follow the script, and was like, "I'm the writer, I can do whatever I want." And it was like, "I know you're the writer, but you know what? You are also one of twelve actors in this show. . . . I don't care that you're the writer, that doesn't mean that you can [do] whatever the fuck you want!" Honestly, most of the trouble with him happened when he did the prologue and the closing statement. The stuff in the middle, though inconsistent and often incorrect, was not always on purpose. Paul has never been able to say his lines correctly. He has never been able to do the stuff that he is supposed to do correctly. But in the beginning—it was just—we spent so much time rehearsing, and then just to have it all blown away by him because he doesn't want to do it anymore. He always thought that he should talk to and cajole the audience before the show. And Michael [Greif] spent a great deal of time saying, "No, you need to walk out, say who you are, say you wrote the thing, and start the show. You don't get the audience to talk back, you don't banter with them." If it was his own show, maybe. But it's a giant musical that's waiting for him to start. There was no way to know what he was going to say. . . . It's a testament to the professionalism of the cast that they didn't . . . say, "Something has to be done about Paul Scott Goodman because we are not putting up with this anymore." With him being at the curtain call and spouting off whatever's on his mind before he *finally* says goodnight, you know? So many nights, the cast had to stand there as he went on and on and thanked the audience for being there, and he doesn't care what the New York press says, and that kind of stuff. And the audience, meanwhile, is like, "We don't even know what the New York press said, so why don't you shut up?" Killing the end of the show. *Killing* it.[107]

Assistant director Leigh Silverman agrees that Goodman's habit of digressing during the introduction and conclusion worked to dampen the energy of his show:

When he gets out on stage at the beginning and says, "Hi, I'm Paul Scott Goodman and I wrote this musical version of *Bright Lights, Big*

City" and people start to clap, he doesn't understand that when he bows five times, he kills the moment. That a simple head-nod would be plenty. That with five head nods people are like, "I'm outta here. Who *is* this motherfucker?"[108]

Again, whereas onstage banter and interaction with the audience—especially interaction that allows an audience to gain insight into the emotional state of the songwriter—would be perfectly acceptable in the rock realm, Goodman's behavior in a musical theater setting was inappropriate. Ultimately, a majority of the problems Goodman encountered as a musical theater performer would likely be welcomed in a rock concert setting: he was, as Donaldson and Silverman both described him, a "loose canon" who loved getting carried away when playing music and feeding off the energy of crowds. In short, Goodman was an absolutely fascinating rock performer who, unfortunately, also happened to be an utter disaster as an actor. Although he was roundly rejected, however, one might argue that the only thing wrong with Goodman's performance was its setting.

With the sole exception of *Rent*—which benefited from its low budget, its savvy marketing, and, horrifically, its composer's untimely death before the first preview—many rock-influenced musicals that opened in New York City during the 1990s faced similar difficulties. While Pete Townshend's collaboration with Des McAnuff was pleasant enough, and the result, *The Who's Tommy,* earned critical accolades, that musical never managed to escape comparisons with the concept album from which it was adapted, nor did it succeed in attracting traditional theater audiences. Similarly, the companies of *The Capeman, Hedwig and the Angry Inch,* and *Bright Lights Big City* experienced their own difficulties in bridging the gap between rock and theater worlds.

Further, the differences between Pete Townshend, Paul Simon, Paul Scott Goodman, and Stephen Trask are not as vast as their experiences might make them seem. Paul Simon's and Paul Scott Goodman's rock-influenced idiosyncrasies won out over their ability to adjust to the musical theater realm. Simon's singular obsession with bringing "authentic" music to the Broadway stage and Goodman's passion for the spontaneous, the improvisational, and the rebellious ultimately hurt them in settings where such qualities are dismissed as laughably unprofessional. Trask and Townshend made the transition from one camp to the other more gracefully, but in the case of Trask—who is much younger and less established than Townshend—success came at a price. His band, Cheater, went from laboring in obscurity as an actual rock band to winning praise as the fake Angry Inch, and had to drastically alter its onstage behavior and performance style in the process. Further, Trask had to struggle to reconcile his personal goals with a kind of success that he had not anticipated.

The very difficulties that these men and their productions encountered when crossing from the rock to the theater realm reflect inherent tensions between rock and musical theater aesthetics that have arguably only grown stronger in the decades since *Hair* suggested that their union would revolutionize the American musical. In the following interlude, the approaches to performance in both realms—as well as the ways they come together in musical theater works that utilize rock music—will be examined.

Interlude 5

Merging Aesthetics,
Making Performances

ROCK MUSICALS MAY BE INTERPRETED as attempts to bring a sense of youthful energy and spontaneity to an American performing arts genre that is often perceived to be pitifully behind the times. Yet contributing to the many complexities of blending rock and musical theater aesthetics are wildly divergent approaches to performance. While countless attempts to join these often conflicting performance styles have failed miserably, innovative approaches continue to result in successful productions. The various ways that performance in the rock and musical theater realm may be negotiated thus warrant investigation.

Volume, Timbre, and Instrumentation

When it comes to identifying specific influences that post–World War II American popular music has exerted on the musical theater, the one most often mentioned—usually disparagingly—is amplification. Often cited as a chief culprit in the steady decline of the musical theater since the mid–twentieth century, the soaring volumes at which popular music is often performed and listened to have been loudly lamented in theater realms. Since the late 1960s, increasingly sophisticated amplification systems that disembody—or "cinematize"—the voices of stage actors are regularly criticized as necessary evils that allow performers to be heard over electric instruments, but that simultaneously drive a wedge between audiences and performers.

As indicated by heavy metal guitarist Ted Nugent's oft-quoted statement, "If it's too loud, you're too old," the importance of maximum volume to rock cannot be overestimated. In live settings, loud volumes allow popular music audiences to involve themselves in a variety of ways. Because even the noisiest, most raucous responses tend to be drowned out by amplification, spectators at rock concerts have the freedom to respond more loudly and energetically than traditional theater audiences. For all the complaints about amplification destroying the musical theater, it is, ironically, the resultant energetic response of popular music audiences that keeps the theater industry interested in appropriating rock music in the first place.

Of course, volume is important to rock music not only sociologically, but sonically, as well. As Theodore Gracyk notes, playing music at loud volumes on electric instruments results in specific timbres that have become valued in the popular music world. While microphones were initially implemented simply to make music louder, he argues, "musicians now exploit the microphone, amplification, and resultant technologies for musical effects beside volume."[1] When it comes to rock music, then, timbre and volume are mutually interdependent, defining aspects of the genre.

Rock's relationship with timbre and volume can be problematic when the genre is used in the theater, where instruments playing at loud volumes and vocalists singing unclearly can be seen as detriments to the coherence of a production. In an interview in which he discusses taking over the title role of *Hedwig and the Angry Inch* from John Cameron Mitchell, actor Michael Cerveris touches on some difficulties that he and his fellow company members encountered in attempting to bring a credible rock sensibility to the show:

> I . . . worry less about total intelligibility with *Hedwig:* I'm willing to go on feeling and intensity much more. [But] some audiences have a problem with that; they want to get every word. There's a funny story about that. John [Cameron Mitchell]'s background is much more musical theater, and Stephen [Trask] was encouraging him stylistically to throw it away more, give it more of a rock performance, not over-articulate things. But then [Stephen] sat out and listened one night, and couldn't hear some of the words he was most proud of.[2]

The conundrum described above is not atypical. Cerveris remembers that during rehearsals for *The Who's Tommy,* Pete Townshend and director

Des McAnuff spent long hours fretting over how to preserve the volume levels and timbres that are vital to rock, while simultaneously ensuring that none of the lyrics would be lost on the audience.[3]

At worst, poor sound design results in blaring volumes, muddied lyrics, and a bad overall sound. As discussed in chapter 3, shows like *Jesus Christ Superstar, Via Galactica,* and *Dude* suffered in part as a result of inadequate sound design that drowned out dialogue and lyrics, leaving audiences confused and frustrated. On the other hand, happy mediums can be attained; many rock musicals are designed so that volume levels increase during particular numbers (anthemic finales and post-curtain-call "encores," for example), and decrease during more intimate numbers, or those in which lyrics progress the plot and thus must be heard clearly by audiences. In the case of *Hedwig and the Angry Inch,* not every lyric of every song was clear in performances, and the band had to alter its sound by playing more softly than the musicians were typically accustomed, but the resultant sound allowed the audience to follow the trajectory of the plot on one hand, and, on the other, allowed the characters the chance to more closely emulate rock performance than they otherwise might.

Due to the need for intelligibility in the musical theater, however, it is often the case that the most extreme volumes and timbres heard in the rock world are lost in translation to the theater stage. Many rock musicians who take on musical theater projects complain that, in the words of *Bright Lights Big City* musical director Richard Barone, "the dynamics of rock have to be adjusted to the theater," and almost never the other way around.[4] Because rock's volume levels, and the timbres attained by the resultant distortion, are regularly compromised for the sake of clarity in the musical theater, other aural signifiers of rock music, as well as many visual ones, become that much more important.

In *Performing Rites: On the Value of Popular Music,* Simon Frith writes,

A good rock concert . . . is measured by the audience's physical response, by how quickly people get out of their seats, onto the dance floor, by how loudly they shout and scream. And rock performers are expected to revel in their own physicality, too, to strain and sweat and collapse with tiredness. Rock stage clothes (like sports clothes) are designed to show the musician's body as instrumental (as well as sexual), and not for nothing does a performer like Bruce Springsteen end a show huddled with his band, as if he'd just won the Super Bowl. Rock acts conceal not the physical but the technological sources of their sounds; rock audiences remain uneasy about musical instruments that appear to require no effort to be played.[5]

It is in large part the importance of physicality in live rock performance that often results in the decision to set the accompanying musicians on the stage of a rock musical, instead of tucked away beneath the stage in the orchestra pit.

When musicians are confined to an orchestra pit, as most tend to be when accompanying musicals, the visual aspects of live music performance are denied. Guitarist Mark Stewart, who played in the Broadway pit band of *The Who's Tommy,* argues that the physical distance between the orchestra pit and the audience has important psychological consequences, as well:

> When you're onstage, the exchange is really direct. You are aware of a kind of dialogue between you and the audience—aware of who it is you are "speaking" to, and when they "speak" back, they're looking right at you. When you're in a pit, there's a big wall. The audience doesn't know who you are and you don't know who they are. It's especially profound in this day and age, because it's very similar to them sitting in their living rooms or in a movie theater, where the music is coming out of speakers. Now, when they are at home or at a movie theater, they know that it's is recorded music. And on Broadway, most people know that it's *not* recorded music. But phenomenologically, it's the same thing— they're hearing music coming out of speakers, and not seeing any musicians. So they are relating to what's on the stage, but there is a separation from the band. So when you're onstage, your exchange is clear. When you're in a pit, you can be doing a great job . . . you're sending it out to the audience, but it's secondhand. And in the end, when the audience is clapping, they don't know who I am, and I don't know who they are.[6]

So strongly does Stewart believe in a visual connection between rock musicians and audience members that he remains convinced that one of the biggest flaws Des McAnuff made in directing *The Who's Tommy* was in confining the band to the orchestra pit, instead of placing them, as in most rock musicals, on the stage with the actors, where their presence would have brought a vital aspect of live rock performance to the theater stage.

A related reason for making musicians visible to the audience when staging rock musicals lies with the fact that instruments tend to function quite differently in the rock realm than they do in the theater realm. Throughout the history of the musical theater, instruments are used primarily to accompany human voices, which are the most important aural aspect of a theater piece. Instrumentalists who work in the theater are expected to bring out the best aspects of a musical score while almost always remaining invisible beneath the stage, thereby never distracting the audience from characters or plot.

Of course, there are obvious similarities: like theater music, rock is usually vocal music with instrumental accompaniment. A rock band usually features a lead singer, who often becomes the mouthpiece for the band, both on and off the stage. As the spokesperson, the lead singer thus tends to become more of a household name than other band members. Such a regularly recurring phenomenon can cause rock to be viewed as a genre that, like theater, places primary importance on the voice and grants secondary status to all other instruments. Yet to define rock as such is to deny the importance of particular instruments that have helped characterize the genre.

Although instrumentation varies slightly from group to group and sound recording to sound recording, rock generally utilizes electric guitar, electric bass, and drums. These instruments are important to rock music largely because of their unique timbral qualities.[7] The electric guitar, in particular, has been so closely associated with rock 'n' roll and its many offshoots that it, and not the human voice, is arguably the style's defining instrument. A successful rock guitarist is held in particularly high esteem among fans of the genre, especially ones who—like Jimi Hendrix or Eddie Van Halen—are virtuosic, technically savvy, or compelling enough performers to attain "guitar god" status.

Because its loud volumes and harsh timbres threaten to drown even the strongest singers, the electric guitar is generally reserved, in the theater, for instrumental interludes or to accompany highly melodramatic, wordless scenes, especially those that feature particularly intense subject matter. For example, the score of *Godspell* features a single electric guitar solo, which accompanies the death throes of Jesus after he is crucified at the end of the musical; the thirty-nine lashes administered to Jesus at the end of *Superstar* are similarly accompanied by a recurring riff on the electric guitar, which gradually disintegrates into improvisational licks before stopping abruptly at the last lash. An electric guitar solo accompanies the lead character's cocaine-induced emotional collapse near the end of *Bright Lights Big City;* squealing, distorted riffs also accompany the title character's breakdown at the end of *Hedwig and the Angry Inch.*

Lighting

Lighting is often used during live popular music performance to highlight the connection between fans and performers. At many concerts, lights are primarily focused on the musicians onstage, but will often scan the crowd, especially between songs. This use of lighting allows for various kinds of watching during a live show: as the lights travel through the house and back to the stage, the musicians can watch the audience and the audience can watch itself shouting, cheering, dancing, pounding the air with fists, and otherwise reveling in group mentality, in the music, in the moment, and in one another.

Many contemporary rock and pop-based musicals thus emulate concerts, as well, through creative use of lighting. During the second act of *The Who's Tommy,* for example, one scene made a visual reference to the 1960s West Coast psychedelic scene, during which bands performed while swirling, colored lights were projected onto the walls of the concert venue, thereby illuminating both the musicians and their gyrating audiences. During the "Pinball Wizard" number in *Tommy,* flashing lights and video projections covered the walls of the darkened St. James Theater, thereby temporarily transforming the house into a giant pinball machine, and bathing both performers and audience members in brightly colored, spinning lights. A similar use of lights was employed during the curtain call for the 1999 stage adaptation of the 1977 film *Saturday Night Fever.* As the orchestra thumped out reprises of the Bee Gees hits performed in the show, a glittering disco ball descended from the ceiling, temporarily transforming the Minskoff Theater into a giant discotheque. The cast members took their bows and then broke into several choreographed disco dance numbers, while an onstage DJ encouraged the audience to get up and dance along.

One of the most straightforward uses of lighting-as-unifier occurred during the anthemic finale of *Hedwig and the Angry Inch*. During the last number, "Midnight Radio," the cast appealed directly to the audience to "lift up your hands" and wave them slowly back and forth in time with the music. During this number, the auditorium was bathed in bright, white lights, allowing performers and audience members to see one another clearly, and to thereby enjoy a heightened emotional connection before the curtain call.

Visual Signifiers

In many cases, a rock musical is self-identified, or becomes identified as such in the press or among theatergoers, specifically because one or more of its characters is a rock musician. Musicals that feature such characters include *Bye Bye Birdie,* which revolves around the guitar-twanging rock 'n' roll idol Conrad Birdie; *Your Own Thing,* in which a four-man rock group called the Apocalypse figures in the plot; *Soon,* which follows the rise and fall of a rock band; *Bright Lights Big City,* which features an electrified-acoustic guitar-strumming narrator; *Hedwig and the Angry Inch,* in which the members of the New York City–based rock band Cheater posed as the fictional Angry Inch; and *Rent,* in which the HIV-positive rock musician Roger, who has responded to his illness by shutting himself off from the world, spends most of his time in his East Village squat struggling to write "one great song" on his electric guitar before dying.

Many staged rock musicals borrow as heavily from the visual aspects of rock music as from the aural ones. Martha Banta, the assistant director of *Rent,* remembers that in staging Roger's big solo number, "One Song, Glory," director Michael Greif drew specifically from rock's visual aesthetics in instructing actor Adam Pascal to infuse his performance with exaggerated physical gestures—such as deep knee bends and raised fists—as if he were a rock star singing the song during a concert in a huge venue.[8] During rehearsals for *Hedwig and the Angry Inch,* too, cast members spent a great deal of time with director Peter Askin discussing ways not only to *sound,* but also to *look* convincingly like a gigging bar band.[9]

It is no coincidence that all of the characters mentioned above are played by men. One aspect of rock culture that seems to have transferred quite well to the musical stage, for better or worse, is its gender construction. As it has developed in the Western world, rock has become strongly culturally identified with heterosexual, white men. The roles that both black and white women have played in the creation and perpetuation of the style have largely been dismissed as secondary. As sociologist Barbara Bradby writes, if "women have had an acknowledged role in rock and pop it has been as performers, even though this has been mainly limited to vocal rather than instrumental performance, and has been circumscribed by ideologies that do not generally allow women's performances to be 'authentic' in the way that men's are."[10]

Musical theater, like rock, is a performing arts genre that tends to emulate the dominant culture that fuels it. It should thus come as no surprise that central characters in rock musicals who play instruments are overwhelmingly white, male, and heterosexual. Even a prominent exception, Hedwig, is transformed at the end of *Hedwig and the Angry Inch,* when the character strips away all hints of artifice (read: femininity) and stands nearly naked (and clearly male) before the audience. Simultaneously, Hedwig's cross-dressing husband, Yitzak, is transformed into a role that is expected of women in rock: a backup singer in a blonde wig and a slinky black dress.

However, because the musical theater is not strongly associated with heterosexual masculinity, because it is a performing arts genre that places a great deal of emphasis on the human voice, and because many theater actors do not play the electric bass or guitar, rock musicals on the whole tend to borrow more from postwar popular styles that emphasize voices than they do from those that emphasize instrumental performance. The result is the frequent emulation of the sound of 1950s male doo-wop groups, which were central to long-running musicals like *Grease* and the Lieber and Stoller revue *Smokey Joe's Café,* and particularly of 1960s girl-groups, which have exerted particularly profound influence on musical theater.

While the girl-group sound and image are discussed in relation to *Little Shop of Horrors* and *Dreamgirls* in chapter 4, it should be noted here that girl groups have continued to work their way into a number of contemporary Broadway and Off Broadway musicals. For example, the girl-group sound and image were playfully evoked in *Mamma Mia!* (2001). During one scene, set at a drunken bachelorette party, three close friends giddily perform "Super Trouper" in a tightly choreographed sequence; in an earlier scene, the same three women amuse themselves by dancing around a hotel room to "Chiquitita" and "Dancing Queen," while singing into a hairbrush, a hair dryer, and a deodorant stick.

While not a rock musical, the Jeanine Tesori–Tony Kushner musical *Caroline, or Change,* which opened Off Broadway at the Public Theater in October 2003 before moving to Broadway in April 2004, made clever use of the girl-group sound to evoke the place and time during which the musical is set: New Orleans in the early 1960s, just before and after the assassination of John F. Kennedy. The title character, an African American maid, habitually listens to pop music on the radio while doing the laundry of the Jewish family she works for. The music keeps Caroline company, but also, at times, informs her decisions, influences her opinions, and reinforces her moods. The radio thus becomes Caroline's friend and confidant; in keeping with this idea, "The Radio" is an important character in *Caroline, or Change.* Ingeniously, the part is written for a trio of black women whose musical numbers all feature the same bouncy rhythms and tight harmonies typical of the girl groups of the time, despite the occasionally heavy lyrics directed at the title character.

Performance Space

In his absorbing *Places of Performance: The Semiotics of Theatre Architecture,* Marvin Carlson writes that almost any space may be made into a place for performance, since the performance will allow the space to "take on certain of the semiotic expectations of the theatre itself, but, at least equally important, it will bring to the theatrical experience its own spatial and cultural connotations, which the sensitive producer will seek to draw on to maximum effect in the work presented to a public."[11] Indeed, as theater groups that transform parks, restaurants, or places of worship into performance spaces have repeatedly proven, arguing that theater performance should be limited to theaters is as ridiculous as arguing that live rock performance should be limited to stadium-sized arenas. Nevertheless, both rock and the musical theater have become associated with different performance spaces. Thus, bringing one genre into a space more commonly associated with the other can pose problems.

A musical can arguably be staged, within reason, in any space or location in the world. Yet the history of the American musical is most closely connected with Broadway, the grand old theaters of which played frequent hosts to the genre as it developed through the twentieth century. Due in large part to the obvious commercialism of the Broadway district—with its huge billboards, bright lights, and atypical concentration of large theaters with flashing marquees—the American musical has, like Broadway itself, come to carry with it the type of overt connection to commerce that proves troublesome in the rock realm. The original production of *The Rocky Horror Show,* for example, was right at home in a gritty, rundown London theater, but was a mismatch for the ornate old Belasco Theater on Broadway, where it managed only forty-five performances in 1975. The 2000 revival of *The Rocky Horror Show* fared far better in the Circle in the Square, a smaller, less adorned Broadway theater-in-the-round.

An additional problem that can be encountered when bringing rock into spaces associated with the musical theater lies with the fact that successful live rock performances are designed to cultivate a sense of intimacy, even in the largest of venues. Accepted venues for rock concerts may be far larger than those for the musical theater. It is, after all, more likely that one would see the Rolling Stones perform at Shea Stadium than the cast of *Rent.* Yet the musical theater's typically presentational style—in which plots that are clearly fictitious are presented in a slightly exaggerated performance style, and the expression of emotions tends to be more formulaic than realistic—can drive a wedge between performers and audiences that is never quite as pronounced in the rock realm.

Despite experiments in the 1960s and 1970s by directors like Tom O'Horgan, the presentational style has proven very difficult to negate, especially on Broadway, where it is deeply ingrained, not only as a result of history but also as a result of the performance venues themselves. Majestic as most of them are, Broadway's theater houses tend to exacerbate the distance between audiences and performers due to their sheer size, proscenium arches, thousands of seats, and tiers that extend great distances from cavernous stages. Intimacy has proven easier to cultivate in smaller, alternative performance spaces like those Off and Off-Off-Broadway, where the rock musical was born and has since remained most comfortable.

Most theaters Off and Off-Off-Broadway differ from those on Broadway not only in terms of size, but also in terms of their unadorned facades and the distance at which they are typically set from other theaters. These aspects can help to create a sense of intimacy that is much harder to attain at larger, more centrally located venues. While Broadway houses serve an ever-renewing, always ephemeral mass of commuters, urban dwellers, and international tourists, Off and Off-Off-Broadway are more closely associated with a smaller, more intimate public; the fact that many smaller theaters eschew the huge, flashy external signs typical of Broadway can help to reinforce "intimacy, exclusiveness, and focus on the internal event," and thereby to create "a conscious and striking contrast to the traditional commercial house with its flashing lights, billboards, and lavish displays of quotes from favorable reviews."[12] It is this very sense of exclusiveness and intimacy that press agent Tom D'Ambrosio evokes in discussing the hard-to-reach location of the Jane Street Theater, former home of *Hedwig and the Angry Inch:* "the location doesn't stand in your way of going, and if it does, then you're square and that's *your* problem."[13]

Further, Off and Off-Off-Broadway theaters—if they were originally built to be theaters at all—are generally much smaller and less ornate than those on Broadway, and their performance spaces thus more easily adaptable to fit the needs of a specific production. Carlson writes that neutral spaces devoid of decorative features have been "enormously influential in modern experimental theatre design," since they allow for decoration that is unique to each production. Audiences who attend particular productions are easily "encompassed not within the semiotics of a theatre auditorium, but within those of the fictive world of the play itself."[14]

For example, the site of the 2001 musical *Love, Janis* was easily made to evoke a late-1960s nightclub. A two-character musical based on the witty, highly descriptive letters that Janis Joplin wrote home to her family between 1966 and her death in 1970, *Love, Janis* interspersed monologues fashioned from Joplin's letters with songs from her repertoire. Staged at the Village Theater, a well-known downtown concert venue formerly known as the Village Gate, *Love, Janis* set the mood of the production long before the performance began. As audience members descended a narrow flight of stairs, which brought them from the unadorned street-level entryway into the dark, nondescript house, they were confronted immediately with Day-Glo period posters advertising late-1960s Bay Area–based happenings, be-ins, and rock concerts. A tiny stage, preset with instruments, sat directly in front of them once they took their seats.

Neither the posters nor the instruments had to compete with such traditional theater trappings as crystal chandeliers or wall and ceiling murals for the audience's attention. While not every Off and Off-Off-Broadway theater is quite as nondescript as one having *Love, Janis,* a majority are certainly smaller, less adorned, and thus arguably more versatile than their Broadway counterparts

Of course, productions like *Hair* and *Rent* prove that it is possible to create a sense of intimacy and cultivate connections between actors and audience members in larger theaters. Yet as shows like *Dude* demonstrate, such an achievement is exceptionally challenging. In general, smaller and comparatively undistinguished performance spaces, set far from the glaring lights and obvious commerce of Broadway, allow for more intimacy and exclusivity than their larger, more traditional counterparts. Because these spaces promote a sense of intimacy similar to that cultivated in live rock performances, they are often the most effective spaces for rock musicals.

6 🎸 Rock-Influenced Musicals at the Millennium: The Dawning of the Age of . . . the Revival

THE RISING COSTS OF PRODUCTION since the 1980s, coupled with the increased "corporatization" of Broadway in the 1990s, has resulted in an increased interest among producers in theatrical properties that are most likely to appeal to the broadest possible audience, thereby making the largest amounts of money. Since the turn of the millennium, especially, "risk-free" properties—including staged versions of films, television shows, and novels, as well as lots and lots of revivals—have sprung up all over town. While some of these "risk-free" productions have failed to win audiences despite the lure of familiarity, many others are of interest here because they manage to breathe new life into old forms. In the following pages, some of the more successful rock-influenced productions that have opened around the turn of the century, and that combine the familiar with the original, will be contrasted with a few productions that relied on familiarity at the expense of originality.

The Donkey Show

Developed and directed by Diane Paulus and Randy Weiner, co-creators of the experimental Project 400 Theater Group, *The Donkey Show* followed Antonin Artaud's philosophy that theater should be ritual and transformative rather than simply entertaining. The result was an hour-long adaptation of Shakespeare's *A Midsummer Night's Dream* with a pre-recorded disco score, set in a discotheque in the mid-1970s. Performed in an actual dance club located in the westernmost reaches of Manhattan's Chelsea neighborhood, *The Donkey Show* premiered on August 18, 1999, and ran for seven years.

The Donkey Show integrated audience members directly into the action, thereby entrusting them to sustain the mood created by the actors. This mood was cultivated long before the staged action began. Ticket holders for *The Donkey Show* were advised to arrive a half-hour early; when they did, they were asked to wait in a long line in front of the club, the entrance to which was guarded by velvet ropes and an actor playing a bouncer. In keeping with the exclusivity rituals that have been enacted nightly at dance clubs since the heyday of the famous nightclub Studio 54, the actor playing the bouncer occasionally allowed some of the ticket holders to enter the club, and insisted that others continue to wait in the line. Meanwhile, members of the cast, who had been standing on line along with the audience members, began to walk up and down the queue, interacting with ticket holders and occasionally begging the unyielding bouncer to let them in.

The entire audience was granted entry into the club about fifteen minutes before the start of the staged performance. Once inside the club, which was replete with smoke machines, flashing lights, and mirror balls, the audience was confronted by the sound of familiar disco hits of yore, which were amplified over the loudspeakers. Dancing vigorously to these recorded songs were still more actors, many of whom took occasional breaks from dancing to interact with audience members as they filed into the club, thereby working to lower the crowd's inhibitions. By the time the staged production commenced, the audience and the cast had mingled enough that despite the actors' period costumes, it became difficult to tell who was a cast member and who was a spectator.

The staged portion of *The Donkey Show* began without much in the way of theatrical convention. The actor playing the disc jockey, who had been introducing and spinning records from a booth set up in one of the balconies, would suddenly announce a very special appearance by Oberon, the club owner. The character, lit by a spotlight, would appear next to the disc jockey's booth and wave, only to have his attention drawn away by Titania, the fairy queen, standing across the room in the guise of a raven-haired disco dancer wearing an eye mask, thigh-high boots, hot pants, and butterfly pasties. As she is carried toward Oberon by her attending fairies (here, a group of well-built men wearing more glitter makeup than clothing), the disc jockey cued Alicia Bridges's 1978 hit "I Love the Nightlife (Disco 'Round)." Titania would look up at Oberon and begin to sing along with the track.

The Donkey Show progressed much in this manner. Few words were spoken in the piece, save for brief snippets of dialogue used to set up the relationships between the characters. The story was instead recounted almost entirely through actions accompanied by disco-era sound recordings, each representing the changing moods of the characters as they argued, chased one another, fell in and out of love, and—in keeping with this particular period, subculture, and setting—became progressively befuddled as a result of the endless supply of cocaine ("fairy dust") provided by a roller-skating Puck.

The Donkey Show allowed its audience and its performers to revel collectively in music that is by now highly familiar to much of the Western world, simply by allowing it to take center stage. Because there was no traditional narrative to follow—just lights, action, lip-synching, and prerecorded songs combined to tell a very basic love story—the audience was allowed to remain absorbed in the music, as well as to behave much more freely than they would at a more traditional theatrical production. Through the show, audience members danced, talked, whistled, applauded, and sang along. In this rare case, such commotion only enhanced the performance. Both entertaining *and* transformative, as Artaud advocated, *The Donkey Show* relied on the familiar, but presented it in a way that was refreshingly unique.

Jesus Christ Superstar Redux

The creative team of the April 2000 Broadway revival of *Jesus Christ Superstar* also attempted to breathe new life into an old form by turning Tom O'Horgan's original staging on its head. Unfortunately, the resultant production implies that had Rice and Lloyd Webber gotten what they initially claimed to have hoped for—a sparser, more intimate staging of their album—just as many spectators would have been unsatisfied with the result. The Broadway revival of *Superstar* that opened in the spring of 2000 at Broadway's new Ford Center for the Performing Arts was even more disappointing than O'Horgan's version.

With the exception of a few flashy costumes, some graffiti-scrawled pillars, and a huge video screen that dropped from the wings to provide a grotesque close-up of Jesus's bloody face during the crucifixion scene, the revival of *Superstar* was simpler, more straightforward, and not nearly as visually busy as the first. The result was a thuddingly flat production, in which a majority of the actors seemed to have no idea what they were supposed to be doing at any given time, save to bend at the waist or raise a fist to show passion, or to rub a chin or scratch a head to reflect pensiveness. The flat feel of the revival implies, once again, that staging a concept album—especially one that emphasizes the thoughts and feelings of its characters—is particularly tricky business. Spectacle-laden or not, there is ultimately nothing terribly interesting about watching a group of people think their way through the last days of Jesus' life.

Like its predecessor, the 2000 revival of *Jesus Christ Superstar* received mixed-to-poor notices. Tellingly, many of the reviews this time around focused on just how difficult the piece is to stage. Ben Brantley, who panned the show in the *New York Times,* acknowledged that *Superstar* "works better as a chain of virtuosic songs than as a sustained piece of theater. It doesn't fully follow through on most of its themes, and the disjunctiveness is much more evident in performance."[1] Like the critics, audience members interviewed at random during intermission and after the final curtain of the performance on April 12, 2000, were largely unimpressed by the production. On the one hand, theatergoers who said that they were familiar with the album felt that the voices featured in the staged version paled in comparison. On the other, theatergoers who were unfamiliar with the score complained that the poor sound design, lack of action onstage, and the rock opera's lack of adherence to historic detail, caused them to become confused as to what was happening onstage, despite the familiar subject matter. Poor ticket sales reflected such tepid responses. On September 3, 2000, the revival of *Superstar* closed in the red after 161 performances.

The Rocky Horror Show

Like *The Donkey Show,* the Broadway revival of *The Rocky Horror Show*—which opened at the Circle in the Square on November 15, 2000, for 437 performances—attempted to break down barriers between performers and audience members by drawing spectators directly into the action.

This rowdy rock 'n' roll musical, with a book, score, and lyrics by British actor Richard O'Brien, had made the rounds before. It premiered at London's Royal Court Theatre Upstairs in June 1973, and was so successful that producer Lou Adler snapped up the American rights and opened productions at the Roxy in Los Angeles in 1974 and the Belasco on Broadway in 1975.[2] While the Roxy production was a hit, the one at the Belasco lasted only forty-five performances.

The important role that the audience plays in *The Rocky Horror Show* was cultivated over many years. The musical opened in London less than five years after the abolition of theater censorship in Britain; the original production was thus more invested in breaking theatrical taboos of the time than it was in fostering much in the way of interaction between cast members and the audience.[3] The plot centered around Brad and Janet, a young, virginal, ludicrously priggish couple who seek refuge in a spooky castle when their car breaks down in the middle of the woods during a rainstorm. The castle turns out to be the dwelling of Frank 'n' Furter, a self-described "sweet transvestite from Transexual, Transylvania," and his thoroughly bizarre, ambisexual entourage.

Ignoring Brad and Janet's request for a phone, Frank 'n' Furter instead whisks them up to his lab to see his new creation: Rocky, a scantily-clad, muscular blonde man whom Frank hopes will fulfill his every sexual desire. Rocky, who turns out to be as stupid as he is handsome, rejects Frank in favor of Janet who, midway through the show, succumbs to Rocky's advances. Although initially upset by Rocky's rejection, Frank soon turns his attention to the sexual initiation of both Brad and Janet. Amid the mayhem, a leather-clad biker named Eddie shows up, only to be slaughtered by Frank, who then lies about Eddie's whereabouts when Eddie's uncle, Dr. Scott—who also happens to be a former professor of Brad's and Janet's—shows up in search of him.

Frank's maid and butler, Magenta and Riff Raff, eventually reveal themselves to be, like Frank, aliens from the planet Transylvania. They kill Frank, Rocky, and the other inhabitants of the castle before returning home, leaving Brad, Janet, and Dr. Scott to ponder their future. A narrator, whose role is never clearly defined, wanders in and out of the action to comment on, but never to explain, the musical's twisting, turning plot.

In 1976, the musical was made into a feature film, *The Rocky Horror Picture Show,* which was a critical and commercial disaster in England. It slowly developed into a cult hit in the United States, however, as the result of frequent midnight showings at movie houses across the country. Immediately prior to late-night screenings, it became customary for audiences to dress up like *Rocky Horror* characters and perform informal stage shows. Over time, audiences also developed silly actions and heckles to shout and perform at various points during the film. While these varied from region to region, and even from movie house to movie house, it became fairly standard, for example, for audiences to throw rice during the two wedding scenes; to put newspapers over their heads during the storm scene; to shout, "Asshole!" and "Slut!" respectively, whenever Brad and Janet appeared; to sing along boisterously with the many musical numbers; and to rush into the aisles to join the characters in performing the silly dance known as "The Time Warp."

Riding the wave of interest in adapting films for the musical stage, the recent Broadway revival of *The Rocky Horror Show* was truer to the film than the original stage version in that it actively encouraged the audience to interact with performers in much the same way that moviegoers interact with the film. The 2000 production was staged in the round, and, as in *The Donkey Show,* the lines between spectator and performer were blurred through the use of actors planted in the audience before the show began. For the length of the performance, the television talk-show host Dick Cavett, in the role of the Narrator, was seated in a small box in the middle of the rear aisle, facing the stage. From his seat amid the audience, he bridged the gap between spectators and performers by engaging the former in witty, unscripted banter about the latter during specific points in the show. The rest of the actors incorporated a great deal of direct address into their performances, and chorus members frequently ran into the aisles during songs, occasionally selecting spectators at random as dance partners.

Theatergoers interested in getting even deeper into the act could buy feather boas, as well as bags of glitter, toast, toilet paper, and newspapers to fling during the show. Each of these prop-bags also contained a list of instructions explaining when to throw the various props and when to shout particular heckles. Thus, as director Christopher Ashley noted, the audience was actively encouraged to interact with the characters and to dance in the aisles—especially during "The Time Warp."[4]

Despite positive reviews and strong word-of-mouth, the revival of *The Rocky Horror Show* suffered in the aftermath of September 11, 2001. A marked drop-off in sales immediately after the attacks forced the producers of the musical to put it on hiatus from late September until late October. When it reopened, *The Rocky Horror Show* could not regain its momentum. It managed to last out the year, but only just; the revival shuttered for good on January 6, 2002.

Saturday Night Fever and *Mamma Mia!*

Unlike both *The Donkey Show* and *The Rocky Horror Show,* several recent Broadway musicals that were heavily influenced by popular music genres of the recent past attempted to draw the audience into the onstage action only during or after the curtain call, so as not to disrupt the narrative flow. Throughout the performance, however, some of these musicals featured "show within a show" segments, during which the imaginary fourth wall remained firmly in place, but actors on the stage served as extensions of the real audience. For example, *Saturday Night Fever,* a recycled version of the 1977 film that ran at the Minskoff Theater from October 1999 to December 2000, was tightly scripted and featured no breaks to the fourth wall. There were, however, several segments in each of the two acts during which characters broke into extended song and dance numbers, while other characters served as spectators. Most of these segments were set in the local discotheque, where lead character Tony Manero and his dance partner competed in weekend disco competitions. During these scenes, set to the most infectiously recognizable of disco tunes, part of the huge cast would sing and dance, while the rest of the cast would stand off to the sides, cheering the dancers, and singing along.

While *Saturday Night Fever* attempted to lure audiences with the promise of familiarity, it offered little in the way of innovation. The stage version was simply a carbon copy of the film, minus most of the cursing and all of the date rape. The Bee Gees songs that filled out the movie's enormously successful soundtrack were simply worked directly into the plot and sung by the characters themselves, while the pit band dutifully pumped out disco accompaniment.

The same "show within a show" tactic attempted in *Saturday Night Fever* has been applied to the much more successful *Mamma Mia!* A smash success in London's West End, where it opened on April 6, 1999, *Mamma Mia!* premiered at Broadway's Winter Garden Theater on October 18, 2001, to enthusiastic reviews and strong ticket sales. Productions have since been staged in major cities around the globe. *Mamma Mia!* is the brainchild of Benny Andersson and Björn Ulvaeus, who, with Agnetha Faltskog and Anni-Frid Lyngstad, comprised the phenomenally successful 1970s Swedish pop group ABBA. *Mamma Mia*'s book (written by Catherine Johnson) recounts the tale of Sophie Sheridan, a young bride-to-be who concocts a zany scheme to find her father by secretly inviting three men who once courted her bohemian mother to her wedding on an idyllic Grecian isle. Woven into this blithe plot is a score made up of twenty-seven ABBA hits that have, over the course of thirty years, become highly recognizable to mass audiences throughout the Western world and beyond. Like *Saturday Night Fever, Mamma Mia!* features a series of familiar pop songs that are sung by actors who remain in character throughout the performance. These songs, however, have not been forced into a preexisting script, as in the case of *Saturday Night Fever;* instead, the humorous book has been crafted around the songs, which makes *Mamma Mia!* seem much fresher and less contrived.

While the plot of *Mamma Mia!* unfolds without any breaks to the imaginary fourth wall, live popular performance is emulated in several sequences during the show. For example, the act 1 finale is set at Sophie's bachelorette party. At the beginning of this scene, Sophie's mother Donna and two old friends who have come in for the wedding dress up in flashy spandex and surprise the guests by performing a jokey rendition of the ABBA number "Super Trouper." The tipsy guests laugh, dance, and sing along exuberantly. Once the number ends, the bachelorette party is crashed by the male wedding guests; dancing, drinking, and, of course, more energetic singing of ABBA tunes continue well into the night (and, thus, until intermission). Although the fourth wall remains intact here, the "show within a show" structure nevertheless allows this scene to function as a modified pop concert, especially during the "Super Trouper" segment, when Donna and her three friends act as pop stars, and the rest of the actors onstage become extensions of the audience. Because the scores of *Mamma Mia!* and *Saturday Night Fever* have been constructed from songs that are now internationally familiar, it is not uncommon, especially during such extended song-and-dance sequences, to observe members of the real audience mouthing—or even quietly singing—along, nodding their heads or bouncing in their seats in time to the rhythm of a musical number.

The beginning of the second act of *Mamma Mia!,* like the second act of

The Who's Tommy, takes its lighting cues from live rock performance, and specifically, the light shows evocative of the 1960s San Francisco scene. At the Winter Garden, as spectators rush to take their seats after intermission, the interior of the house becomes awash in swirling, spinning, purple and green lights, which skim the audience as the band launches into an improvisational jam replete with strange, otherworldly sounds emanating from the synthesizer. Once the curtain rises, the psychedelic light show is worked neatly into the plot: it is representative of a stress-related nightmare that Sophie is having on the morning of her wedding day.

Both *Saturday Night Fever* and *Mamma Mia!* emulate live rock performance—and, specifically, performer-audience interaction—most directly during their carefully choreographed curtain calls, which are clearly influenced by concert encores. Rock concert encores are designed to heighten the experience of live performance, thereby leaving the audience buzzing with excitement at having seen an admired performer or performers live, and having heard their favorite songs. Regardless of the popular genre that a performer represents, encores are almost always structured the same way: after the lead singer introduces the band while singing what is ostensibly the very last song of the evening, the musicians bid their farewells to the crowd and take their leave from the stage. The houselights stay down, while the crowd expresses its desire for a few more songs by applauding, shouting, stomping feet, holding up lit cigarette lighters, whistling, and the like. Once the din in the concert site has reached a fevered pitch, the musicians run back onto the stage, often to an even more passionate explosion of cheers and applause by the crowd. In response to the demand for more songs, musicians tend to play one or two of the most familiar songs from their repertoire during encores; energized by successfully drawing the performers back to the stage, audience members often stand through encores, and many sing and dance along to the music.

At *Saturday Night Fever* curtain calls, the entire cast broke into disco dances choreographed to songs that had already been performed during the show—"Stayin' Alive," "Boogie Shoes," and "Disco Inferno"—while an onstage deejay instructed the audience to get up and dance along. At *Mamma Mia!* performances, the encore becomes a miniconcert in its own right. After the cast members take their initial bows, the leads depart from the stage, and the rest of the cast faces the audience while singing and dancing along to the ABBA song from which the musical derives its title:

"Mamma Mia." The cast is then rejoined by the three female leads (Donna and her "Super Trouper" singing buddies), clad again in ridiculous spandex outfits, for a fully choreographed reprise of "Dancing Queen." Finally, the three male leads, also clothed in whimsical getups, pair off with the three female leads, and the whole cast sings "Waterloo" before taking a final curtain call. Meanwhile, colored lights around the stage swivel in all directions, flashing repeatedly into the house, where audience members can observe each other dancing and singing along while members of the cast wave enthusiastically at them from the stage.

While it is perhaps discouraging to ponder the future of the contemporary American musical in light of so much reliance on familiarity, it is important to note that even old material—pop songs, hit films, musicals that premiered decades ago—can be brushed off, spruced up, and given brand new lives. As the stale and unimaginative stagings of *Saturday Night Fever* and the most recent revival of *Jesus Christ Superstar* demonstrate, true familiarity can indeed breed contempt. Yet shows like *The Donkey Show*, *The Rocky Horror Show* and *Mamma Mia!* imply that old forms and fresh ideas are in no way mutually exclusive.

Conclusion

SINCE THE 1950S, the musical theater has been struggling mightily to regain its foothold in American popular culture, chiefly by emulating stylistic trends that appear in other, more wide-ranging and influential types of media. Throughout its history, but especially since the 1950s, the theater industry has endeavored to appeal to audiences with innovations in both aural and visual spectacle, resulting in productions that imitate the aesthetics of television shows, studio recordings, and films. This is especially true in recent years, since entertainment corporations accustomed to working with film and television properties have taken a new interest in creating and producing musicals. Accordingly, half a century after what is seen to have been the golden age of the American musical, Broadway has fully reversed its position. Whereas it once exerted strong influence on Hollywood, Broadway is, at present, a site for a growing number of big-budget musicals that are based, both thematically and stylistically, on movies.

Such general trends toward the increasingly commercial and risk-free, however, obscure a more complex history of the American musical, in which smaller, less expensive, more specialized ventures can be seen to compete against larger, more commercial, more spectacular ones for the attention of the ticket-buying public. In this respect, the American musical is no different from other, more far-reaching types of media—especially film and popular music—which are often depicted as arenas in which smaller, less commercial concerns struggle to be heard over larger, more corporate-driven ones. Like these other forms of media, the largest commercial musical theater properties are often viewed as posing a serious threat to smaller, less commercial ones.

The American musical is additionally similar to the film and popular music industries in that smaller properties ultimately seem to find ways to adapt and survive in even the most difficult and unfriendly of arts environments. Indeed, just as histories of the American film and popular music industries reveal independent filmmakers and popular groups forever struggling—but surviving—in their increasingly corporate worlds, the death of the American musical at the hands of huge corporations has yet to become a reality. Indeed, constant warnings about the certain death of the musical notwithstanding, this performing arts genre is in fact as diversified and fragmented as all other types of media. Although it tends, most often, to be depicted in linear histories that focus on the ways such luminaries as Kern, Gershwin, Berlin, Porter, Rodgers, and Sondheim built upon one another's contributions, the actual development of the American musical is far messier. New subgenres of American musical have developed in response to the changing times, and either succeed or fail depending on how well they fit sociological needs. Countless composers try their hands at musicals, only to be met with critical and commercial indifference that deems them historically irrelevant. Similarly, many lesser-known composers enjoy success with musicals that enjoy long runs but that are, for whatever reason, forgotten with the passing of time.

Earning a place in the musical theater canon—as in any canon—thus has a great deal to do with a composer's ability to transcend the topical. This is no small feat, since the musical theater has always borrowed heavily from the popular music of its time. In this respect, the staged rock musical may be seen as an evolutionary subgenre, which was born from a desire within the theater industry to keep the American musical alive and attractive to a young generation that had diverged widely, both in tastes and in behavior, from those that had come before it.

The emulation of proven trends in the dominant popular culture, staged rock musicals in particular, is an attempt by the theater industry to keep itself and its art viable and appealing. The history of the staged rock musical thus reveals a great deal about the development of the American musical theater and its industry, especially since the 1950s. In keeping with the notion of the American musical as a great imitator of popular culture at large, rock musicals clearly have followed general trends that developed in popular music. Rock's relationship to the counterculture, for example, was reflected in what is considered to be the first successful rock musical, *Hair,* which premiered at a time when the counterculture had already begun to dissipate. In the early 1970s, Broadway became home to a number of rock musical spectacles that placed flamboyance before narrative flow, and that followed closely on the heels of the larger, ever more spectacular arena shows that were, at the time, being offered in the rock realm.

The "fragmented" rock musicals that opened on Broadway at this time were, for the most part, so poorly received by both critics and audiences that the subgenre was pronounced dead by the end of the 1970s. In reality, however, it was during the 1970s that rock had only just begun to be absorbed into the fabric of the American musical, just as jazz and ragtime had been absorbed before it. The 1980s saw the flowering of megamusicals on Broadway. These borrowed a number of elements from staged rock musicals, but proved far more accessible to mainstream audiences.

Just as there is a wide variety of film, television, and popular music genres, there is no single, defining American musical, nor one definitive style of rock musical. Rather, as has been demonstrated, shows that end up being labeled—by someone, somewhere—"rock musicals" continue to dot the American theatrical landscape. While elements of rock music were absorbed into most Broadway musicals by the 1980s, many smaller, more specialized musicals continue to feature less diluted versions of rock music in their scores, and attempt to emulate more accurately the performance styles that have been cultivated in the rock realm. The tensions that arise between smaller rock musicals that aspire to a more "authentic" rock sound, and larger, more mainstream pop musicals that appeal to broader audiences are similar to the ideological tensions between the pop and rock realms of the music industry.

Yet when it comes to the American musical, individual elements of rock music—the occasional use of its instrumentation, for example, or a nod toward its vocal styles—tend to translate more easily than attempts at direct imitation. Rock resists absorption as a result of its aesthetic qualities, which differ markedly from those in the musical theater, but especially as a result of its ideological values, which maintain a veneer of artistic authenticity and anticommercialism, despite thuddingly obvious evidence to the contrary.

Although rock has been absorbed by the musical theater mainstream in the guise of pop musicals, these are largely rejected by many rock performers, industry members, journalists, and fans. As a result, the rock musical that manages to win the grudging admiration of both the mainstream and the fringe is a rare creation indeed. Nevertheless, as the phenomenal success of both *Hedwig and the Angry Inch* and *Rent*—which are, ultimately, two vastly different musicals, both of which happen to borrow liberally from the sounds and styles associated with rock music—have proven, the staged rock musical, like the American musical itself, has never died, and in fact shows no signs of waning.

Be that as it may, while divergent performance styles and ideologies certainly work against attempts to merge rock music and the American musical, it is possible that the biggest problem inherent in attaining such a union lies in the fact that the popular music world tends to be ephemeral, forward-looking, and accepting of change, while the musical theater realm seems forever to be stepping ahead with one foot, while keeping the other rooted in its canonized, celebrated, illustrious past. For all its parallels to more far-reaching kinds of media, the American musical is, in this respect, most akin to such performing arts genres as the opera or the symphony. Like these, the musical is constantly struggling to remain relevant and viable as a live performing art in an age when electronic media exert the most power and influence.

A problem that the musical and its surrounding industry faces, then, is how to rectify its hundred-year-old history with its need to remain fresh and relevant. The current solution—emulating trends in the dominant popular culture—is, in many ways, also a problem despite the presence of many innovative adaptations, since popular music trends are at often at odds with the traditional (and stubborn) "Broadway sound."

Because it is always chasing the aesthetic and economic developments introduced by more dominant media, the American musical will continue to be seen as derivative and anachronistic, and Broadway, its spiritual home, continue to be saddled with the nickname "the Fabulous Invalid." This is especially the case since stage musicals often take many years to produce, and thus run the risk of appealing to audiences with stylistic trends that have long since passed out of the dominant popular culture. The resultant perception of the American musical as a corny and aging performing art form is, perhaps, even more of a deterrent to those interested in creating rock musicals than the divergence in aesthetics or ideology.

Then again, Off and Off-Off-Broadway have always been slightly more in tune with the times, and thus slightly more hospitable to musicals that borrow from the most recent contemporary popular styles—and the diverse people who make them—than has Broadway. Indeed, far from the bright lights of the Great White Way—aptly named in both senses of the term—hip-hop has recently begun to show signs of theatrical viability, even though its influence remains minimal on Broadway. In contrast, Off and Off-Off-Broadway have become home to a number of hip-hop influenced theatrical ventures in the past few years. Most notable is the New York City Hip-Hop Theater Festival at PS 122, which has been growing in popularity and winning the attention of the press since it first appeared in June 2001. If history is expected to repeat itself—and it almost always is—it is only a matter of time before a small, hip-hop-influenced musical opens in a tiny downtown theater, wins the adoration of audiences and the glowing praise of theater critics, and moves uptown where, more than twenty years since rap music was introduced, it will be hailed alternately as "revolutionary," "anathema," or simply not that big a deal—just as *Hair* was in 1968.

Notes

INTRODUCTION

1. Warfield 2002, 231.
2. Middleton 2001, 485.
3. Warfield 2002, 232.
4. Mast 1987, 7–8.
5. Lamb and Snelson 2001, 453.
6. Filmer, Rimmer, and Walsh 1999, 381.
7. See, for example, Lawson-Peebles 1996; Steyn 1997; Block 1997; Burston 1998; Filmer, Rimmer, and Walsh 1999; Wickstrom 1999; Savran 2002; Most 2004; and Kirle 2005.
8. See, for example, Mates 1985, and Bordman 2001.
9. See, for example, Mordden 1976.
10. Gracyk 1999, 214.
11. Kauffmann 1979, 36.
12. Everett 2000; Bracket 2000; Middleton 2000; Stempel 1992; Mast 1987; Banfield 1996.

CHAPTER 1

1. Warfield 2002, 231.
2. Gottfried 1984, 288.
3. Bordman 1992, 658–59.
4. Bordman 1992, chap. 10.
5. Gottfried 1984, 287.
6. Bordman 1992, 642.
7. J. Jones 2003, 3. Lefkin (1998, 22) notes an increase in attendance at Broadway shows by individuals under the age of eighteen through the 1990s, but adds that even with this increase, the majority of Broadway theatergoers (78 percent) are over the age of twenty-four.
8. Hamm 1986, 63.
9. Bordman 1992, 602.
10. Kronenberger 1958, 336.
11. Atkinson 1957.
12. Kronenberger 1957, 357–58.
13. Funke 1959.

14. Padula 1995, 2–3.
15. Atkinson 1960.
16. Schier 1960.
17. Padula 1995, 2–3.
18. Bordman 1992, 642–43.
19. Warfield 2002, 232–33.
20. Chapman 1964.
21. Gottfried 1984, 288.
22. Hewes 1963, 15.
23. Bordman 1992, 628.
24. Gottfried 1966.

INTERLUDE 1

1. See, for example Frith 1981; Sanjek 1992; Goodman 1998; and Gracyk 1999.
2. Frith 1981, 159–60.
3. Frith 1981, 160.
4. Denisoff 1972, 101.
5. Denisoff 1972, 103–4.
6. Frith 1981, 162.
7. Frith 1981, 162.
8. Bloomfield 1993, 17.
9. Frith 1984, 66–67.
10. Frith 1984, 66–67.
11. Goodman 1998, 8.
12. S. Jones 1992, 3.
13. Frith 1986, 266–67.
14. P. Clarke 1983, 203; Guernsey 1970, 265–75.
15. Frith 1986, 271.
16. Frith 1986, 272.
17. Sanjek 1992, 12–13.
18. McLeod 2001, 47.
19. Bangs 1988, 227.
20. Personal communication, September 30, 1999.
21. Sanjek 1992, 14–15.
22. Sanjek 1992, 16.
23. Goodman 1998.
24. McLeod 2001, 57.
25. Buxton 1983, 428.
26. Goodman 1998, 78.
27. Frith 1984, 65–66.
28. Scudder 1984, 168–69.
29. Gracyk 1996, 220.
30. Grossberg 1992, 209.
31. Gracyk 1996, 220

32. Frith 1987, 140–43.
33. Orgill 1999, 23.
34. Lawson-Peebles 1996, 1–5.
35. Personal communication, September 30, 1999. For more on the association between musical theater and homosexuality in American culture, please see John M. Clum, *Something for the Boys: Musical Theater and Gay Culture* (New York: St. Martin's Press, 1999), 1–26.
36. Personal communication, September 30, 1999.
37. Personal communication, October 6, 1998.
38. Personal communication, July 17, 1998.
39. Wild 1993, 21.
40. Personal communication, November 24, 1998.
41. O. Jones 2000, 17.
42. Personal communication, October 6, 1998.
43. Steyn 1997, 225.
44. Gracyk 1999, 216.
45. Personal communication, August 28, 1998.
46. Personal communication, October 6, 1998.
47. Personal communication, October 6, 1998.
48. Personal communication, July 17, 1998.
49. Personal communication, July 17, 1998.
50. Personal communication, August 28, 1998.
51. Winer 2000.
52. Rich 1993, C1; emphasis added.
53. Bessman 1998.
54. Fricke 1998, 55.
55. Dansby 1999.
56. Borow 1999.
57. Butsch 200, 57–58.
58. Witchell 1991.
59. Brantley, Canby, and Marks 1999.
60. Singer 2000.
61. Fox 1993, 81.
62. Fox 1993, 81.
63. Tommasini 2000.
64. http://www.rollingstone.com/news/newsarticle.asp?nid=13586&cf=855.
65. Ibid.

CHAPTER 2

1. Kauffmann 1979.
2. Simmer 1977, 61.
3. Banham 1995, 647.
4. Horn 1991, 17.
5. Pasolli 1970, 74–75.

6. Pasolli 1970, 75.
7. Personal communication, January 16, 1999.
8. Passoli 1970, 76.
9. Passoli 1970, 76.
10. Richards 1979, 391.
11. Terry 1966, 251.
12. Terry 1966, 261–62.
13. Terry 1966, 21–22.
14. Personal communication, January 16, 1999.
15. Horn 1991, 27, 135.
16. Personal communication, October 22, 1998.
17. Warfield 2002, 233.
18. Horn 1991, 35–36.
19. Personal communication, October 22, 1998.
20. Horn 1991, 41–42.
21. J. Jones 2003, 269–304.
22. Horn 1991, 14.
23. Lamb 1986, 297.
24. Personal communication, January 16, 1999.
25. Barnes 1968.
26. Richards 1979, 389.
27. Personal communication, February 23, 1999.
28. Personal communication, January 3, 1999.
29. Simmer 1977, 61–62.
30. Barnes 1968.
31. Chapman 1968.
32. Personal communication, February 23, 1999.
33. Personal communication, December 15, 1998.
34. Personal communication, December 5, 1998.
35. Personal communication, January 3, 1999.
36. Personal communication, December 15, 1998.
37. Personal communication, January 3, 1999.
38. Personal communication, January 3, 1999.
39. Personal communication, February 23, 1999.
40. Hamm 1986, 64.
41. A "happening" as defined by Kirby is "a purposefully composed form of theater in which diverse alogical elements, including nonmatrixed performing, are organized in a compartmented structure" (1965, 21). The term, however, has been contested as imprecise by many writers. Kostelanetz offers, instead, the label "theatre of mixed means," which "encompasses various strains of activity and yet makes the crucial distinction between this theatre and traditional, predominantly literary mono-mean practice" (1968, xi).
42. Personal communication, January 3, 1999.
43. Personal communication, January 3, 1999.
44. Barnes 1968.
45. Whitburn 1995 and 1996.

46. Personal communication, October 22, 1998.
47. Personal communication, October 22, 1998.
48. Warfield 2002, 231.
49. Horn 1991, 63.
50. Bordman 1992, 643–44.
51. Horn 1991, 133–34.
52. Lefkin 1998.
53. J. Jones 2003, 251–56.
54. Horn 1991, 89–90.
55. A. Green 1970.
56. Horn 1991, 89–90.
57. Personal communication, December 15, 1998.
58. Personal communication, January 16, 1999.
59. Aronowitz 1970.
60. Anonymous review in *Cue*, May 11, 1968.
61. Personal communication, October 18, 1998.
62. Bordman 1992, 659.
63. Anonymous article in *Time* magazine, October 3, 1969, 78.
64. Personal communication, January 16, 1999.
65. Personal communication, January 3, 1999.
66. Online post, archive.jabberwocky.com/lists/hair-list/199910/msg00082.html, October 16, 1999.
67. Personal communication, October 7, 1998.
68. Personal communication, December 5, 1998.
69. Personal communication, December 5, 1998.
70. Personal communication, December 15, 1998.
71. Larkin 1995, 461n.
72. Warfield 2002, 233.
73. Lahr 1969a, 57.
74. Barnes 1969.
75. Sealy 1970.
76. Warfield 2002, 236.
77. Mishkin 1969.
78. Lahr 1969b.
79. Guernsey 1970, 28.
80. Personal communication, October 22, 1998.

INTERLUDE 2

1. Burns 1972, 184–85.
2. Bennett 1997, 86.
3. Manuel 1988, 9.
4. Adorno 1976, 21–38.
5. Canetti 1973, 37.
6. Baker-White 1992, 41.

7. Davies 1999; Young 1995.

8. See for example Croteau 2000; Stempel 2001; Sauter 2000; Stokes and Maltby 1999; Taylor 1999; and Seiter 1998.

9. Personal communication, November 9, 2004.

10. Personal communication, October 6, 1998.

11. See, for example, Bagdikian 1985; Rothenbuhler 1996; and Wollman 1998.

12. Bennett 1997, 2–3.

13. Lancaster 1997, 76.

14. Bennett 1997, 3.

15. Butsch 2000, 6.

16. Butsch 2000, 106–11.

17. Grossberg 1990, 116.

18. Buxton 1990, 428.

19. Schroeder 1970, 41–42.

20. Gracyk 1996, 78.

21. Carla Bianco, personal communication, April 7, 1999.

CHAPTER 3

1. Quoted in J. Jones 2003, 270–71.

2. J. Jones 2003, 271.

3. J. Jones 2003, 272–73.

4. J. Jones 2003, 273.

5. Suskin 1992, 571.

6. MacDonald 1994, 171.

7. Kealy 1982, 105.

8. Branscomb 1993, 29.

9. Macan 1997, 21.

10. Rockwell 1992, 1365.

11. Rockwell 1992, 1365.

12. Strauss 1998, E5.

13. http://www.5years.com/faq.htm, October 26, 2004.

14. Bordman 1992, 665.

15. Personal communication, October 22, 1998.

16. Mandelbaum 1991, 24.

17. Bosworth 1972, D5.

18. Bosworth 1972, D5.

19. Guernsey 1973, 9.

20. Watt 1972.

21. Anonymous article in *New Yorker,* September 23, 1972.

22. Mandelbaum 1991, 22.

23. Anonymous article in *New Yorker,* September 23, 1972.

24. Bosworth 1972, D5.

25. Bosworth 1972, D5.

26. Mandelbaum 1991, 22.

27. Personal communication, October 22, 1998.
28. Mandelbaum 1991, 23.
29. Gottfried 1972.
30. Kroll 1972.
31. Mandelbaum 1991, 23.
32. Goodwin 1984, 20–21.
33. Guernsey 1973, 10.
34. Mandelbaum 1991, 23.
35. Kerr 1972b.
36. Barnes 1972.
37. Guernsey 1973, 7 and 343.
38. Personal communication, August 3, 1998.
39. Barnes 1972.
40. Kerr 1973.
41. Guernsey 1973, 389.
42. Guernsey 1970, 361.
43. Guernsey 1971, 30.
44. Guernsey 1971, 321.
45. Guernsey 1971, 301.
46. Guernsey 1978, 398.
47. Guernsey 1978, 399.
48. Isserman and Kazin 1989; repr. in Griffith 1992, 491.
49. Morrow 1973, 155–56.
50. J. Jones 2003, 282–83.
51. Personal communication, January 26, 1999.
52. Barnes 1971.
53. Warfield 2002, 237.
54. Suskin 1992, 537.
55. Whitburn 1996, 256.
56. Personal communication, May 4, 2000.
57. Bergman et al. 1981, 396.
58. Bergman et al. 1981, 396.
59. Singer 1999, AR5.
60. Gracyk 1996, 1.
61. Nassour and Broderick 1973, 1.
62. Nassour and Broderick 1973, 20.
63. Nassour and Broderick 1973, 20.
64. Nassour and Broderick 1973, 20.
65. Nassour and Broderick 1973, 20.
66. Denisoff and Romanowski 1991, 204.
67. Denisoff and Romanowski 1991, 204.
68. Denisoff and Romanowski 1991, 205.
69. Denisoff and Romanowski 1991, 205.
70. Nassour and Broderick 1973, 48.
71. Denisoff and Romanowski 1991, 207.
72. Whitburn 1995, 367.

73. Denisoff and Romanowski 1991, 203–07.
74. *Forbes,* July 10, 1978, 42.
75. Denisoff and Romanowski 1991, 209.
76. Nassour and Broderick 1973, 99–100.
77. Anonymous article in *Variety,* October 13, 1971, 48.
78. Nassour and Broderick 1973, 95.
79. Anonymous article in *Variety,* October 13, 1971, 48.
80. Denisoff and Romanowski 1991, 210.
81. Suskin 1992, 594.
82. Nassour and Broderick 1973, 212.
83. *Joseph and the Amazing Technicolor Dreamcoat, Great Performances,* PBS, April 5, 2000.
84. Nassour and Broderick 1973, 37–38.
85. *Joseph and the Amazing Technicolor Dreamcoat, Great Performances,* PBS, April 5, 2000.
86. Personal communication, May 4, 2000.
87. Nassour and Broderick 1973, 209.
88. Personal communication, May 4, 2000.
89. Simmer 1977, 64.
90. Kerr 1971c.
91. Scholem 1971.
92. Nassour and Broderick 1973, 34–35, 177.
93. Pearson 1971.
94. Pearson 1971.
95. Personal communication, May 4, 2000.
96. Huffman 1972, 266.
97. Bender et al. 1971.
98. Bender et al. 1971.
99. Personal communication, May 4, 2000.
100. Personal communication, May 4, 2000.
101. Kane 1972.
102. Kane 1972.
103. Nassour and Broderick 1973, 48, 62.
104. Nassour and Broderick 1973, 48, 118.
105. Barnes 1971.
106. Ken Mandelbaum, personal communication, August 3, 1998.
107. Larkin 1995, 4535.
108. Larkin 1995, 1375.
109. Larkin 1995, 1375.
110. Rosenberg and Harburg 1993, 61.
111. Kerr 1979b.
112. Kerr 1979a.
113. Walsh 2000, 9.
114. Prece and Everett 2002, 246.
115. Tom O'Horgan, personal communication, February 23, 1999.
116. Simmer 1977, 65.

117. Personal communication, May 4, 2000.

118. Gaines 1974, 11.

119. Tom O'Horgan, personal communication, May 4, 2000.

120. Pacheco 1975, 56.

121. Pacheco 1975, 56.

122. Tom O'Horgan, personal communication, May 4, 2000.

123. Peter Blake, the artist who designed and staged the photography of the cover, discusses his work in the liner notes to the compact disc release of the Beatles' *Sgt. Pepper's Lonely Hearts Club Band,* EMI Records, 1987, 7.

124. Gottfried 1974.

125. Gottfried 1974.

126. Tom O'Horgan, personal communication, May 4, 2000.

127. Gaines 1974, 11.

128. Denisoff and Romanowski 1991, 247.

129. Kalem 1974.

130. See, for example, reviews by Gaines (1974), Gussow (1974), Probst (1974), and Gottfried (1974).

131. Woll 1989, 250.

132. Woll 1989, 249–50.

133. Woll 1989, 248.

134. J. Jones 2003, 215–18.

135. Woll 1989, 263.

136. Surowiecki 1999, 176.

137. Gussow 1972.

138. Gussow 1972.

139. See, for example, Kroll 1971; Watt 1971; and Topor 1972.

140. Kerr 1971c.

141. Abelman 1971.

142. Riley 1971.

143. Gottfried 1971

144. Oppenheimer 1971.

145. Riley 1971.

146. Barnes 1971a.

147. Hewes 1971.

148. Watts 1971.

149. Gottfried 1971.

150. Topor 1972.

151. Gussow 1972.

152. Woll 1989, 259.

153. Topor 1972.

154. Woll 1989, 259.

155. Topor 1972.

156. Potter 2001, 143.

157. Potter 2001, 143–44.

158. Warfield 2002, 236.

159. All titles, dates, and run information from Bordman 1992, 683–99.

160. Salzman 1991, 243.
161. Mordden 1976, 309–15.
162. Guernsey 1972, 29 and 1973, 25.
163. Guernsey 1978, 25.

INTERLUDE 3

1. Rosenberg and Harburg 1993, 7.
2. Rosenberg and Harburg 1993, 18.
3. Rosenberg and Harburg 1993, 7.
4. Rosenberg and Harburg 1993, 18–23.
5. Rosenberg and Harburg 1993, 12.
6. Rosenberg and Harburg 1993, 12.
7. Burston 1998, 205–06.
8. Larkin 1995, 745.
9. Rich 1998, 7.
10. Rosenberg and Harburg 1993, 59.
11. Information provided by The Really Useful Company.
12. Auslander 1997, 5.
13. See, for example, Kerr 1982; Canby 1994; Rich 1998; and Walsh 2000.
14. Warfield 2002, 236.
15. Burston 1998, 207.
16. Théberge 2001, 4.
17. Personal communication, March 4, 1999.
18. Burston 1998, 208.
19. Burston 1998, 208–9.
20. Prece and Everett 2002, 246–47.
21. Hewitt 1970.
22. Personal communication, October 6, 1998.
23. Burston 1998, 206.
24. Rosenberg and Harburg 1993, 59.
25. Bordman 1992, 665–66.
26. Rich 1998, 7.
27. Rosenberg and Harburg 1993, 109.

CHAPTER 4

1. Guernsey 1982, 21–22.
2. Duka 1982.
3. Crossette 1982.
4. Kerr 1982.
5. Kerr 1982.
6. Warfield 2002, 238.
7. Rich 1981.

8. Rich 1981.
9. Brustein 1982.
10. Crouch 1981.
11. Brustein 1982.
12. Gaar 1992, 34.
13. Gaar 1992, 69–84.
14. Frith 1987, 142–43.
15. J. Jones 2003, 305–08.
16. Rich 1982.
17. Larkin 1995, 712.
18. Mandelbaum 1991, 5–9 and 348–54.
19. Larkin 1995, 712.
20. Mandelbaum 1991, 351.
21. Rich 1988
22. Larkin 1995, 712.
23. Mandelbaum 1991, 351.
24. Gänzl 1994, 1361.
25. Rosenberg and Harburg 1993, 28.
26. Whitburn 1996, 279.
27. Warfield 2002, 240.
28. Bordman 1992, 766–79.

INTERLUDE 4

1. See, for example, *Drama Review* 42, no.1 (1998), a special issue devoted to exploring the nature of public space in the "new" Times Square.
2. See, for example, Nelson 1995 and Wickstrom 1999.
3. Nelson 1995, 83.
4. Nelson 1995, 83.
5. Wickstrom 1999, 286.
6. Wickstrom 1999, 286.
7. Nelson 1995, 72–74.
8. According to the ESPN website (www.ESPN.com), 80 percent of the ESPN cable network is owned by ABC, a subsidiary of Disney; the other 20 percent is owned by the Hearst Corporation.
9. Nelson 1995, 72–74.
10. Sorkin 1999, 9.
11. Wickstrom 1999, 288.
12. Nelson 1995, 72; and Evans 1997a, 71.
13. Dominguez 2001.
14. Personal communication, November 24, 1998.
15. Evans 1997b, 71.
16. http://www.broadway.org/, January 11, 2005.
17. Demographic studies by the League of American Theaters and Producers, 1997, 1999, and 2003.

18. Personal communication, August 3, 1998.
19. Rose 1998, C1; Pogrebin 1998, 3.
20. Pogrebin 1998, 3.
21. Personal communication, November 11, 1998.
22. Gold 1999, 7.
23. Personal communication, November 24, 1998.
24. Mardenfeld 1999, 21.
25. Mandelbaum 1991, 112.
26. Personal communication, November 24, 1998.
27. Personal communication, October 6, 2000.
28. Cox and Evans 1997, 1.
29. Personal communication, October 20, 1998.
30. J. Simon 2000, 88.
31. Personal communication, November 24, 1998.
32. Tommasini 1998, 24.
33. Cameron 2000, 10.
34. Study conducted by the League of American Theatres and Producers, http://www.livebroadway.com/bwaystats.html (November 22, 2004).
35. Personal communication, November 24, 1998.
36. Rich 1998, 7.
37. Personal communication, October 20, 1998.
38. Cameron 2000, 10.
39. Singer 1998, 5.
40. Pogrebin 2000b.

CHAPTER 5

1. Personal communication, August 28, 1998.
2. Personal communication, October 6, 1998.
3. Hinckley 1993, 16.
4. Pareles 1993, 18.
5. Townshend and Barnes 1977, 113.
6. Somma 1969, 138.
7. Denisoff and Romanowski 1991, 214.
8. Denisoff and Romanowski 1991, 214.
9. Pareles 1993, 5.
10. Grode 1993, 29
11. Personal communication, October 20, 1998.
12. Fox 1993.
13. S. Green 1996, 294.
14. Personal communication, October 20, 1998.
15. Morehouse 1995, 37.
16. Morehouse 1995, 37.
17. Morehouse 1995, 37.
18. Morehouse 1995, 37.

19. Personal communication, October 20, 1998.
20. McAnuff 1993, 12.
21. McAnuff 1993, 12.
22. McAnuff 1993, 12.
23. McAnuff 1993, 19.
24. Grode 1993, 29.
25. Personal communication, August 28, 1998.
26. Rich 1993.
27. Pareles 1993, 18.
28. Maslin 1993, 27.
29. Personal communication, August 28, 1998.
30. Personal communication, August 28, 1998.
31. Stock 1993, 29.
32. Personal communication, August 28, 1998.
33. Personal communication, October 13, 1998.
34. DeCurtis 1993.
35. Personal communication, October 13, 1998.
36. Personal communication, October 6, 1998.
37. Kroll 1996, 57.
38. Lipsky 1996, 103, 129.
39. Rich 1996.
40. Bordman 2001, 806.
41. *Rent* assistant director Martha Banta, personal communication, November 24, 1998.
42. See, for example, Istel 1996, 14.
43. Shapiro 1996, 52.
44. Riedel 1996, 35.
45. Kroll 1996, 54–60; Pluchino 1996, 14–17; O'Brien 1996, 54–58.
46. Kroll 1996, 56.
47. Personal communication, November 24, 1998.
48. Personal communication, October 6, 1998.
49. Rosenberg and Harburg 1993, 92.
50. Personal communication, October 6, 1998.
51. Personal communication, October 6, 1998.
52. Sussman 1998, 40–41.
53. Personal communication, August 25, 1998.
54. Dubner 1997, 46.
55. Dubner 1997, 45–47.
56. Dubner 1997, 65.
57. Dubner 1997, 44.
58. Dubner 1997, 48.
59. Dubner 1997, 44.
60. Dubner 1997, 48.
61. Dubner 1997, 56.
62. Personal communication, April 15, 1999.
63. Manning 2001.

64. Brantley 1998, 1.

65. Canby 1998, 4.

66. Dubner 1997, 83.

67. Lyman 1998.

68. Personal communication, August 28, 1998.

69. Eisenbach 1998.

70. Eisenbach 1998.

71. McDonnell 1998, 51.

72. Marks 1998.

73. Evelyn McDonnell, personal communication, September 30, 1999.

74. Tom D'Ambrosio, personal communication, July 17, 1998.

75. E. Smith 1999.

76. Kendt 1999.

77. Personal communication, July 29, 1998.

78. Personal communication, July 29, 1998.

79. Personal communication, July 17, 1998.

80. Fricke 1998, 54–55.

81. McDonnell 1998, 51.

82. http://content.gay.com/channels/arts/musicorner/stephentrask_000217 .html.

83. Dansby 1999.

84. Wilson 1975.

85. Galtney 1999, 13.

86. Galtney 1999, 14.

87. Walters 1999, 58.

88. Stephen Trask, personal communication, July 29, 1998.

89. Kendt 1999.

90. McInerney's novel, *Bright Lights, Big City,* included a comma in its title; Paul Scott Goodman's musical adaptation, *Bright Lights Big City,* did not.

91. Paul Scott Goodman, personal communication, March 14, 1999.

92. W. Smith 1999, 14.

93. Nicola 1999, 7.

94. P. Simon 1998, 28.

95. Personal communication, March 14, 1999.

96. Personal communication, March 25, 1999.

97. Personal communication, March 25, 1999.

98. Paul Scott Goodman, personal communication, March 14, 1999.

99. Richard Barone, personal communication, March 25, 1999.

100. Personal communication, March 14, 1999.

101. Personal communication, March 25, 1999.

102. Personal communication, March 11, 1999.

103. Personal communication, March 31, 1999.

104. Marks 1999, 7.

105. Whitehead 1999, 148.

106. http://www.sondheim.com/comedy/columna/past/77.html.

107. Personal communication, March 25, 1999.
108. Personal communication, March 11, 1999.

1. Gracyk 1996, 109.
2. Kendt 1999, 2.
3. Personal communication, August 25, 1998.
4. Personal communication, March 25, 1999.
5. Frith 1996, 124–25.
6. Personal communication, October 13, 1998.
7. Davies 1999, 203.
8. Personal communication, November 24, 1998.
9. Stephen Trask, personal communication, July 29, 1998.
10. Bradby 1993, 156.
11. Carlson 1989, 36–7.
12. Carlson 1989, 125–27.
13. Personal communication, June 17, 1998.
14. Carlson 1989, 196–97.

CHAPTER 6

1. Brantley 2000.
2. Larkin 1995, 3539.
3. Larkin 1995, 3539.
4. Lemon 2000, 22.

Bibliography

Abelman, Lester. "The Black Life 'Tunes' Are Slowly Emerging." *New York Daily News,* September 24, 1971.

Adorno, Theodor, *Introduction to the Sociology of Music.* Trans. E. B. Ashton. New York: Seabury, 1976.

Aronowitz, Alfred G. "Hair's Happy Birthday." *New York Post,* April 27, 1970.

Atkinson, Brooks. "Tired Blood." *New York Times,* March 2, 1957.

———. *"Bye Bye Birdie." New York Times,* April 15, 1960.

Auslander, Philip. "Ontology vs. History: Making Distinctions Between the Live and the Mediatized." Paper presented at the Third Annual Performance Studies Conference, Atlanta, April 1997.

Bagdikian, Ben H. "The U.S. Media: Supermarket or Assembly Line?" *Journal of Communication* 35, no. 3 (1985): 97–109.

Baker-White, Robert. "Crowds, Audiences, and the 'Liturgy of Irreverence': Rethinking the Altamont Concert as Participatory Theatre." *Studies in Popular Culture* 14, no. 2 (1992): 37–49.

Banfield, Stephen. "Sondheim and the Art That Has No Name." In *Approaches to the American Musical,* ed. Robert Lawson-Peebles. Exeter: University of Exeter Press, 1996.

Bangs, Lester. *Psychotic Reactions and Carburetor Dung.* Ed. Greil Marcus. New York: Vintage, 1988.

Banham, Martin, ed. *The Cambridge Guide to Theatre.* Cambridge: Cambridge University Press, 1995.

Barnes, Clive. "'Hair': It's Fresh and Frank." *New York Times,* April 30, 1968.

———. "The Theater: 'Salvation.'" *New York Times,* September 25, 1969.

———. "The Program: *Tarot." New York Times,* December 12, 1970.

———. "'Jesus Christ Superstar' Billed as Rock Opera." *New York Times,* October 13, 1971.

———. "Blacks Move Through Gauntlet of the Slum." *New York Times,* October 21, 1971a.

———. "The Theater: 'Rainbow.'" *New York Times,* December 19, 1972.

Baugh, Bruce. "Prolegomena to Any Aesthetics of Rock Music." *Journal of Aesthetics and Art Criticism* 51, no. 1 (1993): 23–29.

Bell, John. "Disney's Times Square: The New American Community Theatre." *Drama Review* 42, no. 1 (1998): 26–33.

———. "Times Square: Public Space Disneyfied." *Drama Review* 42, no. 1 (1998a): 25.

Bender, Bill, et al. "The Gold Rush to Golgotha." *Time,* October 25, 1971.

Bennett, Susan. *Theatre Audiences: A Theory of Production and Reception.* 2nd ed. New York: Routledge, 1997.

Bergman, J. Peter, et al. "Preserving the Heritage: The Aural Record." In *Musical Theatre in America: Papers and Proceedings of the Conference on the Musical Theatre in America,* ed. Glen Loney. Contributions in Drama and Theatre Studies, no. 8. Westport, Conn.: Greenwood, 1981.

Bessman, Jim. "On Stage: *Hedwig and the Angry Inch.*" *Billboard* 10, no. 4 (1998): 66.

Block, Geoffrey. *Enchanted Evenings: The Broadway Musical from "Show Boat" to Sondheim.* New York: Oxford University Press, 1997.

Bloomfield, Terry. "Resisting Songs: Negative Dialectics in Pop." *Popular Music* 12, no. 1 (1993): 13–31.

Bordman, Gerald. *American Musical Theatre: A Chronicle.* 2nd ed. New York: Oxford University Press, 1992.

———. *American Musical Theatre: A Chronicle.* 3rd ed. New York: Oxford University Press, 2001.

Borow, Zev. "Glam Slam: The Star of the Hit Musical *Hedwig* Muses on Previous Rock Opuses." *Spin,* January 1999.

Borrow, Edith. "Origin of Species: Conflicting Views of American Musical Theater History." *American Music* 2, no. 4 (1984): 101–11.

Bosworth, Patricia. "'Dude' . . . An $800,000 Disaster: Where Did They Go Wrong?" *New York Times,* October 22, 1972.

Boyd, Malcolm. "'Jesus Christ Superstar': A Priest Says 'It Doesn't Have a Soul.'" *New York Times,* October 24, 1971.

Brackett, David. *Interpreting Popular Music.* Berkeley and Los Angeles: University of California Press, 2000.

Bradby, Barbara. "Sampling Sexuality: Gender, Technology, and the Body in Dance Music." *Popular Music* 12, no. 2 (1993): 155–76.

Branscomb, H. Eric. "Literacy and a Popular Medium: The Lyrics of Bruce Springsteen." *Journal of Popular Culture* 27, no. 1 (1993): 29–42.

Brantley, Ben. "A Broadway Battle: Stars vs. Spectacle." *New York Times,* August 28, 1995.

———. "The Lure of Gang Violence, to a Latin Beat." *New York Times,* January 30, 1998.

———. "Superstar or Not, 'Jesus' Returns." *New York Times,* April 17, 2000.

———. "How Karaoke Conquered Broadway." *New York Times,* February 25, 2001.

Brantley, Ben, Vincent Canby, and Peter Marks. "London—New York: A One-Way Street?" *New York Times,* February 21, 1999.

Brustein, Robert. "Arguing with a Tank." *New Republic,* January 27, 1982.

Burns, Elizabeth. *Theatricality.* London: Longman, 1972.

Burston, Jonathan. "Theatre Space as Virtual Place: Audio Technology, the Reconfigured Singing Body, and the Megamusical." *Popular Music* 17, no. 2 (1998): 205–18.

Butsch, Richard. *The Making of American Audiences: from Stage to Television, 1750–1990.* Cambridge Studies in the History of Mass Communication. Cambridge: Cambridge University Press, 2000.

Buxton, David. "Rock Music, the Star-System, and the Rise of Consumerism." In *On*

Record: Rock, Pop, and the Written Word, ed. Simon Frith and Andrew Goodwin. New York: Pantheon Books, 1990.

Cameron, Ben. "Broadway: Devil or Angel for Nonprofit Theater? Finding the Right Way to Cross the Divide." *New York Times,* June 4, 2000.

Canby, Vincent. "Spectacle and Special Effects Aren't All Bad." *New York Times,* January 16, 1994.

———. "Capeman Doesn't Fly, Despite the Music." *New York Times,* February 8, 1998.

Canetti, Elias. *Crowds and Power.* Trans. John Willett. New York: Farrar, Straus and Giroux, 1973.

Carlson, Marvin. *Places of Performance: The Semiotics of Theatre Architecture.* Ithaca: Cornell University Press, 1989.

Chapman, John. "*Cambridge Circus* Diverting." *New York Daily News,* October 7, 1964.

———. "'Hair' Is Itchy, Twitchy & Dirty: The Company Dances with Zest." *New York Daily News,* April 30, 1968.

Chase, Gilbert. *America's Music, from the Pilgrims to the Present.* 3rd ed. Urbana: University of Illinois Press, 1987.

Clarke, Gary. "Defending Ski Jumpers: A Critique of Theories of Youth Subculture." In *On Record: Rock, Pop, and the Written Word,* ed. Simon Frith and Andrew Goodwin. New York: Pantheon, 1990.

Clarke, Paul. "'A Magic Science': Rock Music as a Recording Art." *Popular Music III: Producers and Markets,* ed. Richard Middleton and David Horn. Cambridge: Cambridge University Press, 1983.

Conard, Robert C. "Bertolt Brecht's Dramatic Theories and Their Relationship to Rock Music: Another View." *University of Dayton Review* 7, no. 3 (1971): 103–10.

Considine, J. D. "R.E.M.: Subverting Small Town Boredom." In *The R.E.M. Companion: Two Decades of Commentary,* ed. John Platt. New York: Schirmer, 1998.

Cox, Dan, and Greg Evans. "B'way Rules Rewritten to Heed 'Lion's' Roar: Megahit Puts Mouse in Catbird's Seat." *Variety,* December 22, 1997–January 4, 1998.

Crossette, Barbara. "Making a Plant Grow: A Hidden Art on Stage." *New York Times,* October 8, 1982.

Croteau, David. *Media/Society: Industries, Images, and Audiences.* 2nd ed. Thousand Oaks, Calif.: Pine Forge, 2000.

Crouch, Stanley. Review of *Dreamgirls. Village Voice,* January 30, 1981.

Dansby, Andrew. "Hedwig Unleashed: The Creators of the Groundbreaking Glam Rock-Opera Are Getting Miles Out of Their Angry Little Inch." *Rolling Stone,* February 18, 1999.

Davies, Stephen. "Rock versus Classical Music." *Journal of Aesthetics and Art Criticism* 57, no. 2 (1999): 193–204.

DeCurtis, Anthony. "Opinion: Broadway Production of *Tommy.*" *Rolling Stone,* June 24, 1993.

DeCurtis, Anthony, James Henke, and Holly George-Warren, eds. *The Rolling Stone Album Guide.* New York: Random House, 1992.

Denisoff, R. Serge. *Sing a Song of Social Significance.* Bowling Green, Ohio.: Bowling Green University Popular Press, 1972.

Denisoff, R. Serge, and William D. Romanowski. *Risky Business: Rock in Film.* New Brunswick, N.J.: Transaction, 1991.

Diamond, Lisa. "The World According to Blue Man." *Theater* 24, no. 1 (1993): 116–19.

Dominguez, Robert. "Films are the Thing on Broadway." *New York Daily News,* March 21, 2001.

Dotter, Daniel. "Rock and Roll Is Here to Stray: Youth Subculture, Deviance, and Social Typing in Rock's Early Years." In *Adolescents and Their Music: If It's Too Loud, You're Too Old,* ed. Jonathon S. Epstein. New York: Garland, 1994.

Dubner, Stephen. "The Pop Perfectionist on a Crowded Stage." *New York Times Magazine,* November 9, 1997.

Duka, John. "The Ego and the Art of David Geffen." *New York Times,* October 3, 1982.

Ehrenstein, David, and Bill Reed. *Rock on Film.* New York: Delilah, 1982.

Eisenbach, Helen. "Pretty Boy: Cavorting Onstage in Pumps and a Fright Wig, John Cameron Mitchell Has Become One of the City's Most Wanted Leading Men." *New York Magazine,* May 11, 1998.

Erlewine, Michael, Vladimir Bogdanov, Chris Woodstra, and Stephen Thomas Erlewine, eds. *The All Music Guide: The Experts' Guide to the Best CDs, Albums, and Tapes.* 3rd ed. San Francisco: Miller Freeman, 1997.

Evans, Greg. "'Lion' Roars at Broadway B.O.: Mouse Tuner Hits Sales, Hoopla Highs." *Variety,* November 17, 1997a.

———. "'King' Takes Daily B.O. Title." *Variety,* November 24, 1997b.

Everett, Walter, ed. *Expression in Pop-Rock Music: A Collection of Critical and Analytical Essays.* Studies in Contemporary Music and Culture. New York: Garland, 2000.

Filmer, Paul, Val Rimmer, and Dave Walsh. "'Oklahoma!': Ideology and Politics in the Vernacular Tradition of the American Musical." *Popular Music* 18, no. 3 (1999): 381–95.

Flanagan, Bill. *Written in My Soul.* Chicago: Contemporary, 1987.

Fox, Margalit. "Not the Usual Broadway Crowd: Audience Who's Who at 'The Who's Tommy.'" *Newsday,* April 30, 1993.

Fricke, David. "Sex & Drag & Rock & Roll: 'Hedwig and the Angry Inch' Is the First Rock Musical that Truly Rocks." *Rolling Stone,* December 10, 1998.

Frith, Simon. "'The Magic That Can Set You Free': The Ideology of Folk and the Myth of the Rock Community." In *Popular Music,* vol. 1, ed. Richard Middleton and David Horn. Cambridge: Press Syndicate of the University of Cambridge, 1981.

———. "Rock and the Politics of Memory." In *The 60s Without Apology,* ed. Sohnya Sayres, Anders Stephanson, Stanley Aronowitz, and Frederic Jameson. Minneapolis: University of Minnesota Press, 1984.

———. "Art Versus Technology: The Strange Case of Popular Music." *Media, Culture and Society* 8 (1986): 263–79.

———. "Towards an Aesthetic of Popular Music." In *Music and Society: The Politics of Composition, Performance, and Reception,* ed. Richard D. Leppert and Susan McClary. Cambridge: Cambridge University Press, 1987.

———. *Performing Rites: On the Value of Popular Music.* Cambridge: Harvard University Press, 1996.

Funke, Lewis. "The Girls Against the Boys." *New York Times,* November 3, 1959.

Bibliography

Gaar, Gillian. *She's a Rebel: The History of Women in Rock & Roll.* Seattle: Seal Press, 1992.

Gaines, Steven. "'Sgt. Pepper': A Milestone on the Road of Rock." *New York Sunday News,* October 27, 1974.

Galtney, Smith. "Double Fantasy: Can an Off Broadway Musical About a Transsexual Prostitute Become a Classic Rock Album? *Hedwig's* John Cameron Mitchell and Stephen Trask Dream That It Will." *Time Out New York,* January 28–February 4, 1999.

Gänzl, Kurt. *The Encyclopedia of the Musical Theatre.* New York: Schirmer, 1994.

Gold, Sylviane. "Where Did Our Dreams Go?" *Soho Weekly News,* January 12, 1982.

———. "Giving Mouth-to-Mouth to 'The Pimpernel.'" *New York Times,* January 31, 1999.

Goodman, Fred. *The Mansion on the Hill: Dylan, Young, Geffen, Springsteen, and the Head-on Collision of Rock and Commerce.* New York: Vintage, 1998.

Goodwin, John. *Peter Hall's Diaries: The Story of a Dramatic Battle.* New York: Harper and Row, 1984.

Gottfried, Martin. "A Joyful Noise." *Women's Wear Daily,* December 16, 1966.

———. *Opening Nights: Theatre Criticism of the Sixties.* New York: Putnam, 1969a.

———. "Salvation." *Women's Wear Daily,* September 25, 1969b.

———. Review of *Ain't Supposed to Die a Natural Death. Women's Wear Daily,* October 22, 1971.

———. *"Dude." Women's Wear Daily,* October 11, 1972.

———. "'Sgt. Pepper' on Stage." *New York Post,* November 18, 1974.

———. *Broadway Musicals.* New York: Abradale/Harry Abrams, 1984.

Gracyk, Theodore. *Rhythm and Noise: An Aesthetics of Rock.* Durham, N.C.: Duke University Press, 1996.

———."Valuing and Evaluating Popular Music." *Journal of Aesthetics and Art Criticism* 57, no. 2 (1999): 205–20.

Green, Abel. "L'Affaire *Hair* and the Astronauts Who Walked Out: Slur to the Flag." *Variety,* June 18, 1970.

Green, Stanley. *Broadway Musicals Show by Show.* 5th ed. Revised and updated by Kay Green. Milwaukee: Hal Leonard, 1996.

Griffith, Robert, ed. *Major Problems in American History Since 1945: Documents and Essays.* Lexington, Mass.: D.C. Heath, 1992.

Grode, Eric. "Tommy's Mommy: Marcia Mitzman on the Highs and Lows of Starring in a Rock Opera." *Theater Week,* August 9–13, 1993.

Grossberg, Lawrence. "Is There Rock After Punk?" In *On Record: Rock, Pop, and the Written Word,* ed. Simon Frith and Andrew Goodwin. New York: Pantheon, 1990.

———. *We Gotta Get Out of This Place: Popular Conservatism and Postmodern Culture.* New York: Routledge, 1992.

Guernsey, Otis L., Jr., ed. *The Best Plays of 1969–1970.* New York: Dodd, Mead, 1970.

———. *The Best Plays of 1970–1971.* New York: Dodd, Mead, 1971.

———. *The Best Plays of 1971–1972.* New York: Dodd, Mead, 1972.

———. *The Best Plays of 1972–1973.* New York: Dodd, Mead, 1973.

———. *The Best Plays of 1977–1978.* New York: Dodd, Mead, 1978.

————. *The Best Plays of 1978–1979*. New York: Dodd, Mead, 1979.

————. *The Best Plays of 1981–1982*. New York: Dodd, Mead, 1982.

Gussow, Mel. "The Baadasssss Success of Melvin Van Peebles." *New York Times,* August 20, 1972.

————. "Stage: 'Sgt. Pepper' Goes on the Road." *New York Times,* November 18, 1974.

Hamm, Charles. "Rock." In *The New Grove Dictionary of American Music,* vol. 4, ed. Wiley Hitchcock and Stanley Sadie. London: Macmillan, 1986.

Hannaham, James. "Sweet Transvestite: *Hedwig and the Angry Inch.*" *Village Voice,* February 18–24, 1998.

Hewes, Henry. "The Aints and the Am Nots." *Saturday Review,* November 13, 1971.

————, ed. *The Best Plays of 1962–1963*. New York: Dodd, Mead, 1963.

Hewitt, Alan. Untitled article on theater amplification. *New York Times,* January 18, 1970.

Hinckley, David. "Will 'Tommy' Tilt or Triumph? The Who's Legendary Rock Opera Looks to Light up Broadway," *Daily News,* Sunday, April 18, 1993.

Holland, Bernard. "Theaters Alive with a New Sound of Music." *New York Times,* May 10, 1998.

Horn, Barbara Lee. *The Age of "Hair": Evolution and Impact of Broadway's First Rock Musical.* Westport, Conn.: Greenwood, 1991.

Huffman, James R. "*Jesus Christ Superstar*—Popular Art and Unpopular Criticism." *Journal of Popular Culture* 6, no. 2 (1972): 259–69.

Isserman, Maurice, and Michael Kazin. "The Failure and Success of the New Radicalism." In *The Rise and Fall of the New Deal Order, 1930–1980,* ed. Steve Fraser and Gary Gerstle. Princeton: Princeton University Press, 1989.

Istel, John. "Did the Author's Hyper-Romantic Vision Get Lost in the Media Uproar?" *American Theatre,* July–August 1996, 13–17.

"'J.C. Superstar': Biggest All-Media Parlay in Show Business History." *Variety,* October 13, 1971.

Jones, John Bush. *Our Musicals, Ourselves: A Social History of the American Musical Theatre.* Hanover, N.H.: University Press of New England, 2003.

Jones, Oliver. "On the Road Again: The Monsters of Rock Are Flying High on Summer Tours." *Us Weekly,* July 31, 2000.

Jones, Steve. *"Rock Formation": Music, Technology, and Mass Communication.* Foundations of Popular Culture, no. 3. Newbury Park, Calif.: Sage, 1992.

Kalem, T. E. "Contagious Vulgarity: 'Sgt. Pepper's Lonely Hearts Club Band on the Road.'" *Time,* December 2, 1974.

Kane, John. "The Mike Is Mightier Than the Word." *Sunday Times,* February 6, 1972.

Kauffmann, Stanley. "New York: The City and the Theatre." *Theatre Quarterly* 8, no. 32 (1979): 34–40.

Kealy, Edward R. "Conventions and the Production of the Popular Music Aesthetic." *Journal of Popular Culture* 16, no. 2 (1982): 100–115.

Kendt, Rob. "Rocks in His Hedwig: Most Rock Musicals Are a Drag—Actor/Singer Michael Cerveris Headlines Ones That Actually Rock." *Backstage West,* October 21, 1999.

Kerr, Walter. "Why Make St. Matthew Dance? For the Fun of It." *New York Times,* May 30, 1971a.

————. "Kerr on 'Superstar.' " *New York Times,* October 24, 1971b.

————. "Maybe Even a Third Act . . . Maybe Even a Third Act, Please." *New York Times,* October 31, 1971c.

————. Untitled review of *Dude. New York Times,* October 22, 1972a.

————. Untitled review of *Via Galactica. New York Times,* December 10, 1972b.

————. "Is That the Way to End the Vietnam War?" *New York Times,* January 7, 1973.

————. "*Evita.*" *New York Times,* October 7, 1979a.

————. "*Evita:* A Bold Step Backward." *New York Times,* October 7, 1979b.

————. " 'Little Shop of Horrors' and the Terrors of Special Effects." *New York Times,* August 22, 1982.

Kirby, Michael. *Happenings: An Illustrated Anthology.* New York: E. P. Dutton, 1965.

Kirle, Bruce. *Unfinished Show Business: Broadways As Works-in-Process.* Carbondale, IL: Southern Ilinois University Press, 2005.

Kloman, William. " '2001' and 'Hair'—Are They the Groove of the Future?" *New York Times,* May 12, 1968.

Kostelanetz, Richard. *The Theatre of Mixed Means.* New York: RK Editions, 1968.

Kroll, Jack. "Black Bombshell." *Newsweek,* November 1, 1971.

————. "Bombs Away: *Dude.*" *Newsweek,* October 30, 1972.

————. "A Musical for the '90s Jumps a Generation Gap: Love Among the Ruins." *Newsweek,* May 13, 1996.

Kronenberger, Louis, ed. *The Best Plays of 1956–1957.* New York: Dodd, Mead, 1957.

————, ed. *The Best Plays of 1957–1958.* New York: Dodd, Mead, 1958.

Lahr, John. "On-Stage." *Village Voice,* October 2, 1969a.

————. "On-Stage." *Village Voice,* November 20, 1969b.

Lamb, Andrew. "Musical." In *The New Grove Dictionary of American Music,* vol. 3, ed. Wiley Hitchcock and Stanley Sadie. London: Macmillan, 1986.

Lamb, Andrew, and John Snelson. "Musical." In *The New Grove Dictionary of American Music,* vol. 17, ed. Stanley Sadie. 2nd ed. London: Macmillan, 2001.

Lancaster, Kurt. "When Spectators Become Performers: Contemporary Performance-Entertainments Meet the Needs of an 'Unsettled' Audience." *Journal of Popular Culture* 30, no. 4 (1997): 75–88.

Landesman, Rocco. "Broadway: Devil or Angel for Nonprofit Theater? A Vital Movement Has Lost Its Way." *New York Times,* June 4, 2000.

Larkin, Colin, ed. *The Guinness Encyclopedia of Popular Music.* 2nd ed. Middlesex: Guinness, 1995.

Lawson-Peebles, Robert, ed. *Approaches to the American Musical.* Exeter: University of Exeter Press, 1996.

Lefkin, Marian. *The Audience for New York Theatre: A Profile of the Broadway and Off Broadway 1997 Theatre Season.* New York: Theatre Development Fund and the League of American Theatres and Producers, 1998.

Lemon, Brendan. "Audiences Today Are Getting in on the Act." *New York Times,* October 8, 2000.

Leverence, John. "Promoting *Tommy.*" *Journal of Popular Culture* 8, no. 3 (1974): 465–76.

Lipsky, David. "Impossible Dream." *Us,* November 1996.

Loney, Glenn M. "Musical Comedy." In *The Reader's Encyclopedia of World Drama*, ed. John Gassner and Edward Quinn. New York: Thomas M. Crowell, 1969.

———, ed. *Papers and Proceedings of the Conference on the Musical Theatre in America*. Westport, Conn.: Greenwood, 1984.

Lyman, Rick. "After Rocky Run, 'Capeman' to Close." *New York Times*, March 6, 1998.

Lyons, Donald. "Ungodly Mess." *New York Post*, April 13, 2000.

Macan, Edward. *Rocking the Classics: English Progressive Rock and the Counterculture*. New York: Oxford University Press, 1997.

MacDonald, Ian. *Revolution in the Head: The Beatles' Records and the Sixties*. New York: Henry Holt, 1994.

Mandelbaum, Ken. *Not Since "Carrie": Forty Years of Broadway Musical Flops*. New York: St. Martin's, 1991.

Manning, Kara. "You Can't Always Get What You Want." *National Endowment for the Arts: Art Forms' Musical Theatre Features*. April 2001.

Manuel, Peter. *Popular Musics of the Non-Western World: An Introductory Survey*. New York: Oxford University Press, 1988.

Mardenfeld, Sandra. "Celluloid Into Song." *Stagebill*, June 1999.

Marks, Peter. "Briefly, a New Hedwig, but the Same Self-Discovery." *New York Times*, July 24, 1998.

———. "The Clubs! The Snorts! The Rhymes! (Last Resorts)." *New York Times*, February 25, 1999.

Maslin, Janet. "The Man Who Reinvented the Who's 'Tommy.'" *New York Times*, May 9, 1993.

Mast, Gerald. *Can't Help Singin': The American Musical on Stage and Screen*. Woodstock, N.Y.: Overlook Press, 1987.

Mates, Julian. *America's Musical Stage*. Contributions in Drama and Theatre Studies. Westport, Conn.: Greenwood, 1985.

McAnuff, Des. "See Me, Feel Me, Touch Me: How the Design Team of 'The Who's Tommy' Reinvented a Rock-and-Roll Classic." *American Theatre*, November 1993, 12–19.

McClary, Susan, and Robert Walser. "Start Making Sense! Musicology Wrestles with Rock." In *On Record: Rock, Pop, and the Written Word*, ed. Simon Frith and Andrew Goodwin. New York: Pantheon, 1990.

McDonnell, Evelyn. "The Angry Inch Monologues: How John Cameron Mitchell and Stephen Trask Created *Hedwig*, the Rockingest Musical Since Nothing." *Village Voice*, March 10, 1998.

McDonnell, Evelyn, and Katherine Silberger, eds. *Rent*. New York: William Morrow, 1997.

McKinley, Jesse. "Original Stars Returning to 'Producers' at a Price." *New York Times*, November 5, 2003.

———. "Plays Without Music Find Broadway Harsh." *New York Times*, December 7, 2004.

McLeod, Kembrew. "* 1/2: A Critique of Rock Criticism in North America." *Popular Music* 20, no. 1 (2001): 47–60.

Meyer, Leonard B. *Emotion and Meaning in Music*. Chicago: University of Chicago Press, 1956.

Middleton, Richard. *Studying Popular Music.* Milton Keynes: Open University Press, 1990.

———. "Rock." In *The New Grove Dictionary of Music and Musicians,* vol. 21, ed. Stanley Sadie. 2nd ed. London: Macmillan, 2001.

———, ed. *Reading Pop: Approaches to Textual Analysis in Popular Music.* New York: Oxford University Press, 2000.

Miller, Arthur. "On Broadway: Notes on the Past and Future of American Theater." *Harper's,* March 1999, 37–47.

Miller, D. A. *Place for Us: Essay on the Broadway Musical.* Cambridge: Harvard University Press, 1998.

Mishkin, Leo. "Everybody Gets into the Act in 'Stomp.'" *Morning Telegraph,* November 18, 1969.

Mordden, Ethan. *Better Foot Forward: The History of American Musical Theatre.* New York: Viking, 1976.

Morehouse, Ward, III. "Who Killed 'Tommy'?" *New York Post,* June 21, 1995.

Morrow, Patrick. "*Sgt. Pepper, Hair,* and *Tommy:* Forerunners of the Jesus-Rock Movement." In *Mystery, Magic, and Miracle: Religion in a Post-Aquarian Age,* ed. Edward F. Heenan. Englewood Cliffs, N.J.: Prentice-Hall, 1973.

Most, Andrea. *Making Americans: Jews and the Broadway Musical.* Cambridge: Harvard University Press, 2004.

Nassour, Ellis, and Richard Broderick. *Rock Opera: The Creation of "Jesus Christ Superstar" from Record Album to Broadway Show and Motion Picture.* New York: Hawthorn, 1973.

Nelson, Steve. "Broadway and the Beast: Disney Comes to Times Square." *Drama Review* 39, no. 2 (1995): 71–85.

"New Musicals: A Guide to Modcom." *Time,* October 3, 1969, 78.

Nicola, James. Program notes for *Bright Lights Big City,* January–March 1999.

O'Brien, Patti. "*Rent* Strikes." *Rolling Stone,* May 16, 1996, 54–58.

O'Grady, Terence J. "Kingston Trio." In *The New Grove Dictionary of American Music,* vol. 2, ed. H. Wiley Hitchcock and Stanley Sadie. London: Macmillan, 1986.

Oppenheimer, George. "Stage: A Curse of Boredom." *Newsday,* October 21, 1971.

Orgill, Roxanne. "From Hard Facts Comes Comfortable Music." *New York Times,* April 18, 1999.

O'Toole, Lawrence. "Theater Is Discovering a New Voice." *New York Times,* January 22, 1995.

Pacheco, Patrick. "Review with Pictures: 'Sergeant Pepper's Lonely Hearts Club Band on the Road.'" *After Dark,* January 1975.

Padula, Edward. *Bye Bye Birdie: A Musical Memoir.* N.p., 1995.

Palmer, Gareth. "Bruce Springsteen and Masculinity." In *Sexing the Groove: Popular Music and Gender,* ed. Sheila Whitely. London: Routledge, 1997.

Palmer, Robert. *Rock & Roll: An Unruly History.* New York: Harmony, 1995.

Pareles, Jon. "'Tommy' and His Father Reach Broadway." *New York Times,* March 28, 1993.

———. "Damping 60's Fire of 'Tommy' for 90's Broadway." *New York Times,* April 27, 1993.

Pasolli, Robert. *A Book on the Open Theatre.* Indianapolis: Bobbs-Merrill, 1970.

Pearson, Ladley K. " 'Superstar' Reaches Youth." *Newark Evening News,* May 22, 1971.

Pluchino, Joseph. "Bohemian Rhapsody." *Time Out New York,* April 24–May 1, 1996.

Pogrebin, Robin. "The Magic Is in the Marketing: Theaters Go Around the Critics and Straight to the People." *New York Times,* November 19, 1998.

———. "Nary a Drama on Broadway; Straight Plays are Thriving, but Elsewhere in Manhattan." *New York Times,* December 28, 1999.

———. "A Drive to Turn Children into Avid Theatergoers." *New York Times,* April 18, 2000a.

———. "Cameron Mackintosh: A Theater Maverick Isn't Fretting Over His Lean Spell." *New York Times,* July 17, 2000b.

———. "The Princes to the Rescue: Director and His Children Nurture Theater's New Composers." *New York Times,* November 9, 2000c.

Potter, Russell A. "Soul Into Hip-Hop." In *The Cambridge Companion to Pop and Rock,* ed. Simon Frith, Will Straw, and John Street. Cambridge: Cambridge University Press, 2001.

Prece, Paul, and William A. Everett. "The Megamusical and Beyond: The Creation, Internationalisation and Impact of a Genre." In *The Cambridge Companion to the Musical,* ed. William A. Everett and Paul R. Laird. Cambridge: Cambridge University Press, 2002.

Probst, Leonard. *"Sgt. Pepper's Lonely Hearts Club Band on the Road."* Television review broadcast on NBC, November 17, 1974.

Rich, Frank. " 'Dreamgirls,' Michael Bennett's New Musical, Opens." *New York Times,* December 21, 1981.

———. "A Theatrical Mystery: The Missing Balconies." *New York Times,* September 9, 1982.

———. "Basic Training: *Starlight Express.*" *New York Times,* March 16, 1987.

———. "I Just Want to Set the World on Fire: *Carrie.*" *New York Times,* May 13, 1988.

———. "Capturing Rock-and-Roll and the Passions of 1969." *New York Times,* April 23, 1993.

———. "East Village Story." *New York Times,* March 2, 1996.

———. "A Detour in the Theater That No One Predicted." *New York Times,* October 18, 1998.

Richards, Stanley. *Great Rock Musicals.* New York: Stein and Day, 1979.

Riedel, Michael. "Available at Bloomies: The 'Rent' Rags Can Be Yours—For a Price." *New York Daily News,* April 30, 1996.

Riley, Clayton. "A New Black Magic—And They Weave It Well." *New York Times,* November 7, 1971.

Rockwell, John. "Rock Opera." In *The New Grove Dictionary of Opera,* vol. 3, ed. Stanley Sadie. London: Macmillan, 1992.

Rose, Lloyd. " 'Footloose': Musical Chore." *Washington Post,* August 31, 1998.

Rosenberg, Bernard, and Ernest Harburg. *The Broadway Musical: Collaboration in Commerce and Art.* New York: New York University Press, 1993.

Rothenbuhler, Eric W. "Commercial Radio as Communication." *Journal of Communication* 46, no. 1 (1996): 125–43.

Rothstein, Mervyn. "A Season of Graying Crowds and Whitening Stars." *New York Times,* January 27, 2002.

Salzman, Eric. "Whither American Musical Theater?" *Musical Quarterly* 75, no. 4 (1991): 235–47.

Sanjek, David. "Pleasure and Principles: Issues of Authenticity in the Analysis of Rock 'n' Roll." *Tracking* 4, no. 2 (1992): 12–21.

Sauter, Willmar. *The Theatrical Event: Dynamics of Performance and Perception.* Iowa City: University of Iowa Press, 2000.

Savran, David. *Breaking the Rules: The Wooster Group.* New York: Theatre Communications Group, 1988.

———. "*Rent*'s Due: Multiculturalism and the Spectacle of Difference." *Journal of American Drama and Theatre* 14, no. 1 (2002): 1–14.

Schier, Ernie. "*Bye Bye Birdie* Musical Bows Prior to New York." *Evening Bulletin,* March 17, 1960.

Scholem, Richard J. "*Jesus Chris Superstar.*" Radio review broadcast on WBGM–New York, October 13, 1971.

Schroeder, Robert. "The 1969–70 Off-Off-Broadway Season." In *The Best Plays of 1969–1970,* ed. Otis L. Guernsey Jr. New York: Dodd, Mead, 1970.

Scudder, David F. "On Buxton: Structuralist Logic and the Conspiracy of Latent Functions." *Telos* 59 (1984): 167–71.

Sealy, Robert. "Sing Unto the Lord." *Episcopal New Yorker,* January–February 1970.

Seiter, Ellen. *Television and New Media Audiences.* Oxford: Clarendon, 1998.

Shapiro, Ellen. "*Rent* Strike: Broadway Advertising Takes a New Direction." *Print,* 1996, 52–55.

Simmer, Bill. "The Theatrical Style of Tom O'Horgan." *Drama Review* 21, no. 2 (1977): 60–78.

Simon, John. "Pyramid Scheme." *New York,* April 10, 2000.

Simon, Paul. "Highbrows and Hits: A Fertile Compound." *New York Times,* April 30, 1998.

Singer, Barry. "The New Musical: Will Corporate Money Call the Tune?" *New York Times,* August 30, 1998.

———. "Trying to Keep the Sound of Musicals Alive." *New York Times,* August 29, 1999.

———. "'Youngsters' Reach Broadway Bearing Gifts: Musical Scores." *New York Times,* August 27, 2000.

Smith, Ethan. "Glamorama: Theater and Rock Have Made an Ill-Fated Match, but the Cast Album of the Off-Broadway Glam-Rock Musical *Hedwig and the Angry Inch* Proves a Thrilling Exception." *New York,* February 22, 1999.

Smith, Wendy. "Turning a Touchstone of the 80's Into a Musical for the 90's." *New York Times,* February 21, 1999.

Somma, Robert. "Rock Theatricality." *Drama Review* 14, no. 1 (1969): 128–38.

Sorkin, Michael. "The Big Peep Show: The Media Have Invented a New Kind of Pornography for Times Square." *New York Times Magazine,* December 26, 1999.

State of New York. Press release, February 2, 1994.

Stempel, Larry. "The Musical Play Expands." *American Music* 10, no. 2 (1992): 136–69.

Stempel, Tom. *American Audiences on Movies and Moviegoing.* Lexington: University Press of Kentucky, 2001.

Steyn, Mark. *Broadway Babies Say Goodnight: Musicals Then and Now.* London: Faber and Faber, 1997.

Stock, Jeffrey. "Eminence Front: Has Pete Townshend Pulled a Quick One on Broadway?" *Pulse,* October 1993.

Stokes, Melvyn, and Richard Maltby. *Identifying Hollywood's Audiences: Cultural Identity and the Movies.* London: BFI, 1999.

Strasberg, Lee. *A Dream of Passion: The Development of the Method.* Ed. Evangeline Morphos. Boston: Little, Brown, 1987.

Strauss, Neil. "The First Rock Opera (No, Not 'Tommy')." *New York Times,* September 3, 1998.

"Supermogul in the Land of Opportunity." *Forbes,* July 10, 1978.

Surowiecki, James. "Making It: A Conversation with Melvin Van Peebles." *Transition* 79 (1999): 176–92.

Suskin, Steven. *Show Tunes, 1905–1991: The Songs, Shows, and Careers of Broadway's Major Composers.* New York: Limelight, 1992.

Sussman, Mark. "New York's Facelift." *Drama Review* 42, no. 1 (1998): 34–42.

Taylor, Lisa. *Media Studies: Texts, Institutions, and Audiences.* Oxford: Blackwell, 1999.

Terry, Megan. *Viet Rock and Other Plays.* New York: Simon and Schuster, 1966.

"Theatrics." *New Yorker,* September 23, 1972.

Théberge, Paul. "'Plugged In': Technology and Popular Music." In *The Cambridge Companion to Pop and Rock,* ed. Simon Frith, Will Straw, and John Street. Cambridge: Cambridge University Press, 2001.

Tommasini, Anthony. "A Composer's Death Echoes in His Musical." *New York Times,* February 11, 1996.

———. "A Crowd of Old Musicals Squeezes the New." *New York Times,* August 16, 1998.

———. "He's a Singing Star, but Not in Quite the Way He Planned." *New York Times,* March 22, 2000.

Topor, Tom. "Melvin Van Peebles: The Show That Was Supposed to Die." *New York Post,* February 5, 1972.

Townshend, Pete, and Richard Stephen Kent Barnes. *The Story of Tommy.* Twickenham: Eel Pie, 1977.

Trapido, Joel, Edward A. Langhans, James R. Brandon, and June V. Gibson, eds. *An International Dictionary of Theatre Language.* Westport, Conn.: Greenwood, 1985.

Walser, Robert. *Running with the Devil: Power, Gender, and Madness in Heavy Metal Music.* Hanover, N.H.: Wesleyan University Press, 1993.

Walsh, Michael. "Lloyd Webber: Now, but Forever?" *New York Times,* April 9, 2000.

Walters, Barry. "*Hedwig and the Angry Inch:* Original Cast Recording." *Rolling Stone,* February 18, 1999.

Warfield, Scott. "From *Hair* to *Rent:* Is 'Rock' a Four-Letter Word on Broadway?" In *The Cambridge Companion to the Musical,* ed. William A. Everett and Paul R. Laird. Cambridge: Cambridge University Press, 2002.

Watt, Douglas. "Van Peebles' Musical Misses Poetic Mark." *New York Daily News,* October 21, 1971.

———. "'Dude': Much Ado About Nothing." *New York Daily News,* October 10, 1972.

Bibliography

Watts, Richard. "Life in a Black Ghetto." *New York Post,* October 21, 1971.

———. "A Young Man Named Dude." *New York Post,* October 10, 1972.

Whitburn, Joel. *Billboard Book of Top 40 Albums.* 3rd ed. New York: Billboard, 1995.

———. *Billboard Book of Top 40 Hits.* 6th ed. New York: Billboard, 1996.

Whitehead, Sam. "Reviews: *Bright Lights, Big City.*" *Time Out New York,* March 4–11, 1999.

Wickstrom, Maurya. "Commodities, Mimesis, and *The Lion King:* Retail Theatre for the 1990s." *Theatre Journal* 51 (1999): 287–98.

Wild, David. "Who's on Broadway? Pete Townshend Discusses Bringing the Rock Opera to the Great White Way." *Rolling Stone,* March 18, 1993.

Wilson, John S. "Recordings View: 'The Wiz' Is Not a Subtle Soul." *New York Times,* June 1, 1975.

Winer, Linda. "Time Warp Redux: 'Rocky Horror' Is Original Again, on Broadway." *Newsday,* November 16, 2000.

Witchell, Alex. "At the Theater: The Manners to Mind." *New York Times,* October 11, 1991.

———. "An 'Aida' Born of Ecstasies and Explosions." *New York Times,* March 19, 2000.

Woll, Allen. *Black Musical Theatre from "Coontown" to "Dreamgirls."* New York: Da Capo, 1989.

Wollman, Elizabeth. "Men, Music, and Marketing at Q104.3 (WAXQ-FM, New York)." *Popular Music and Society,* vol. 22, no. 4 (1998): 1–23.

———. "The Economic Development of the 'New' Times Square and Its Impact on the Broadway Musical." *American Music* 20, no. 4 (2002): 445–65.

Young, James O. "Between a Rock and a Harp Place." *Journal of Aesthetics and Art Criticism* 53, no. 1 (1995): 78–81.

Index

Index

Index

Text design by Mary H. Sexton

Typesetting by Delmastype, Ann Arbor, Michigan

Text Font: Minion
Designed by Robert Slimbach, the first version of Minion was
released in 1990. Inspired by classical, old style typefaces of the late
Renaissance, it is a versatile, highly readable typeface.
—Courtesy www.adobe.com